STEVE MARTIN
THE MAGIC YEARS

by

Morris Wayne Walker

For further information, contact:

S.P.I. Books
99 Spring Street
New York, NY 10012
Tel: 212/431-5011
FAX: 212/431-8646

10 9 8 7 6 5 4 3 2 1
First Edition

Library of Congress Cataloging-in-Publication Data available.

S.P.I. Books World Wide Web address: spibooks.com

ISBN: 1-56171-980-3

*Dedicated to my wonderful mother,
Marjorie Grace Walker,
without whom Steve would never have
discovered his special purpose*

ACKNOWLEDGEMENTS

There are so many people to thank in regard to this manuscript. Without their help, love and support, this book never would have materialized. These are just a few of those I would like to mention who encouraged and inspired me over the years. You know who you are and what you did! My heartfelt thanks goes out to each and every one of you.

Marjorie Walker, Steve's other mother, who epitomized the phrase "unconditional love." Marsha O'Brien, my twin, who vamped for Steve in the late 1950s, and Lesley, my older sister, who gave Steve his first mashed potato facial. Glenn and Mary Lee Martin, Steve's parents. My other brother, Doug Rowell, and his wonderful folks, Ed and Bette Rowell. Kathy Westmoreland. Rick Kendall. Lloyd and Betty Maxwell. Dr. Ellen Tart. Art Jensen. Dorothy and Jim Foisy. Ned, Sally and Brooke Simonds. Dr. Eileen LaBarthe. Donna Allen-Nelson. Toni Attell. Bud Cook. Clyde and Gladys Johnson. Chester Hooks. Franceska Sanders. Pasquale DeMaria. John McEuen. Doug and Mark Ericson. Melanie Boone. Chris, Fawn and Tim Damitio. Denny and Linda Taylor. Guy Sparks. Ted and Sis Knight. Cynthia Lurton. Suzanne Pierson. Linda Summers. Dr. Susan Smith-Jones. Ryn and Alicia Reavis. Dr. Lon and Mary Jensen. B. Stanford and Caroline Day. George Walton. Dr. Dee Wallace. George and Bobby Goodspeed. Dr. Dennis Steigerwald. Dave and Bodil Anderson. Ronnie and Melba Bolet Murphy. Norm and Robin Sancho. Al and Gretchen Cecere. Kirk Whistler. The Bears, the Settlers, and the Fools. Sunshine Lofton. Carl Gottleib. Richard and Angela Palmer. Dr. Bernard Jensen. Herb Shapiro & Rainbow. Lynn Bell. Owen Phairis. Dana Shaw Prophet. Jim Ryerson. Doug Rhodes. Karla Alfano. Lee McCourry. Larry and Halie Loren Smith. Tim and Becky McCullough. Billy Bob Lanham. Michael Diogo. Constance Brooks. Scott Wallace and his clan. Amrita Whitman. Kanta for her prayers. My attorney, Clark Willes. The unforgettable Garden Grove Class of '63.

Special thanks, Ilene Waterstone, L.A. Films. DaScribe Literary Agency (thanks R.T.). Shelia Smith for her T.L.C., my publisher, Ian Shapolsky, who never lost his sense of humor; and last but not least, my very talented children, Skye and Amoris, who were my inspiration.

I

COVER DESIGN
Richard Syfert
Skye Walker

BOOK DESIGN
Angela Middleton @ Atomic Communications, Inc.

PHOTOS
L.A. Films
Greg Gorman Photography
Ned Simonds
Lynn Walker
Photos of young Steve, thanks to Glenn and Mary Lee Martin
Garden Grove Argonauts Yearbook '62 and '63

ILLUSTRATIONS
Skye Walker

FOOLS INDEX
Amoris Walker

MARTIN MANIACS
L.A. Films

My very special thanks and eternal love
and gratitude to my divine partner Lynn Walker
without whom this book would not exist

PREFACE

This twenty-year project has been a labor of love. It is biographically accurate, but it is not a typical biography; it contains my personal memories of Steve Martin, acquired over the last few decades. Biographers might have spent more time researching and included more statistics. They would have documented their findings and moved on to another job. That's not my purpose. I possess a different perspective. I can't separate myself from Steve. I've witnessed a series of events that are historical in nature, because Steve is not only an example of genius, he is the obvious incarnation of his own desires. He is, in the truest sense of the word, a self-made man, a one-of-a-kind. I have envied him, resented him, admired him, and loved him. We freely exchanged intangible intellectual property as kids and developed tools for dealing with life in our own school of camaraderie.

I've laughed with Steve, cried with him, berated him, thanked him, and shared vicariously in his success—like a brother. My wise father passed on to me the old adage, "If you can count all your true friends on the fingers of one hand before you die, then you are a lucky man." Steve's place is as secure as the hand itself, and I am a lucky man to have known and been a friend of Steve Martin's for all these years. I owe him this book.

TABLE OF CONTENTS

*"The years tell a story
the days never knew."*
—Ralph Waldo Emerson

Chapter 1

BOY WITH A SPECIAL PURPOSE

"Babies are such a nice way to start people"
—Don Herold

Deep in the heart of Waco, Texas, Mary Lee Martin, sporting her tight but fashionable Eisenhower jacket, returns from the hospital with her new baby boy. She notices a large bump on his forehead and decides that she should take the child back to have the bump removed surgically. Grandma Martin gently picks up the infant and cuddles him delicately. "Ya'll don't need to worry about this li'l ol' bump," she whispered. "We'll just give little Stevie a bath and rub that li'l ol' bump and in a few days it will be gone. Little Stevie is going to have a wonderful life, and he's going to be a famous actor like his daddy wants to be."

She snuggled him gently against her breast, stroking her frail, bony finger down his soft bubble nose as she gazed upward and reverently spoke to her Maker. "Dear God, please take care of this baby and give him a special purpose in life." With that, a tear welled up in her eye, and she passed the baby to Glenn, kissing him gently on his bump (the baby's, not Glenn's; Glenn was the father).

The bump eventually went away, just like Grandma said, but God never forgot that precious prayer uttered by Grandma Martin. The year was 1945. Boris Karloff signed with RKO for three horror movies and made less money on all three than entertainer Steve Martin would make in one show at the MGM Grand in Las Vegas thirty years later—scary.

Glenn Martin's mind still lingered on his recent performances with Raymond Massey for the USO in Europe, where he'd been working only weeks before. Acting was his passion, and even though he had taken a position as resident actor and drama instructor at Baylor University, he knew he could do better for his family elsewhere. By 1954, his priorities and prayers were changing to succeeding in real estate; that's where there was money to be made. Soon the Martins would move to the land of golden opportunity, Southern California, where real estate was going crazy and Glenn Martin would make his money—and his mark on Orange County real estate history.

Steve adored his father, but Glenn was "too busy" to spend much time with his son, and as the years rolled by, they became more and more distant. All Steve cared about during his early years was tumbling—he loved his tumbling classes. He enjoyed watching Dean Martin and Jerry Lewis movies and Milton Berle and Red Skelton on TV. He would imitate their routines for "show and tell" time in school. But before he knew it, he and his older sister, Melinda, were on their way to the land of promise. More promise than anyone could have possibly imagined.

Steve called his father "Glenn," not "Dad" or "Pop," just "Glenn." Mother was called neither "Mom" nor "Mommy," but simply by her name, "Mary Lee." There were few hugs in this family once they moved away from the warmth of Grandma Martin, who chose to remain behind in Waco. Sister Melinda was rarely conversational with Steve, and vice versa.

Even as a child, Steve earned the money for what he wanted or needed. As the Martins didn't believe in doling out money to their kids, Steve started working at age seven. He was willing to work hard to ensure that he had cash on hand to buy the things he wanted. When fate placed Steve near the newest and greatest theme park in the history of the world, he wasted no time getting a job selling 25-cent guidebooks at Disneyland.

It was the summer of 1956, and Steve was almost eleven years old. Disneyland had been open little more than year. Although the Martins had been living in Inglewood, Glenn decided to buy a small tract home on Brookside Drive, only two miles from the Magic Kingdom. The Soviet Union was preparing to launch the first man-made satellite (Sputnik One) into orbit, but the American public was, by nature, more entertainment-oriented, so Disneyland received far more attention than the forthcoming satellite (after all, what possible good could a satellite ever serve?). Walt Disney himself was not impressed with Russian accomplishments or Russian dignitaries. In fact, he made headlines when he refused to let Premier Nikita Khrushchev visit his park.

No one was more impressed with, or more excited about, Disney's boldest venture than the young Steve Martin. His summer was alive with action as he sold guidebooks at the main gate and became a fan and friend of Aldini, the man behind the tricks at the Magic Castle Magic Shoppe. Aldini also ran the Frontier Magic Shoppe and the Main Street Magic Shoppe.

Before Steve knew it, the summer of 1956, had ended. It was September—time for school and higher education. As if anything could qualify as a higher education than watching Aldini or the sur-real scenes that composed the little seventeen-acre park known as Disneyland. Aldini was an expert with sleight-of-hand magic tricks; he was also a mock con man, a slick talker, the kind of guy who would have been doing "bean under the shell" tricks in the days of the frontier carpetbaggers. He was "great" in Steve's mind, and the feeling was mutual. Aldini would be remembered, as Steve began formulating his character for the lead role in his 1991 movie *Leap of Faith*. Steve, in those early days, had more respect for magic than for organized religion and more interest in collecting coins than going to church—or school. Steve knew what he liked. He liked "D-Land," Red Skelton, Abbott and Costello, and being free to explore the world of magic and entertaining.

Even as he gazed out the window of the stubby, yellow school bus on his way to Palm Lane Elementary school for the first day of the sixth grade, Steve couldn't get his mind off Disneyland, magic tricks, and the evening fireworks display he viewed, courtesy of Disney, every night. He'd been able to stay at Disneyland, enjoying its wonders after his work, before hitchhiking home every night. He was so enamored by the world of Disney that he daydreamed about the place and only partially paid attention on the playground as the other kids screamed and hollered, renewing their friendships from the past year. It was Steve's first day at this new school, and all he could think about was Disneyland.

A commotion nearby snapped Steve out of his daydream, as a small crowd of children gathered around a boy with glasses standing near the tether ball game. I was also new at Palm Lane and was faced with a crowd of strange kids who just could not believe that the bolo tie I was wearing had a real silver dollar as its centerpiece. I don't know why they doubted the authenticity of that bolo tie. After all, silver dollars were commonplace at that time, especially in Las Vegas, where my father had purchased the tie. I liked being the center of attention, but I was outnumbered, outvoted and losing the debate over the authenticity of the coin when another strange kid entered the group, holding his large hand slightly above his head in an attention-getting manner. He gently lifted my tie and scrutinized the coin. Hand still held high, he authoritatively announced to the group, "I'm a numismatist, and this is definitely a real silver dollar."

The bell rang, the crowd of kids dispersed quickly, and I looked at him with a curious expression and asked, "What's a numiswhattist???"

"A numismatist," he said politely, "is a coin collector."

He then smiled.

"I'm Morris," I said, offering my hand.

"Hi, I'm Steve...Steve Martin."

We shook hands. His hand was large for a sixth-grade kid, and his grip was firm. We were instant friends. It was comedy at first sight. There was humor lurking behind every lesson, and an immediate chemistry between two boys that kept us together through thick and thin during those formative years.

My father was in the oil business and was away most of the time, primarily in Iraq then. Steve's father was there...but not really there (he was too busy with real estate). Until we graduated from high school, rarely a day passed that Steve and I were not together.

We were closer than brothers, and rapid-fire creativity was a way of life for us. We could read each other's minds, and even as the years have flown by and Steve has grown to be a world-class entertainment superstar, things still happen between us that seem uncanny.

Since my father worked in and around Baghdad for many years and he would come home for a month only, once a year, he would fill our heads with exotic stories of Arabs in black veils and oilmen, who mocked their holy city of Mecca and were then chased out of the country at dagger point. When the Gulf War broke out in 1991, Steve volunteered to travel to Asia and entertain the troops for the USO. He wrote me a letter telling me how strange it was to be where my dad had been and what an "eerie" feeling he had, sitting there writing a letter to me about my father from the same place my father had talked about so many times. My father had passed away by that time, but an "eerie" feeling also shot up my spine when I noticed that Steve's letter was written and dated on my dad's birthday.

Glenn Martin was a tall, handsome man, always a gentleman, polite but aloof. What it boiled down to for Steve and me was that we were two rookie comedians with fathers who were not our role models or our pals. We loved them, but we never saw much of them. We were each other's role models. I was entertained by Steve and Steve was entertained by me, and entertainment was our purpose and delight. What's more, we lived to entertain everyone in our path—whether or not they knew us, or wanted us.

In class, we were the clown princes of comedy, and our poor old sixth-grade teacher, Mrs. Miller, was too often the butt of our antics. As alphabetical seating would have it, Steve was much closer to the front row than I, and when Mrs. Miller's huge old body started quivering with anger, she would grab her yardstick and start for Steve. It didn't matter which one of us had been the perpetrator of the "schtick." We got the stick for our "schtick," and she often hit Steve over the head with her handy yardstick. He buried his face and his laughter under the hinged, wooden top of his desk as the class roared.

Little could Mrs. Miller realize that she was attempting to clobber a boy who would one day reach the status of her favorite star, Humphrey Bogart. Bogart died that year, but Steve lived on, with a mind like a computer—programmed to analyze, absorb, and record everything that could possibly be used in his vocation as a comedian and, eventually, a dramatic (never without comedy) actor. There finally came a time when the venerable (or should I say vulnerable) Mrs. Miller decided to bypass Steve in her raging anger and, waving her yardstick like Conan the Destroyer wielding his mighty sword, came barreling down the isle towards me, screaming, "I'm going to come down on you like a ton of bricks!" A little foot found its way into her path (not one of ours) and she truly came down—most impressively—like a ton of something.

But practical jokes were not our forte, and although everyone else laughed at the poor old defeated and deflated Mrs. Miller, Steve and I looked at each other and saw a sympathetic response in each other's eyes that, moments later, brought us to her side, helping her get to her feet and regain her balance and composure—whereupon she started whacking us with the yardstick again, and our sympathy was quickly replaced with mock agony.

On Columbus Day that year, Mrs. Miller had left a message on the blackboard (as was her way) for the class to analyze and be prepared to answer when she entered the room. The question was "WHAT HAPPENED 458 YEARS AGO TODAY?" It gave Steve and me just enough time to organize the class so that by the time she walked in, the entire room was standing up, singing, "Happy Birthday to you, Happy Birthday to you, Happy Birthday, Mrs. Miller, Happy Birthday to you!"

We needed each other and filled a gap in one another's lives in those precious years. Steve was at our house most of the time, but he wasted no time at all in introducing me to the wonders of "The Park" or "D-land," as we called it. By the time the summer of '57 arrived, I (with Steve's help) had nabbed a job at Disneyland's main gate next to him. He sold his guidebooks, and I sold balloons. Steve wore the designated attire: 1890s-style straw hat, vest, and bow tie. My outfit varied a bit: I wore a derby.

We saved most of our antics for off-duty hours, but we did do our best to entertain anyone who ventured into the Magic Kingdom. Business was business, and we were usually busy taking care of it. But if we didn't take breaks together, then one of us would sit and watch the other "work the gate." I was his audience or he was mine.

What a life! Disneyland was the most popular amusement

park in the country, and often they would close the main gates before noon because of the volume of people who had already entered. Steve held the record for guidebook sales, once having sold 600 in a single day. He was neat, clean, articulate—and Walt Disney's ideal turn-of-the-century, main-street kid hawking his wares. He was the most frugal kid in Orange County, and, like so many other burning desires that were heating up in his complex mind, being rich was at the subconscious forefront. Where others prayed for love or friendship or fame, Steve just visualized. He had the determination to be wealthy (extremely wealthy), no matter how much work it took. I believe that desire was second in importance only to comedy for the sake of fun at that time in his life.

In his own home, Steve was uncommonly quiet—he seemed almost reclusive—but he was truly euphoric at work, in transit, at school, and almost everywhere we went together. He loved spending time at our house with me, my mother and my two sisters, Lesley (my older sister) and Marsha, (my twin). He especially enjoyed Marsha, because she was extremely well-developed at a very early age and had a way of getting close enough to Steve to scratch his back and tickle his imagination. That youthful foreplay later became much more.

Sex, at that early time in our lives, was a mystery. Those days were quite different than the 90s. We knew little, saw little, and our fathers were not accessible, so we had to discover many of the mysteries of sex through our own conversations and debates. One such debate was quite memorable. In discussing the way people actually "did it," Steve suggested that a man would put his "thing" in the woman and move it in and out. I objected to this theory, and expressed my belief that one should just insert "it" and leave "it." Well, Steve was right (except in rare cases); nevertheless, his only description of "it" was simply "it."

Since he apparently had one hand up on me in this in-depth biological debate (no pun indented), I then had to explain to him that the real terminology for this "thing" we were discussing was given to me by my mother when I was but a mere child. "It's called your special purpose," I told him proudly. His face widened with a wild and crazy grin, which from that point on was instantly plastered upon his countenance whenever anyone would say "special purpose"—whether it was a teacher or an innocent bystander at

Disneyland (we would break up and nobody knew why).

God gave Steve his "special purpose," but I told him what it was, and he told me how to use it! With all this (and more) deep and meaningful dialogue, we continued on as the best of friends for many years. Steve carried his special purpose (the terminology, that is) well into his adult life, and it made for several of the funniest sequences in his first feature film *The Jerk*. Steve invited me to the screening of *The Jerk* in Hollywood in 1979. Like everyone else in the audience, I found it outrageously funny, and no one was more entertained by his "special purpose" comedy lines than I.

By the time Steve made *The Jerk*, he had become one of the highest paid comedians in the country. He was in such demand that Universal Pictures struck an unprecedented deal with him, whereby, he would receive fifty percent of the movie's gate. He made millions on that picture, and quickly became one of the most sagacious businessmen in Hollywood. His training at Disney's main gate paid off. People don't talk about how wealthy Steve is these days, and he likes it that way. He's a very private person, so you won't ever see much in print about his monetary success. But his greatest wealth is his enormous heart. I know that if Steve spent a week with a group of homeless people, he would soon not have any money left! But that's just not going to happen—go figure.

I have received dozens of letters from Steve over the years, and there remain precious memories of two boys with two "special purposes"—but one specific purpose: entertainment. "Martin and Walker" they called us in school, and before we knew it, we actually had quite a reputation.

I have also pursued a career in entertainment and believe that it was the years of our basic training with each other that have been the cornerstone of our vocational aspirations and accomplishments. The spirited and delightfully humorous magician I grew up with was a kid I'll never forget. I hold those early days as very dear memories. As we all know, the weight of life gets heavier with the years. And even considering all of the great things that have happened over the years for Steve, I believe that he would relinquish all that he has acquired to go back to those days in and around Disneyland and relive those true "magic years" again, in the precious innocence and anonymity he has lost forever.

Steve with his mother, Mary Lee, and a bump on his head

Chapter 2

THE TALE OF
"THE HAND"

*"One of the effects of fear is to disturb the senses and
cause things to appear other than what they are."*

—Cervantes

B ig hands, Steve had big hands. From the day I met him,
his most notable characteristics were his big hands and
his nose...Oh, and big feet: size twelve in the seventh grade.

Steve's nose was always "rather large," as was noted in his hit
movie *Roxanne*. Maybe it was Steve's cognizance of his own
slightly large nose that kept him spellbound when he and I sat in
front of the old black and white TV and watched a rerun of the
1950 version of Edmond Rostand's *Cyrano de Bergerac*, starring
José Ferrer (who, by the way, won the Academy Award for that
performance). We were mesmerized, and watching that movie
could very well have planted the seed that would eventually give
birth to the movie *Roxanne*.

Although Steve told me he rewrote the script forty times before it became a hit, I believe its essence was discovered while we were still kids. I'm not laying claim to any creative input in the final product, but a seed planted in Steve Martin's mind at any time in his life was always destined for growth. With a "Midas Touch", Steve has managed to tap into the most minute fleeting moments in his life experience with phenomenal success. Not only have the ideas come to fruition in a creative/artistic manner, but always with a strong financial bottom line as an integral part of the final product. I believe the process all blended together until a creative bug in Steve's head—buried deep beneath his symbolic silver locks—amalgamated that synergism and produced the magic of Steve Martin. And magic was always a part of it.

In the August 1987, issue of *Time* magazine, Steve recalled some of the weird merchandise available at the Magic Shoppe at Disneyland: "We sold rubber vomit, shrunken heads, finger choppers, nails through the head, and skulls that glowed in the dark." Somewhere down the line among these unique items was our "hand." And what a hand it was! The fingers were twelve inches long, it was green and blood-vessel red, the enormous knuckles bulged wickedly, and the long, ragged nails were filthy, as if from scraping the inside of a forgotten coffin. Just the kind of thing a kid loves to play with. But the hand was pure inspiration to Steve Martin. I remember the hand distinctly and how we flashed it around on several occasions to grab onlookers' attention. You see, "attention" was the purpose for living for young Steve Martin and me. It's important to know this in order to understand the complex character of Steve Martin. This hand was an extraordinary prop. At that precious time, the "Midas Touch" was not a part of Steve's persona—fun for the sake of fun was all that mattered. And yet, the early seeds were being planted. It was inevitable that he would become funny for money in the long run.

It was late one fall evening, and we had been at Steve's house on Brookside Drive. We were thirteen years old and full of mischievous energy. As we strolled up the street, we conceived a plot. Steve leaned over and said, "Let's go hold 'the hand' up in front of someone's window!" I choked back a sneaky laugh at the thought of it and said, "Okay, let's do it!" This was not really meant to be a practical joke. We had this ugly, oversized monster hand, and we needed desperately to find someone to entertain with it. We know now who we were really entertaining.

Suddenly there was an air of mystery in the evening breeze. We stooped down and creeped behind a hedge towards an unsuspecting neighbor about a block away from Steve's house. From our vantage point, we could see a man was in the kitchen. He was a middle-aged man, apparently standing at the sink doing the dishes and staring out the window. He had a distant look in his eyes, as if his body was going through the motions of doing the dishes, but his mind was elsewhere. Before we knew it, we were next to the wall by the kitchen window, bending low to avoid being seen. Suppressing our giggles, Steve slipped the enormous hand over his own. The bumpy alligator texture of the rubber wrist came halfway up Steve's forearm. Slowly, ever so slowly, he began raising the horrid hand directly in front of the window the innocent dishwasher stared through. The tension was heavy for both of us— which made the situation even more difficult to cope with. It wasn't fear, it was imprisoned laughter, forcing its way up out of our throats like so much regurgitation.

Slowly, Steve raised the fingers up to the window in front of the poor, unsuspecting dishwashing husband. Higher and higher— and still no response. How could he *not* see it? He must have been totally mesmerized by his subconscious distractions. Steve slowly inched the hand up higher and higher, until soon the entire hand was exposed directly in front of the man—and still no response.

Our eyes locked on each other, our choked-back laughter almost beyond our control as the tense seconds turned into minutes. Then, suddenly, we heard a terrified, trembling voice from inside the kitchen: "Oh, God, I'll never do it again! Sweet Jesus, forgive me. Oh, God, don't hurt me— pleeeeassse don't!" he screamed.

The man babbled on like an idiot, begging mercy from above and recoiling from the window in a state of total panic and fear! He, evidently, turned and bolted towards an interior door, bonking his head into something and yelping like a wounded animal. More screams of terror, and now pain, were heard inside the kitchen. We wanted to look, but we were locked in fear, and we had a frantic need to burst into uncontrollable laughter. We gazed at each other one last time, our eyes bulging, and the smothered laughter finally began to escape from our throats. We just couldn't believe this guy was as frightened as he sounded—but it was very, very real to him. And, therefore, to us.

Finally, after a few seconds more of panic, I looked straight at Steve. Knowing that our mission was accomplished, we went from forced smirks to blasts of laughter. We both lost control and broke loose, laughing hysterically and running. Steve was in the lead, hauling ass ten feet in front of me—the silhouette of a happy kid running in the moonlight, his big right hand dangling down to his knee.

Steve (8 months) with sister Melinda

Chapter 3

STEVE FOR STEW

"An onion can make people cry, but there has never been
a vegetable invented to make them laugh."

—Will Rogers

There were mornings in Orange County, California when Disneyland was young and you could smell the orange blossoms. It was never too cold, sometimes very warm, but there were only two seasons: winter and summer. At least that's the way it seemed to me and my best friend. It really wasn't the seasons that captivated our curious minds; it wasn't the burgeoning real estate market in Garden Grove or the fins on the new Fords and Chevys; it wasn't even the fact you could get a hamburger for 15 cents at the Pink Spot near the Garden Grove Square. We weren't concerned with politics...we were still unadulterated. And we didn't care about sex, except in schoolyard debates. Such earthy matters were not of paramount importance to two aspiring comedians in the heartland of California in 1957.

Several years ago, over coffee somewhere on Hollywood Boulevard, Steve reminded me about this story. He was in good spirits, as always, but especially elated because he had just won the UCLA student body's annual Jack Benny Award for entertainment excellence as a result of his first film, a short piece he had done for Paramount called *The Absent-Minded Waiter*. He adored Benny.

Steve reminded me that once, as we were walking through the morning mist to our bus stop, he told me that he'd heard a ridiculous story about a man who peeled an onion, and it made him cry. "It's true," I said to Steve (having pulled kitchen detail in our home on several occasions).

Steve knew a tremendous number of facts and was always impressing me with pertinent details about coin collecting and sleight-of-hand magic tricks. He was an amazing source of information. Nevertheless, he had never peeled an onion, or spent more time in the kitchen than it took to walk through it from the living room to his bedroom. I felt I was not as knowledgeable about as many things as Steve. I was only full of off-the-wall responses that seemed to delight him equally as much as his knowledge and expertise entertained me. In this particular matter of onions, I was an expert, and I began planning my approach to catch Steve unaware, while proving my "theory" to him about raw onions and the effect they have upon the human eye. He just didn't believe it.

The sixth grade was an exciting time. It was a time of continually testing old Mrs. Miller. It was a time for entertaining our classmates, at anybody's expense. It was a time to practice humorous techniques for future reference. We were like verbal athletes, bouncing experimental puns and one-liners around the classroom like little Rodney Dangerfields. And when the day was over, a very tired Mrs. Miller heard the last bell ring and buried her head in her arms on the desk. We were off on the bus, down the palm-lined lanes of Palm Lane School and south on Katella Avenue to Dallas Drive.

We always sat together, and I had a plan to teach Steve about the power of onions that day. He was filled with his usual excitement for life and working at Disneyland. He was excited about everything—except going home. I knew that, and it was always easy to talk him into coming to my house for a while.

My little scheme came together quite easily while my sister,

Marsha, scratched Steve's back. He paid her five cents an hour for the service, which he referred to as "vamping." Marsha didn't mind; she loved Steve, and that was more than enough to buy a postage stamp in those days. I conferred with my mother, and shortly thereafter she asked Steve and me to peel onions and potatoes for stew. I suggested that Steve peel the onions. I began on the potatoes and observed him gleefully cut into a large, yellow Orange County onion. Our conversation rattled on, as always, until there was a lull in Steve's ever quick response, and I turned around and faced him. As our eyes met, tears welled in his. Huge tears, happy tears, reverent tears. They poured forth a flood of cognizance, an ocean of realization.

"This is great!" he said solemnly, staring at me. His reaction was priceless; it was akin to a religious experience or a vision. And then loudly, he again said, "This is great!" In Steve's vocabulary, there was no term more all-encompassing and as explicit as the word "great," and he said it over and over again. Tears poured forth as if they had been held back in joy and sorrow for the eleven years of his life. He cried as if he had wanted to cry and never could before that moment. He cried for being happy, and he cried for being sad. And he was thoroughly pleased with the tears because he needed to cry, and he was able to attribute all the sudden saline to the onions. The vegetable tears just kept coming.

Oh, I saw Steve cry on many occasions after that, when we were boys. Tears were not an uncommon occurrence in our relationship. We cried because we couldn't help it. We cried the best kind of tears—tears of laughter. We laughed until we cried. Maybe that's why Steve remembers our times together as the best days of his life.

When Steve's career was really taking off in the late '70s, the pressure on him was overwhelming. One escape he opted for, periodically, was the long drive back to his home in Aspen, Colorado. He told me that he would listen to tapes in his car, usually lectures or poetry readings by esoteric writers such as e.e. cummings. Those deeply personal moments could sometimes bring him to tears. But in recent years, there has been no time for tears—just for the unflappable Steve and the unrelenting, grinding schedule of a superstar.

Steve doesn't peel his own onions now. Such domestic chores

are not a part of his domain. I don't know about the joys associated with being rich, but the nice thing about struggling is that emotions run closer to the surface and the tears of joy and sadness are distinguishable. Tears of too much stuff...I don't know about. But I'm sure they must be heavy. The precious tears of laughter are like priceless gems, lost but not forgotten, and they can only be discovered in mysterious places and at unexpected times in life. They cannot be purchased at any price.

If you aren't with someone constantly for years, and yet you knew them well at one time, things between you inevitably change. But some things never changed with Steve. He has a heart. He is not a well-known philanthropist in most people's minds, although he has donated a lot of money to things he believes in, such as the Los Angeles Art Museum. He has helped friends in need and his family more than a few times. But Steve is also purposely generous with his talent. He feels if he makes people happy that is the greatest gift he can give them. And he's right. Few people can leave a heritage of happiness such as his. But the pressure and pain of success are greater than most of us realize. Even though Steve's public persona is always as calm and cool as a cucumber, I personally believe that, from a therapeutic point of view, it would probably be good for my old friend to peel a few onions every now and then.

Steve & sister Melinda with ol' St. Nick

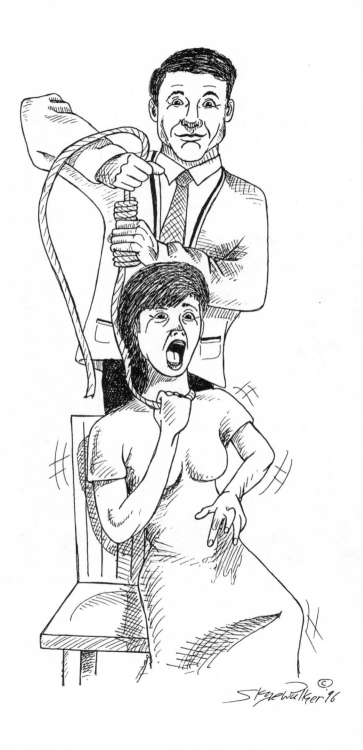

Chapter 4

THE TRIAL OF MISS STEPP

"This a court of law, young lady, not a court of justice."
—Oliver Wendell Holmes

In 1964, I performed a concert at Savanna High School in Buena Park, California with my folk-singing group, the Settlers. There was a singer/song writer named John Denver performing that same night. He had just changed his last name to Denver. He had an old 12-string guitar that he told me he'd reconstructed, working endless hours to convert it to an 18-string guitar. And it was surely equipped with 18 pegs, tuners, a new bridge, and so forth, but he only had 12 strings on it, I was a curious nineteen-year-old comedian/bass player and felt myself obliged to ask why he only had 12 strings on his innovative 18-string guitar.

"I just finished rebuilding it today," he said dejectedly, "and when I put eighteen strings on it, I couldn't hold them down, so I guess I'll just have to play it with twelve until I can afford another 12-string. This is the only guitar I have right now."

Nine years later, John Denver had made it big. I was on the road with my wife, Lynn, performing three or four shows a day at schools across the country when I reminded Lynn of the following story. I asked her where we'd been when it happened, and she told me, "Somewhere between Oregon and New York." That was true, but wherever it was, it was cold—we both remembered that. We were snuggled in bed in yet another cheap motel room for the night and were preparing to watch "John Denver's Rocky Mountain Christmas Special." Steve was going to be a guest star on the show.

The special was filmed live, inside a large glass dome near Aspen, Colorado where Steve and John were both living at the time. When Steve was introduced, he appeared with banjo in hand and a magnificently colored butterfly on his nose. He did quite a bit of "nose humor" in those days. I assumed it was a prop. The show was great; Steve's comedy was a howl. Two years later, I mentioned that special to him.

"That phony butterfly was a great touch Steve!" I told him. "It wasn't phony!" he responded in all sincerity. "That thing landed on my nose and sat there the whole time without moving. It flew away when I went off camera."

Then, as we reminisced about the trials and tribulations of our youth, he reminded me about the following incident.

We were as close as ever in the seventh grade. Steve was always at my house. My family loved him. We attended Lampson Junior High school and worked at Disneyland together.

We were also in most of the same classes together. And our elementary school friends, Steve Szalay and Greg Magedman, still hung around with us periodically. We were all in the same science class, which was quite a collaboration. Our teacher was a young, attractive, and personable single woman named Ann Stepp. She was friendly and had a laudable sense of humor. Naturally, this was a genuine reason to take advantage of her. We created our little science projects with a great deal of enthusiasm, however oblique.

Steve and I presented one project that absolutely befuddled Miss Stepp and all the other students and teachers who witnessed it. I held a copper pointer attached to a little metal box, and Steve explained the purpose of our "invention."

"We have created a heat ray that will transmit through human flesh without damage to the epidermis or other tissue. Furthermore, this is the only apparatus of its kind in the world."

With that, Steve would place a wadded-up piece of tinfoil in the volunteer's hand. He would then instruct the volunteer to close his or her hand while I pointed the copper antennae. After a few seconds of my waving the rod in small circles at the hand, the tinfoil would become so hot that the person holding it would have to drop it. Naturally, this amazed all spectators—especially the person holding the tinfoil, who still felt the sting of a genuinely hot burn.

We had everyone believing that we'd invented a scientifically valid, heat-transmitting device. We were invited to enter our project in the county science fair, but we were too young to appreciate how valuable such a spoof would have been. Furthermore, according to Steve, we felt bad about fooling everybody. Finally, we went to Miss Stepp and admitted that it was a hoax. She had been so taken in that she had to ask how we did it. Steve had acquired a chemical from Disney's Fantasyland Magic Shoppe. Ultimately, the effect of the chemical was to make metallic paper heat up when put in contact with the heat of the hand. But it was the staging and presentation that made it so "amazing."

For us, it was just a good gag. Miss Stepp appreciated our sense of humor and admired our ability to pull off the "fake." She must have sincerely appreciated our project, because she allowed us to go to the science fair anyhow, even though participation was supposed to be a prerequisite for attendance.

The majority of the students rode a bus to the fair, since it was being held at another school. Steve and I had a better idea, and talked Miss Stepp into taking us with her in her new Volkswagen. Halfway to the fair, as she accelerated to catch up with the bus, we were stopped by the Highway Patrol! The ticket was inevitable. She took it with a smile and proceeded toward our destination under complete assault from her erstwhile passengers.

The fair was interesting, but only of second interest to Steve and me, who were already planning "The Trial of Miss Stepp."

Class began right after lunch the next day, as usual. Lunch period had given us just enough time to cast the characters and "set the stage," so to speak. She opened the door of her classroom and was suddenly met by the bailiff, who apprehended her by the arm and took her to the side of her desk—now presided over by Judge Even Steven (Steve Szalay). Steve Martin was the prosecuting attorney, and I was the defense counsel. She was speechless...but not defenseless. And she seemed to enjoy it all, with an absolutely bewildered look.

We bantered back and forth in front of the jury, with Steve, insisting on her guilt in the speeding ticket incident and I begging for mercy on her behalf. The class rolled with laughter. Miss Stepp could not suppress a smile. Finally, the verdict. Our summations were brief (class was almost over):

"We, the jury, find Miss Stepp guilty of speeding," announced the head juror.

"Mercy," I pleaded.

"Is there anything you wish to say before we deliver the verdict, Miss Ann Stepp?"

She sat there, not believing the extent to which we were carrying on the antics. "No," she giggled.

Judge Even Steven announced slowly, "You are hereby ordered by this court to hang by the neck until dead." And he smacked his wooden mallet on her desk with a resounding bang, accidentally launching her teaspoon into a window pane causing a chilling *crack!*

Steve didn't hesitate; he slipped around behind her and pulled out a hangman's noose appropriately tied with thirteen knots. He laughed his best hideous laugh and gingerly slipped it over her neck. As humor gave way to stress, a bit of fright and a cracked window, she gave a startled shout. Everyone broke up. Even in the midst of all this levity, we finally got to her. She blushed and looked confused, angry, happy, and entertained all at once. The class was over, and the attorneys, jurors, judge, hangman, and audience were truly "saved by the bell."

When Steve would start reminding me of one of our old stories, they would tend to be actually two or three tales rolled into one big one, like the story I've just related. Even after Steve and I moved on to high school, we would periodically drop in unexpectedly on Miss Stepp's class at Lampson Junior High. On one such occasion, we dropped in at the beginning of the period to say "Hi," and she instantly introduced us to the class as young instructors (with extremely high IQs) who were visiting from a local college. She told the class that we would offer information on the advantages of higher education. We gladly accepted the challenge, but soon Steve's dialogue turned to humans transmuting into alien beings while I designed an alien named Phlegm Swartstout on the blackboard.

This was a sheer delight for the old "Gopher Boys." We were in front of an audience and, like the good Reverend Schuller at the Garden Grove Community Church, it was all we needed to demonstrate our ad-lib abilities. By that time, we had performed hundreds of impromptu shows together. I really loved Steve; nobody stimulated my imagination like he did.

Steve has acknowledged that he had little or no communication with his family during those days. He says he always drew a ring around himself and made room inside the circle for only a few people. Almost everyone else, including his parents, were outside of that ring except me. I don't know that I felt honored at that time, because I didn't yet see Steve as a future superstar; but I did always believe in his spectacular talent and his potential greatness. I knew Steve would do really well at whatever he eventually decided to do with his life. Of course, at that time there was only one reason for living: comedy.

Years later in a magazine article, Ann Stepp recounted her impressions of the day of the trial. "The organization and spontaneity of that silly trial were exquisite. The leadership over the other students was overwhelming," she said. "I was immediately reduced from teacher to dependent."

She said, "Steve was to Morris what Bud Abbott was to Lou Costello; they were humorous, happy, well liked, and inseparable."

The most accurate of these compliments was "inseparable." The last day of the eighth grade, Ann Stepp had an 8mm movie camera at school. Steve and I showed up in matching, hand-painted shirts. We bowed deeply for the camera. Maybe it was because of those uniformed days at Disneyland, but it seems we wore matching shirts a lot. Guess why? We thought it was funny, and in our young minds, "being funny" was the qualifying factor for a satisfying existence on planet earth. Actually, people probably thought we were geeks, but as long as they laughed, what did we care? I've often thought it was preordained in some misty, cosmic, in-between realm before we arrived in this incarnation that Steve and I should be together—if you believe in that sort of thing.

Another magazine article published a few years back quoted Steve as saying, "I was never popular in high school; all I had was my friend, Morris." In retrospect, I feel privileged to have been drawn into that very small circle of friends. And even as I write, I know that the circle is still very small today; whereas, the circle of influence and stardom is beyond my cognizance. As *Father of the Bride II* became a box office hit in America, I had several conversations with Ilene, Steve's personal assistant in Hollywood. She explained that shortly after the movie was released in America it was also released abroad. Steve was then currently touring numerous countries in Europe, whereupon, he would finish that tour and fly to Japan, where the movie was also a hit. The sort of awesome, worldwide promotional responsibilities and pressures Steve was saddled with suddenly dawned on me.

We are all entertainers. We all love the thrill of a response from an audience. Some of us are brazen enough to pursue this dubious goal as a profession. But there are those of us out there singing songs and telling jokes that aren't any different than so many others who have specific titles like preacher, politician, professor, or the greatest performers of them all, lawyers!

Had Steve chosen to be an attorney, he would have been one of the best. He would certainly have made himself into a major success, earning lots of money, for achievement was his destiny no matter what his vocation. As a lawyer, I'm sure Steve would have become famous for his court room performance and his obvious charisma. But I don't believe he would ever have fallen into the stereotypical lawyer trap of behaving callously towards his clients. It is not in Steve's character to be impervious or without compassion, like sour barristers. He would have been an exception to the rule regarding lawyers: "As long as there is room for one more in hell, there will never be a lawyer in heaven."

After that memorable trial in Miss Stepp's science class, we never talked about the law again until Steve played a mad judge in our Senior Play, "Ten Little Indians." Lawyers and the law were too serious for us, and we both respected rules and regulations within the hallowed walls of our little institutions of learning. We would never break them. But stretching them…that was the challenge.

I remember a day when practically everyone in school was grimacing with pain before noon. First, the agonized looks became apparent to us in our classmates' expressions, and we looked at each other and winked, knowing that our prank was working. At our first break, we noticed that even the teachers seemed to look as if their usual burdens were doubled. By noon, we were called into the principal's office. We sat there innocently, pretending we had no idea about what had been going on that day. She just glared at us icily. Then she reached into her middle drawer and pulled out a stack of signs (each about a foot long), laying them on her desk.

"Morris." She gave me a stern look and then turned slowly and muttered, "Steve." Then, in a very patronizing and exaggerated fashion, she said, "Do either of you know who came here bright and early today and placed these lovely signs on every bathroom before school started?"

At that point she held up one of the signs which simply read "CLOSED" in bright red, block lettering. We pointed at each other. She lost her "cool" and began laughing at our humorous prank; in fact, we all had a good laugh. "We'll have no more of this," she said as she slapped the sign back on her desk. "Excuse me!" she then added in a more dignified manner, as if suddenly remembering something rather urgent. "I have to go to the rest room!"

This might seem a little out of context, but it's important. The late, great John Denver left a wonderful legacy in music, and it was a real pleasure to have had the privilege of meeting him a few times over the years. As this book goes to press, we are currently on the road hosting and performing a number of concerts entitled "*Never Ending Song*, A Tribute to John Denver." People like Steve Martin and John Denver have the ability to leave an abundance of memories on tapes, records, videos, CDs and movies.

But for those whose accolades are not as great, their contributions are no less valuable. Our dear science teacher, Ann Stepp, recently passed away after a long bout with cancer. Her legacy is in the minds and memories of the many students whom she gracefully coached through those junior high classes so many years ago. No life is any greater or more important than another. This is a fact. But in truth, we all know that some lives are a little more "wild and crazy." By the way, Ann Stepp never reported us for breaking the window. She said she was guilty. What a gal!

Chapter 5

GOGGLES AND GOOGLEE EYES

"All my life I have loved a womanly woman and admired a manly man,
but I never could stand a boily boy."

—Archibald Primrose

The summer after our seventh-grade initiation into higher
education found Steve and me working at Disneyland
again. Before we returned to our jobs at the "Wonderful World of
Disney," my mother arranged for us to attend YMCA Camp. Although it can be traumatic for a young boy to venture off to camp
alone, with your best pal it's just another wonderful adventure.

As usual, my mother was our transportation. The night before
we were to depart for the local Y, she took us to the Gem Theater
on Euclid Boulevard in Garden Grove. The movie was *Tammy*,
starring Debbie Reynolds, a young and vivacious actress (Carrie
Fisher's mother for the uninitiated under 40). It was a musical,
corny and hokey, but we were not into criticizing the movies too
much in those years. They were just entertainment to us. Mom
picked us up promptly at the conclusion of the flick. I recall us sitting

in the backseat of our '56 Oldsmobile, singing together, "I hear the cottonwoods whispering above...Tammy, Tammy, Tammy's in love." Youth, friendship and the prospect of adventures at camp had us in the highest of spirits.

Steve once told me he remembered that we went to a lot of trouble to make sure that the last song we heard before our vacation was a good one. He said we didn't want to go to camp for a week without a radio and have a bad song haunting us. How complex that Martin mind was even at an early age. "Computer-like," said Carrie Fisher, who, coincidently, was an intimate of the original *Saturday Night Live* crowd. I can look back now and agree with Carrie's observation. "Calculating" might be another appropriate term, but not in a negative sense. Ultimately, as wild and crazy as Steve might have appeared to the public, his stage and movie material has always been extremely well planned. Even when he did tricks at the Disneyland Magic Shoppe, Steve made notes about his routines. He still has those notes. And on that "American as apple pie" night in Garden Grove before vacation started, he had been planning to make sure we heard the right song to take with us to camp.

So, the next morning as the two-and-a-half-ton, canvas-covered truck departed from YMCA headquarters, we gazed over the tailgate at my mother. Obviously, she was feeling more desolate than we, watching her two favorite boys being shipped out like a couple of recruits, drafted and forced into servitude in a distant and strange place. We waved and happily began our latest excellent adventure.

As the truck, loaded to the hilt and slowly grinding through its gears, maneuvered up the winding road toward Camp Oceola, several boys began complaining of motion sickness. Three or four of them rushed to the back of the truck and began regurgitating across the tailgate. "I'm gonna puke," screamed a fat, red-headed kid.

"Upchuck city," sallied forth another.

"They're all barfing," Steve said, as he looked at me with a wild enthusiasm for the surprise beginning of our adventure. And so they were...spewing last-minute snacks in groups of twos and threes. I remember seeing a car full of nuns behind the truck. They were turning their windshield wipers on, only to smear the onslaught into a homogenized gunk, obstructing their vision as they quickly applied their brakes to avoid a second volley. Everyone laughed. We sat close to one another enjoying the show for a change. What warm, wonderful memories boys cherish. That was the first we ever knew there was a different meaning for the term honking!

The towering pines and fir trees of the San Bernardino Mountains finally relieved our nostrils with delightful aromas as we climbed out of the truck, carefully avoiding the residual droppings on the tailgate. Steve and I were partners, and it was no time at all before everyone at camp was aware of us. We were a team. Just the two of us. We didn't really eliminate anyone from hanging around with us, but it just didn't seem to happen.

We wound up bunking in a room with one other kid named Ivan. He seemed strange and shy, so we tried to be his friend. On the first day, we both noticed that he had a strange rash on his face. By the second day, it was looking pretty weird, so we were polite but a little more distant than we would have been under ordinary circumstances. Nevertheless, he became our friend, and we enjoyed talking with him in the evenings.

All the boys hung out in small cliques. Most of the groups were five or more. The head of the largest group of kids was "Mugsy." He was big for his age and had a thousand freckles. For some unknown reason he singled us out as the main target for his verbally pugnacious attacks. He tagged me with the nickname, "Goggles," because of my glasses, no doubt. Steve, on the other hand, was given the curious title of "Googlee Eyes" for no logical reason whatsoever. Because Ivan's rash was getting worse by the day, the others began to call him "Ivan the Terrible" or "Scarface." We didn't appreciate that and felt sorry for him. Ivan ended up staying in his room for the better part of the days and avoided the others as much as possible.

One of Mugsy's gang hit a baseball toward Steve in the afternoon of the third day. It was rolling slowly when it got close to him, and just as he was bending over to retrieve it, one of the bigger boys ran over and swooped it up, looking Steve directly in the eye. Sneering, he said, "I saved your life!" (as if in all sincerity). We laughed out loud thinking he must have been kidding. We immediately went into a routine reenacting his life-saving catch. I rolled the ball slowly on the ground as Steve—in typically exaggerated, slow-motion movements—finally picked it up and stated in a dramatic but goofy tone, "I saved your life!" I repeatedly thanked him loudly until we both began laughing uncontrollably. Our reenactment was really quite entertaining to us. We agreed that it would have worked better on the streets of "D-land." However, Mugsy's gang was not at all entertained by us making a fool of their guy in front of the rest of the campers.

We told Ivan the story of how we made fools of the older bullies. He smiled a little, but when we actually reenacted the scenario again, he laughed loud and hard and forgot his condition for the rest of the evening. All three of us spent the reminder of the night telling spooky stories. With kids, fear and humor are always a stimulating combination that teases and tempts emotion. Otherwise, there would be no explanation for why kids on a roller coaster are usually laughing away in hysterical happiness instead of peeing in their pants. Sometimes the simultaneous release is satisfying too, so I've heard.

The next day, Mugsy and his buddies were giving us the evil eye whenever we encountered them. We felt something was brewing but ignored it, laughing most of the time (and probably a little louder when we were around Mugsy and his bullies). Camp was a unique experience for us. Its regimen was probably the closet thing to military life Steve experienced until he filmed *Sergeant Bilko*. Of course, we both liked Phil Silver's *Sergeant Bilko* television show of the time, but neither Steve nor I were inclined to play soldier or army or anything like that. It just didn't fit with our personalities.

On the morning of the fifth day at camp, Ivan looked like he had wet leprosy. He had huge, oozing sores all over his face and was ashamed to even step outside our bunkhouse. We brought him his meals, and a counselor said his parents would be picking him up before camp was over. Then, in the mess hall, we heard the rumor that Mugsy and his gang were going to "get Googlee Eyes and Goggles after supper."

It became obvious from their clandestine whisperings and odd actions that there was some sort of plot in progress. We were a little concerned because we were not fighters; we were comedians, and this wasn't funny. After lunch, Mugsy and some of his crew strolled up to our table and leaned over, looking down at Steve in a menacing way. Mugsy's eyebrows knitted and his lips curled as he asked sarcastically, "Been sleeping with Scarface, Googlee Eyes? You know you're going to look like him pretty soon!"

Mugsy's gang laughed, and Steve boldly stood up and said loudly, "Well excuuuuse me!"—which attracted the counselors' attention, dispersing Mugsy's group. We laughed.

After the evening campfire, Steve and I decided it would be best for us to get back to the room immediately. When we got to the steps of the cabin, Mugsy and four other cronies were waiting. It was five big bullies against two small comedians, and they were forming a circle around us, allowing no escape. It looked like something out of an *Our Gang* movie. We stood there, speechless for a change, as Mugsy moved closer with his biggest buddy beside him. "Think you're real funny, huh?" He stood there with his hands on his hips and then reached over and shoved me.

Steve shouted, "Wait a minute, Mugwump!" causing Mugsy to spin around and face him. At this point, Steve was backed up against the bottom of the three steps leading into the cabin.

"Okay, you guys, we don't want trouble with you," I said as loudly as I could without shouting for help, but still hoping there were some counselors around to save us.

When no one came to help us, we knew that it was between us and them. It was showdown time. We didn't know what to expect next. We were hopelessly outnumbered and expecting the worst.

Just then, our roommate, Ivan, stepped out onto the porch holding a flashlight against his chest and pointing the light upward at his horrible scabby face. We were all mesmerized as he stood there in the eerie light, the oozing, pus-filled lesions now covering his entire face and neck. It was staggering. Just since that morning, his condition had taken a turn for the worst, and Mugsy and his goons were visibly shaken at the gruesome sight. Ivan then shouted menacingly, "Get away or I'll...touch all of you!" He boldly started down the steps, reaching out with his left hand and holding the flashlight up closer to his face with the right.

The effect couldn't have been better with Freddy Krueger himself. As soon as Ivan got within a foot of Mugsy, the bully backed away, making a guttural sound like an animal being tortured. Then he and his bewildered bully boys took off like so many little bats out of hell, their tails between their legs, Mugsy screaming and another boy bursting into tears. They ran in all directions and were gone in a few seconds.

We turned to Ivan, who had lowered the flashlight and was standing there laughing with us. He had spooked the hell out of those guys, but after the laughter there was a sadness about him. He looked alone and scared. We knew he was frightened about his condition. Steve reached out to shake his hand in thanks and demonstrate that we weren't afraid of his condition, that we considered him one of our friends. But the boy recoiled, not wanting Steve to touch him. Steve reached down fearlessly, took his hand and shook it anyhow, saying, "Thanks, Ivan. That was…great!" We all laughed ourselves to sleep again that night recounting the events of the evening.

The next day, Ivan's parents picked him up, and we thanked him again and waved goodbye as they drove off. I think we believed he was going home to die. He certainly looked like he had risen from the grave just to save us from the punks. Needless to say, the punks stayed completely clear of us for the balance of the time we were there. Even the counselors seemed to treat us as if we were contaminated, avoiding shaking hands with us as we finally headed over to the trucks to return to Orange County. Steve took one last opportunity to settle things with Mugsy by running towards him and reaching out as if to grab him. Mugsy was out of sight before Steve took five steps. Even the other punks laughed at Mugsy's blatant fear of Steve. His reign of terror was over; camp was over.

A day after we returned home from camp, Steve dropped by my house, and we had my mother and sisters rollicking with laughter as we told them about the events at camp. As Steve was leaving, I noticed his face seemed red—as if a rash were beginning to break out. I teased him about it, calling him "Stephen the Terrible." But when he looked in the mirror he said (very seriously), "I've got it!"

That afternoon I went with Steve and his mom, Mary Lee, to the doctor. And sure enough, he had it. Fortunately, it wasn't terminal. We were also relieved of the grief we had been sharing for Ivan. The real name of the affliction Steve and Ivan had contracted was impetigo. I don't know too much about the condition, but I understand that, thanks to modern medicine, it's rare in America these days. Within two days Steve's face was covered with pustules; he stayed home for a couple of weeks to recover. The way he looked, I didn't believe he would ever recover. Of course, like I said, this condition is not fatal; it just looks like it should be. It cleared up eventually, and "Googlee Eyes" was back to his normal, healthy-looking self.

I asked Steve about this incident a few years ago, and he said that had he known he was going to contract the disease, he might not have shook Ivan's hand. But I wonder. Steve was grateful for what Ivan had done, and Steve always pays his debts. That's just the way he has always operated. He's not afraid to voice his gratitude.

Since Steve spent most of his time in his room at home when he wasn't with me or at Disneyland, I thought he might need a little cheering up during his bout with impetigo. I got the old green hand out, and just after dark I stooped down right below his bedroom window and slowly slid the hand into view. It was deathly quiet, and then suddenly, I heard the voice from inside fearfully repeating, "Oh, God, I'll never do anything bad again, don't hurt me, pleeeeeese, don't hurt me!"

Chapter 6

LEAP OF FACE

"The test of a good religion is whether you can joke about it."
—G.K. Chesterton

W hen people in our school referred to me or to Steve, more likely than not they would refer to us in the same phrase: "Martin and Walker." Since we were together all the time, and we were always doing comedy, we gained a kind of dual reputation.

Those times in school are tattooed into my memory banks: "Steve Martin was here." Let me just say I remember well those four-thousand days hanging around with Steve. He would have succeeded at anything if he made up his mind to do it. He could have been a great athlete. He was really quite agile, fast, and muscular as a teenager. But he opted to avoid football and baseball because he was afraid he might break his fingers and not be able to do his magic tricks.

An impressive trick he learned early on was to roll a half dollar over his knuckles, deftly catching it beneath his fingers with his thumb, and pulling it back for repeated rolls over his knuckles. It's a tricky move, like so many sleight-of-hand moves he learned from his ongoing study of magic. He actually used this trick in *Dead Men Don't Wear Plaid*.

As far as being "Thee Steve Martin," I suppose he just has to take that on along with the other stereotypical euphemisms famous people must endure. I say Steve could have been anything he wanted, except a preacher. Although Steve had the stage ability to be a great preacher, I believe that is one occupation where he might not have found success. He would have felt hypocritical in that vocation. As a teenager and a young man, he could have been described most accurately as an agnostic—although, as a small boy he was always prim and proper in his Sunday-go-to-meeting clothes. He looked good but his mind was elsewhere. As a teenager, Steve rarely went to church and was never involved in organized religion of his own volition. He was more like a mystic: very private, intense, and introspective. At the precious age of 14, Steve and I set off on a little train trip. It turned out to be more of a revelation of sorts. From Garden Grove down through the wide-open spaces of El Toro and countless square miles of dry, rolling hills and finally San Diego, it was a true adventure for two young comics on the road for the first time.

We stayed in a dingy hotel Saturday night. Its general ambiance was that of the slums, by our middle class standards, but we had fun and went to bed late after a day of being a couple of "ramblin' guys." Sunday morning found us wandering down a nearby boulevard, when we were approached by a gaunt but polite man of about fifty years of age. He appeared to be ancient. (At the time he looked ancient to us, but as I write this I realize all too well that Steve and I are both in our fifties now. I wonder how we would define his looks today in these older and less critical eyes.) He was seeking young sailors to attend his local church. There were many sailors on the prowl, and they needed saving a lot more than we did. But instead he found us and gently intimidated us into attending his church, which was only blocks away.

My Methodist roots seemed to favor the idea, and Steve was used to being cajoled into attending service with his parents, so we fell right in line. We sat politely in the pew as the preacher began his sermon. Everything seemed pretty normal at first. But before we knew it, the people around us began mumbling "Amen" or "Hallelujah." This was not the kind of Baptist or Methodist sermon we were used to, and it began to make us a little bit uncomfortable. Soon the preacher's message grew louder and more potent, and the folks around us were barking religious praises and phrases from all parts of the room. Steve and I slowly looked at each other out of the corners of our eyes, wondering how the hell we could get out of there. This was not what we expected. Our host had us packed tightly against a huge woman with sweaty armpits and a triple chin (Steve whispered something about her eating Sunday School children). She stood up and started loudly blathering an endless stream of nonsensical goop. We looked directly at each other, now in total shock.We were ready to laugh but afraid. With our eyes wide open, we waited. A moment later, our skinny host grabbed our shoulders and wrestled us to the ground, slamming our knees into the thin layer of carpet over concrete. He was sweating profusely like the fat woman, and he had turned a kind of cherry red. We were scared. I looked up at the man and asked timidly,

"Uh, what's happening?"

"Tongues," he said, looking at me with stern eyes knitted tightly below bushy eyebrows. Then he snapped his head around again to watch the preacher and suddenly hollered, "Hallelujah!" His eyes were blazing. Then Steve looked at the fat woman and asked me,"What is she saying?"

"Either she's got two tongues or I think she swallowed the one she's got," I told him honestly. I really didn't have any idea what was going on or what we'd gotten ourselves into. Her flabby arms were high in the air now, and Steve was pinned tightly against her enormous leg. Suddenly her hand came down, clobbering Steve on the head and slamming it into the mushy cellulite of her large left leg. Then I couldn't help but laugh. "Who's yer girlfriend, Googlee Eyes?" He yanked his head away from her and scooted close to me. We estimate that our entire first "Gospel experience" must have lasted for two days, but in reality it was about an hour and a half. When it was over and we were allowed to step outside again, our host assumed the same warm and gentle manner he had when he first duped us into going to his church. He said, "Did you enjoy Thee sermon boys?" We lied. Then we bid him goodbye and headed for the train station. I wonder now whether the fat woman would have let us out of "thee"church if she had known that "thee" tasty little morsel bumping into her left leg was going to grow up to become THEE Steve Martin. Not long after that, Steve and I saw the movie, *Elmer Gantry*. We loved it, having experienced first-hand (in Steve's case—first-hand, left leg) the more exuberant aspects of a full Gospel Pentecostal church. When Steve starred in the movie entitled *Leap of Faith*, it seemed like a blend of *Elmer Gantry*, vaudeville, and his appreciation for a good carnival shyster, coupled with the memory of our excursion to the twilight side of a real Gospel church. I don't in any way mean to ridicule a Gospel church, but we were young kids and the difference for us was like night and day. We were caught off guard, like vegetarians accidentally eating a bite of meat hidden in a stew! We just bit off more religion than we could chew that day.

Steve with his wonderful grandmother

Chapter 7

ALDINI TO FLYDINI

"When Steve Martin did his Flydini routine on the Tonight Show,
I laughed so hard, the tears rolled down my legs!"
                                                    —Johnny Carson

Aldini, the owner of the Fantasyland Magic Shoppe, was a classic Jewish gentleman: short with a large nose, thin, and balding. He knew he had a prize when Steve worked for him. It was a time in Steve's life when his magnetic mind was demanding—receiving input and processing it at breakneck speed. He was so in tune with appreciating, and then tapping into, people's talents and expertise that I think he deserved the equivalent of a Ph.D. in magic from Mr. Aldini. While most people use perhaps ten percent of their brain, Steve Martin certainly used more. In some ways, he has been a man with two brains: one focused on entertaining and the other on business. Rarely do these two skills emanate from the same cerebral headquarters.

Steve was young, energetic, and willing to work with the public. He actually *loved* interacting with the public. I know. I also learned a lot from Aldini, through Steve. For instance, a lot of kids develop their own little language so they can mumble something to one of their friends around strangers and only their closest comrades will understand what they're really saying. We were no different. We also had a language, just between us. A few "fools" were let in on this sacred secret. (I'll explain "The Fools" later).

I attribute my introduction to "double talk" solely to Steve Martin and Aldini. Do you know what "double talk" is? It's when someone will walk up to a stranger and say, "Do you have an *arbigan?*" or "Can you *ferbin* the *fedelforinstaf?*" (Sounds like talking in tongues.) The stranger stares blankly for a minute and then says, "Huh?" You repeat, "*Arbigan, arbigan.*" Now they know that you are saying arbigan, and they aren't sure whether it's a word or you're nuts or they're nuts. So you say, "Forget it. But how 'bout a *dow* for a *booberday?*"

Well, that throws them right out into left field. We gleaned much from the people who became our double-talking targets. There are experts in double talk, and you will swear they are really saying something, even when you're told it's a sham. I must admit, we acquired quite a skill by mastering the art of double talk. Of course, the true experts are so good that you can't distinguish which words are real and which ones are gibberish. There were moments when we mastered that dubious talent. Phrases like "*dow for a booberday*" and words like "*arbigan,*" "*crebin,*" and "*rebuff*" were words Steve taught me. We made some up and used these ambiguous terms for the best purpose of all: to make people laugh. (Mostly at each other!)

High above the pristine orange groves and mundane tract houses of Orange County, towered the three-hundred-foot Materhorn mountain of Disneyland. It was, clearly, the most discernible landmark in Anaheim. There was no Tower of Power, no Angel Stadium, no massive hotels lining the roads on both sides of the Magic Kingdom. There was just a replica of the mighty Swiss Materhorn, with all its artificial snow and a twinkling warning light for small aircraft at night. The only objects in the clear Anaheim sky that reached higher than the Materhorn in those days were the nightly fireworks. Like clockwork, every evening at 9:00 p.m. they would thrill thousands of D-land guests, residents for miles away, and, of course, Steve and Morris.

There was always a long line to ride the Materhorn during business hours. It was a fun ride, like a roller coaster, only with the reassurance that it was built by Walt Disney and, therefore, was safe and sound. When we got off early from our jobs, we would wander through the wonderland Disney had created. With warm, Southern California breezes and mystical fantasies of life throbbing in our blood, night after night we would set out to "follow some chicks." We were pretty lousy at picking them up, but, God, could we follow! Every once in a while we would go to the dance in Tomorrowland. I remember dancing with everybody's dreamboat, Annette Funicello (one of the original Mouseketeers). In retrospect, we must have been exceptionally obnoxious. Years later, I was delighted to see Dan Akroyd and Steve do the "Czech Brothers" routine on *Saturday Night Live*. It reminded me so much of us in those days. There we were, early teens with fresh pimples. We had embarrassingly humorous hormones dictating our every move. Inevitably, after we were tired of following chicks, we would focus on something we had real aptitude at: serious double talk.

One night, in the long winding line to the entrance of the Materhorn ride, Steve began to tell me a story. He spoke loud and clear and other folks in line squeezed closer to hear what was obviously going to have a good punch line. They pushed in even tighter as the story went on its merry way. Finally, when the crowd was fraught with anticipation, Steve burst out with, "He looked at her and she said, 'I'm a *dow* for a *booberday*!'" Of course, this brought me to the ground with guffaws. Steve, at this point, could not control himself and laughed in a manner that was, clearly, the beginning of the wild and crazy phenomenon that he eventually innovated: slapping his legs joyously.

The people surrounding us stood lamely looking on, wanting to enjoy this punch line. Some backed away, some smiled at our hysterics, and occasionally (we did this prank a lot), someone would venture to inquire of me, "What did he say?"

Gaining my composure swiftly, I would look at the person as if astonished that they would butt into our conversation. Sometimes I would muster up my angry look and say coldly, "What's it to ya?"

Now, to Steve Martin and me, this was funny. Whether anybody—and I mean anybody else—thought it was funny or not, I'm not sure. But we did. We didn't hurt anybody, and it was not a practical joke. It was just our way of doing very funny things that at first hearing weren't really funny. At least not to anyone else. The truth is, if people had known what we were really doing, they too might have thought it was funny. Every once in a while, I could tell someone knew that we were putting them on. A hint of a smile would appear, and they would enjoy it, too.

These were Steve's comedy roots. In the beginning, in the seventies, he would have manic attacks of "happy feet" and he would often do an abstract and uncontrolled dance around the stage. He did hundreds of shows with virtually no response— people sat just in the audience and simply stared. Before Steve was a stand-up star, he would wear props from Disneyland such as bunny ears, a fake nose and glasses, or a ridiculous balloon hat. If they wouldn't laugh, he would say his now famous, "WELL, EXCUUUUUUSE ME!" Absolutely no one would react, and he would follow up with, "We're having some fun now!"

Steve's humor was too off-the-wall and the timing wasn't quite right, then. When people started appreciating his strange approach to humor, you could see them responding in small groups in clubs across the country. They showed up with Steve's trademark arrows through their heads or wearing bunny ears. It was the beginning of a cult following that was unparalleled in comedic history. Men thought he was hilarious, and woman loved him as if he were a James Dean or Brad Pitt. Had he been a womanizer, the lines of groupies would have been long. He was a major hit with the women—quite different from those days when we wandered the park and couldn't get anywhere with any of the girls, no matter what we tried.

We weren't really failures with girls, but at thirteen or fourteen, we didn't know what "scoring" meant. It was that welling, youthful semen forming inside our young, maturing bodies, telling us to "follow!" So follow we did. And there were always cute little *Aardvarks* to follow. By the way, I'm not referring to the African miniature pig variety. *"Aardvarks"* was part of our double talk, and it did have a meaning. You see, we didn't want to be just a couple of regular guys, we wanted to be special. On occasion, to look particularly foxy, we would wear our special matching shirts. They were neat, bright green shirts with black collars and open chests, collars up. We were hot stuff! Flaunting it! Legends in our own minds! My mother hand made the shirts and frankly, we thought we were the coolest thing happening at the Pavilion Dance Floor on Main Street, Disneyland U.S.A.

As with many close friends, we at a young age had fabricated a language with real words but our own meaning; we used them in "special situations." Sometimes we used this vernacular to communicate our thoughts about girls. For instance, if a "well endowed" young girl would walk by us, Steve would turn to me and comment, "Did you notice the *ferbin* at the *graduation*?" Now, we both could see that this girl had large breasts, but having our own code word for them made it a little more fun. Steve knew that he had commented on her boobs, and I knew he had, but the girl smiled glibly and walked on. If a girl was flat-chested, one of us would mention something like, "No *graduation* for that *Aardvark*." Here again, we both knew the facts, but enjoyed talking out loud. The code word "*Aardvark*" meant good-looking girl, and "*Graduation*" meant breasts. Yes, we were clever, witty, young, stupid, immature, sexist, indolent and gloriously happy!

We always loved playing with words. One time, Steve came to me and said, "I've got a great new word Aldini told me. I think it's a Jewish word."

"Great. What is it?"

"*Tookas*," he whispered, devilishly.

"What does it mean?"

"Asssss," said Steve, dragging out the s's to make it sound as dirty as he possibly could. I don't think we could ever quite manage to use the word correctly. Our games were always just for fun. A little "*Aardvark*" would stroll by Steve and he would turn towards me and mumble, "*Tookas* a long time to see the *regal*." "*Regal*" meant legs. All these words constantly wound up surfacing in our daily jabber.

We used our girl-describing secret code all the way through high school. Our language was augmented by new words like "*Heola*" and "*Vignola*." These words became part of a useless ritual while we were in high school. When Steve and I were in our school bus crossing the railroad tracks, there was a sign posted near the tracks that simply read, "*Vignola*." It was here that we would glance about, tip our heads, repeat the word quietly, and quickly touch our right hands to our foreheads, bringing them to our laps in a circular gesture. This, of course, meant absolutely nothing, but if someone saw Steve or me do this, it was our way of letting them know that they should keep their eyes on us—and they did. There were signs like this for the engineers at most crossings, though I still have no idea exactly what they meant.

I have to admit that I do remember these silly antics far better than most of the information drilled into us by our needle-nosed teachers in school.

And you know, in recalling those mystical nights at Disneyland with my pal Steve, I'm surprised how much detail I remember. We walked those brilliantly lit streets so many times. When I close my eyes, I can still see everything as if it were yesterday—the big key shape of Main Street branching off into the many exciting lands of fantasy and adventure. It was here that Steve came up with his ideal of the perfect girl. He summed her up in one phrase: "Pony tails and peddle pushers." As I've mentioned, Steve and I were latecomers to the sex game. It was after high school before either of us were escorted down the "primrose lane." Oh, we both did our share of "humping and bumping" in the drive-ins with hot-blooded female peers, but none of us succumbed. You know how it is. It's not that we didn't want to get into the whole sex thing, but I guess it's all part of a larger plan and happens when fate has ordained the date.

My father was gone for the majority of my school years. The oil fields were his life, and he traveled a great deal to provide sustenance for our family. As I've mentioned, Steve's father wasn't very close to him at that time, which caused Steve to spend most of his time at our house (much to my delight). Therefore, we had no male role-models in our life, but we did have each other. And the truth be told, we didn't know nothin'. Comedy, that's what we knew—and I wouldn't trade those days of humor for anything. It was a rare opportunity to learn and to share the joy of being funny.

Steve's high school sweetheart was Linda Rasmussen or, to her friends, Ratty. Ratty was an energetic girl with a slender, attractive body and short hair, and she thought Steve was very funny. I know Steve really cared for her. After high school, when he was working at Knott's Berry Farm in the Bird Cage Theater, he met Stormie. (Today she is Stormie Omartian, married to a record producer.) She was a provocative blonde, and Steve fell hopelessly in love with her. Unfortunately, it didn't work out and Steve was crushed—I mean really crushed. But what stuck with him was a book she told him to read. It was Somerset Maugham's *The Razor's Edge*, which sent Steve on a journey of his own into the world of philosophy at Long Beach State.

As much as time seemed to stand still when we were kids, life does move forward. But I know that Steve never forgot those times. I often see how he taps into every experience in his life as he boldly steps forward, achieving greater and greater success in every endeavor he focuses on. Although Steve remembers his past, he never goes back. For example, when he finished being a stand-up comedian, he just flat finished. He was *numero uno*, probably the highest paid comedian in the history of Las Vegas at that time. I remember when he did a two-week gig once and made a cool million dollars. But when asked if he would do stand-up comedy again, he said simply, "I've already done that."

As close as we were, there were moments when Steve would just wander off to be alone. These moments were rare, and I remember watching him and wondering how he could possibly pause from our antics and consider doing anything else. As the years moved on, I noticed that these moments of solitude became longer and longer. When he enrolled at Long Beach State, he chose to study philosophy. Although he found great hope and earned straight A's, before long he realized that he was going nowhere with philosophy. He finally came face to face with the reality that studying was endless, with no clear answers or conclusions, just a lot of gray matter. Except for art. Steve believes in art. He dropped out of college when Mason Williams offered him a job writing for the Smothers Brothers.

Steve found great excitement writing comedy. Plus, he made $500 a week. Then, to top it off, he received an Emmy Award at twenty-one for his writing on that show. I, too, received an offer I could not refuse: I got drafted and made $70 a month! Not quite the same as my pal Steve, but it was a regular gig for almost two years and I got to travel abroad and see the world. Ultimately, Steve now finds happiness at the extreme end of the humor stick. He can sit in his spacious mansion and revel in the cool precisionist beauty of his Charles Sheeler canvas or the abstract expressionist passion of his Franz Kline.

Carl Reiner, who feels he "discovered" Steve as a movie star and produced Steve's first movie *The Jerk*, compares him to a character Steve still performs occasionally. I saw Steve do this character one night in the late eighties. I was invited to a taping in Brentwood, near Los Angeles, with Diane Sawyer, who was doing a *60 Minutes* segment about Steve. That evening we went to watch Steve perform at The Magic Castle. This club is a Mecca for magicians from around the world and has a very exclusive clientele. In order to visit the Castle, you must either be a member or be invited by a member. Of course, Steve is one of those loyal magicians and has never lost his love of the *leger domain*.

After an awesome performance by Lance Burton, an outstanding magician, it was Steve's turn to perform. I'm sure the unsuspecting audience felt sorry for the act that had to follow Burton. And then a voice offstage announced, "The Magic Castle is proud to present the amazing Flydini." Instantly, Aldini snapped into my mind, and I told Diane Sawyer quickly about Steve's Magic Shoppe mentor. The similarity stopped, however, when Steve came onstage. The audience went wild as he, with greatly exaggerated care, unzipped his pants and began pulling out a succession of objects from the fly of his trousers. Carefully, and with the poise of a master magician, he withdrew eggs, a telephone book, endless colored scarves tied together (I kept expecting a large green rubber hand), and finally, a Pavarotti puppet that sang *Pagliacci*. It was an extraordinary performance, which I have since seen on television. It will go down in history as one of the great comedy performances of all time.

That night, I met Steve's new wife, Victoria Tennant. Steve originally met Victoria on the set of *All of Me*, the movie in which he created a credible character in an incredible fix. Lily Tomlin had invaded his body, but I think Victoria stole his heart. By the time he made *L.A. Story* with her, he was quoted as saying, "My mature film career started with *All of Me* and ends with *L.A. Story*." But things change.

He introduced me to her that night as his old friend.

"How does it feel to be the new Mrs. Steve Martin?" I asked happily, finding myself pleased that Steve had found a lady to love.

"I would prefer you call me by my real name, Victoria Tennant," she responded with an impertinent smile, looking directly past me.

I leaned over to Steve and said, "This Aardvark is one cool cucumber, Steve. Are you sure you want to keep her?"

"She's alright," he responded with a grin. "You just have to get to know her." (I could tell he was hooked.)

I never did, however, and evidently, when Steve finally did, there were irreconcilable differences. I know he fell head over heels in love with her, and since their split-up Steve has spent countless, lonely hours in the company of his art collection. He is extremely sensitive, and I don't know if he will ever find a soul mate. When I mentioned having kids to Victoria that night, she practically cringed, explaining that they would never have kids. "Kids would ruin our careers."

I hope Steve finds the right woman. Obviously, he could have his pick, but when it comes to women, he is as obsessively discriminating as he is with his art collection. He respects women and holds them all in high esteem, and I don't think romance has ever been a flight of fancy for him. Anyhow, I'm sure that whatever Flydini pulls out of his pants from now on…he won't be pulling anything out for Victoria Tennant.

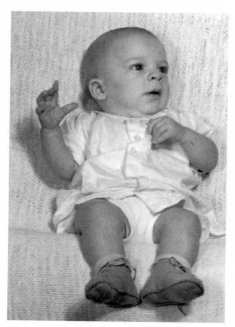

Steve at 3 months

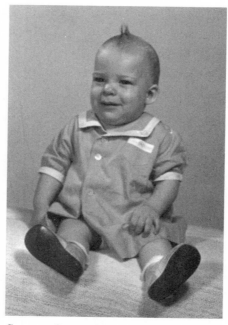

Steve at 8 months

Steve age 3

Steve age 4 in Waco, Texas

Steve with father Glenn

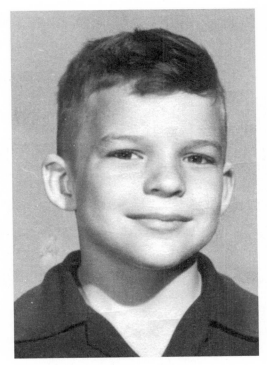

Steve in 4th grade

Steve 6th grade

Morris 6th grade

Morris & Steve, The Gopher Boys, with my sister, Marsha

Morris as Steve's Assist, "Babo of the Orient"

The Gopher Boys: Morris & Steve

The Gopher Boys

Chapter 8

THE GOPHER BOYS

"Man is the only animal that blushes—or ought to."
—Mark Twain

Ayata yata yata, yata yata yata yata, yata yata ya ya ya. Was that a sentence? Hard to say. It's not double talk. Perhaps with a melody, it would make more sense. For us, this was the opening for our debut as "The Gopher Boys." Strictly vaudeville in nature, we were appropriately adorned with bow-ties, vests, and derby hats from (you guessed it!) Disneyland.

Ah yes, The Gopher Boys. "Because all the girls gofer us" was Steve's line.

"Ever been gofered by a girl?" was mine. Nobody ever laughed at that one, except Steve.

It was our freshman year in Rancho Alamitos High School. Great prospects were hidden within the mystery of the eminent decade—the 1960s were upon us. Pat Boone was history, and a group of leather-clad lads were forming a rock band in Liverpool. John F. Kennedy was soon to be president, and a generation of love-ins and druggies was just around the corner. A sick and purposeless war was brewing in a small, unknown, Southeast Asian country. People we would meet in the next four years would die in that war. I would visit that country as a USO performer, and Steve would climb to super-stardom before the decade expired.

We bowed our heads reverently as we crossed the railroad tracks, mumbling, *"Vignola,"* and headed for our first day at Rancho. We were fresh from three years of getting away with murder, in and out of class, and it appeared that the comedy crime wave would continue into our higher education. The difference at this point was that we were beginning to look more like adults and were coming into contact with more opportunities to perform onstage. We had been transferred to a different school and therefore knew even fewer people than if we had gone to Garden Grove High like other students from Lampson Intermediate. I can't say any of this really phased us at all. I only had one friend, and I guess Steve only had me. So we charged on. We were known as "Martin and Walker." We were inseparable.

"Hey, how ya doin', Martin?" people would ask me; or "How's it goin', Walker?" they would ask Steve.

Naturally, we loved it. Recognition for our nonsensical antics. What an opportunity. When we heard there were to be auditions for a school vaudeville show, it only took us a split second to know it was time for Martin and Walker to emerge. Slightly nervous, we did our best. Shortly thereafter, we received word we had been accepted by the drama department to be the leading olio act. Steve came up with some terrific old tunes, and we proceeded to learn them together:

> I was floating down the old green river
> on the good ship Rock and Rye,
> but I floated too far, got stuck on a bar; I was
> there all alone, wishing I were at home....
> The ship went down with the captain and crew,
> there was only one thing left to do:
> I had to drink the whole green river,
> try to get back home to you....

or
On the Old Fall River Line,
On the Old Fall River Line,
I kinda fell for Susie's kinda bunk
And Susie kinda fell for mine;
So we went to see the parson and he tied us tight as twine.
Oh, I wish, oh, Lord, I'd fell overboard on the Old Fall River
Old Fall River, Old Fall River Line.
Not the Atchison, Topeka, or the Santa Fe
But the Old Fall River Line.

Then we would slide into a little soft-shoe routine. I had previously had dance lessons in Long Beach, California from Bobby (the leader of the original Mouseketeers), and, therefore, I actually knew a few steps. Steve hadn't had any formal dance training, but he was exceptionally well coordinated. And when Steve decided to accomplish something, it was academic— a done deal. The world saw his advanced dance steps as he shuffled his way through *Pennies From Heaven* many years later. The movie was a classic failure. However, to watch it now still simply amazes me. Even Gene Kelly would have been proud of Steve's steps.

We managed to put together a great act. Little did we know that it was the seniors' show. We just assumed that all of those who were auditioning just happened to be older. When the drama teacher who had picked us for the show found out that we were only freshman, he acknowledged that it didn't matter. He would break tradition and let Steve and me do our thing in the show— and we surely did.

One of my very favorite routines that emerged from this extremely creative period in our lives dealt with an old college song. A classic fraternity tune entitled, "The Whiffenpoof Song." The lyrics began like this:

"From the tables down at Morrie's, to the place where Louie dwells, to the dear old temple bar we love so well..."

We never professed to be singers then, and it really didn't make any difference since we had no intention of doing a serious rendition. So as I would sing, "From the tables down at Morrie's..." Steve would sing, in unison, "From the tables down at Louie's..."

Then we would pause, look curiously at one another, and continue. We would sing, again in unison, "...to the place where Louie dwells..." And Steve would sing, "...the place where Morrie dwells..." It was a good routine, and from the beginning, it was easy to maintain the audience's attention. I'd sing, "...to the dear old temple bar we love so much..." Steve would sing, "...we love so well..."

Here again, we would pause and stare at each other a little quizzically and just a bit annoyed. As the song goes on, it eventually comes to the part that is probably most recognizable to the general public. I would sing, "We are poor little lambs who have lost our way, baa, baa, baa..." Steve would sing, "We are poor little cows who have lost our way, moo, moo, moo..."

We would nervously glance at one another and, in an attempt to rectify the problem, I would sing, "We are poor little pigs who have gone astray, oink, oink, oink..." At the same time Steve would sing, "...poor little cows, moo, moo, moo, moo..." And then I would sing, "Oink!" And he would sing, "Baa!" And I would continue to Moo!

The confusion would continue until the end, at which point it came out completely wrong. But at no time did we lose the melody, in spite of the blatant mix-ups. Steve and I were delighted with this idea of stumbling through a song and completing it while getting belly laughs the entire time.

Most of our Gopher Boys' material was, as I have mentioned, vaudeville. "And now we'll sing that old favorite, 'Get Out of the Wheat Field, Granny, You're Going Against My Grain.' " Or, "When They Operated On Father, They Opened Mother's Male."

I heard Steve use one of our old lines on TV a few years ago. "It was raining cats and dogs. I know, because I stepped in a poodle." It was part of Steve's "Show for Dogs."

We were well primed for that act by having seen Wally Boag do his vaudeville routine at the Golden Horse Theater in Disneyland, time after time.

Steve has made well over 500 television appearances, perhaps 40 of them on *The Johnny Carson Show* alone. After hosting the show several times, the offer was discreetly made to have Steve take over for Johnny when the time came. This was long before Jay Leno was in the running. Steve wasn't about to commit to a regular schedule like that. It's somewhat of a shame, because Steve's greatest talent in the entertainment arts is his ability to ad-lib. All the prefabricated routines and even his wide range of roles at the box office don't demonstrate the real comedic talent Steve possesses. One night on *The Johnny Carson Show*, Steve read from a phone book, reading average names and getting no laughs. But before long, he put on the old "arrow through the head" and the names became funnier. By the end of his routine, he was waving a rubber chicken and demanding, "Well, excuse me, I didn't write this junk!"

I had a unique perspective on Steve as he slowly grew in fame and fortune. During his early years in show biz, I was on the road with my wife, Lynn, doing three or four shows a day for schools and communities around the country. We were moving from rooms at Motel Six (when they were still six dollars a night) to campgrounds in the back of a handmade camper. I used to laugh to myself how Steve was climbing the ladder of entertainment success, and we were still out there plugging away and broke. On frigid winter highways, making barely enough money to get to the next gig, I watched Steve hundreds of times on TV as he battled his way to the top. I was so happy that his talent and wit enabled him to thrive. Occasionally, I would go to see him in concert. If we were appearing within a hundred miles, we would drive out of our way to watch Steve perform live and would usually visit with him before and after his show.

Every time I caught his act, I would see the "Wild and Crazy Guy" making people laugh insanely over his *schtick*. And the money. Watching Steve make all that money was mind-boggling and somehow gratifying—but not surprising. We both came from similar middle-class upbringings, and we had to work for most of the things we ever bought for ourselves as kids. To see Steve make it—and keep making it, bigger and bigger each season— made me so proud of him. From stage, to television, to movies, nothing seemed to impede his progress. His agents and managers fell by the wayside as he moved beyond them to better and better teams. I don't mean to say he treated them poorly or dumped them; on the contrary, Steve's dealings have always been extraordinarily good with his business associates. But just as he used to drag three or four kids down the Rugby field, he would move forward and upward relentlessly. When the time came to change management teams, he could make those tough changes decisively.

Steve is a marvelously practical individual and a human calculator. I don't mean that in a negative way. Quite the opposite. He calculates his every move and, I might add, his every penny. One doesn't acquire a world-famous, 19th-century American art collection with paintings by Mary Cassatt and Winslow Homer by being slow. One doesn't even acquire such assets by inheritance. Steve's obsession with collecting is merely another indicator of a mind that never rests.

Kathy Westmoreland was a wonderfully attractive and vibrant girl who arrived at school from Steve's home state of Texas. The first day she arrived, she strolled by our classroom window and immediately stole our hearts. Steve and I were equally attracted to her petite form and friendly smile. And believe me, that girl knew how to be friendly. She was sincerely giving and loving to every soul she met. Kathy possessed the most incredible soprano voice I have ever heard. Her father had taught a choir in Texas, and both she and her sister, Melody, could sing like birds. Steve took voice training from Kathy's father for a short time. I recall Mr. Westmoreland telling me that, with a little persistence, Steve could have developed his voice and become a successful opera singer. Kathy did work with the Metropolitan Opera early in her career and performed her first aria when she was 18.

After high school, Steve began doing an act with Kathy. I remember arriving at the Bird Cage Theater one night to see Steve and Kathy. They really were good together. Steve dug some of their material out of an old vaudeville book. One of their routines went like this:

Steve: "It's a beautiful evening."

Kathy: "Righto!"

Steve (*with more fervor*): "It's a great audience!"

Kathy (*even louder*): "Righto!"

Steve (*overflowing with enthusiasm*): "It'll be a great show!"

Kathy (*now shouting*): "Righto!"

Steve would then flash back at her and ask, "What's the matter with you?"

Mimicking great pain, Kathy would point to her foot and stutter, "You are stepping on my right toe!"

I'm sure no one in that antique theater, laughing at Steve and Kathy, would have figured she would become Elvis Presley's lead singer for ten years and Steve would become the "wild and crazy" superstar.

Steve and I had several opportunities to work with Kathy in high school. At one variety show, the three of us did a take-off on Peter, Paul, and Mary. Kathy wore her long black hair piled high on top of her head, and she sported a small goatee. Steve and I wore long blond wigs. I don't remember the songs we did, but I do remember what a great visual effect those costumes had. Everyone called us Peter, Paul, and Almond Joy.

Writers and directors always like to refer to Steve's "physical comedy." He can be more animated on camera than Roger Rabbit. Perhaps this is a reflection of the melodramatic influence we felt as we watched Wally Boag and eventually created our routine as the Gopher Boys. In recent years, Steve has blended his "physical comedy" with a deep desire to perform more dramatic material. *Father of the Bride* was a sensational hit, and four years later, under the direction of Charles Shyer and Nancy Meyers of The Meyers–Shyers Company, he starred in *Father of the Bride II*.

Charles and Nancy wrote the screenplay for *Father of the Bride II*. Charles said this about working with Steve: "Steve Martin is so versatile that he can do physical comedy as well as verbal and emotional comedy, so you're able to write stuff for him you'd never write for other actors."

This movie came about because of the clever writing of Shyer and Meyers and the brainstorming of Steve's co-star and close friend, Diane Keaton. Together, they created the new plot, which was based on *My Little Dividend*, the old sequel to the original *Father of the Bride* with Spencer Tracy.

Chapter 9

BLAST FROM
THE PAST

"May God defend me from my friends; I can defend myself against my enemies."
—Voltaire

We were thirteen, almost fourteen, when puberty began to set in rapidly. I was either at Steve's house or he was at mine. (For the most part, the latter was the situation.) My twin sister was maturing much faster than either one of us. She was built like a woman, and neither man nor boy escaped her charms. Steve was neither man nor boy; he was more "boy-man" at that point. He noticed Marsha as much as anyone did. Steve and Marsha enjoyed one another and were good friends. Steve, being the generous friend he was, would allow Marsha to scratch his back for five cents an hour. Steve had long since planted a seed deep in his ever-active subconscious mind that if he ever acquired great wealth, he would have to be a sagacious businessman and watch every penny.

Money was a constant obsession in those days (because we had none), and the desire to have an abundance of it was at the heart of his craving. Being a coin collector as a young boy was merely the beginning of Steve's life of earning, saving, and collecting money. In the movie, *A Simple Twist of Fate*, Steve plays the part of a miser. Although he claims the movie was based on the book, *Silas Marner*, I did not perceive a great deal of similarity. In any event, in that movie he let gold coins trickle through his fingers as he reveled in his apparent secret wealth. There was an element of truth in those moments: Steve had to be tight to make it as big as he has financially. Money was never given to him as a kid. For every action there is an equivalent reaction, so he made money, a lot of money.

Back in the good old days, however, we had no money. And we had no guns. Except on that fateful day...

My older sister, Lesley, was seventeen and dating a sailor named Larry, who was twenty. Marsha was dating a sailor named Chuck Kendall, who was seventeen. My father was gone at the time, working in Iraq. It might seem like I'm telling more about my family than Steve's, but the truth of the matter is that Steve was like a part of our family and we were his.

God knows, thirteen is a confusing age for anyone. But I was being raised with three women and really didn't have any male companionship other than Steve. Steve and I never played war, guns, shoot 'em up, or even cowboys and Indians. I had never held a gun, toy or real, in my hands before that day.

Chuck had been on a naval cruise and had just arrived from Long Beach. Without delay, he and Larry coaxed a friend to drive them to Garden Grove to visit us. The girls were excited, and I found these guys to be an interesting lot whom I got along with pretty well. It turned out that the friend who brought them to our house was an immense fellow, about six-foot nine inches tall. He was thin, with a ruddy complexion to match his straw-like, red hair. Quite frankly, he was homely. His teeth were crooked, and he smelled bad. His name was "Stretch."

The sailors had a few beers under their belts and were feeling loose. I probably had a few gulps, too. Chuck said to me, "Hey, Morris, you and your buddy, Steve, wanna see my new shotgun?"

"Sure," I said, excited.

"No!" barked Steve, beginning to look very uncomfortable and backing up slightly.

"Just a minute and I'll get it," Chuck drawled, as he casually walked over and picked it up, with a toothpick hanging out of the corner of his mouth.

"Here it is," said Chuck as he withdrew the long-barreled shotgun from its leather case.

Like I said, I didn't care about guns, but here were these "men" showing me this genuine shotgun, and I couldn't help but be interested. Chuck flashed the gun around and slowly opened a box of shells, building the anticipation. "It's a four-ten-gauge shotgun," he mumbled in a macho fashion as he dropped a shell in the chamber.

"I wouldn't do that if I were you," Steve muttered from the other side of the room.

"I've handled lots of rifles in boot camp," Chuck assured him. "Me and Larry and Stretch, we had to learn to be real careful." He raised his eyelid and pushed his bottom lip forward.

"Well, that…that's fine," Steve stuttered, "…but…" he trailed off, and seemed almost paralyzed, standing up against the living room door. It must have been more than the sight of the weapon that backed him up in fear. In retrospect, it looked like a premonition.

Meanwhile, my mother was in the kitchen with Lesley and Stretch. Stretch was making an overstuffed tuna fish sandwich and getting a glass of milk, and my sister Marsha was in the den.

"Well, it's loaded, so you have to be real careful," Chuck stated with all the pride and confidence of a kid with his new toy on Christmas Day. "Would you like to check it out?" he asked me as he held the long-barreled shotgun out with one arm.

"Hey, all right!" I said, as if I knew what the hell I was doing.

"I wouldn't, if I were you," Steve repeated nervously. It's safe to say at this point that Steve was terrified. But not me. I grabbed the rifle. Sorting through my vast knowledge of firearms, I subconsciously retrieved this valuable fact: If you put the safety mechanism on, you cannot pull the trigger. It will not fire with the safety switch on. I knew that. So I slowly slid my hand over the stock and around the trigger area. Finally, I found it—a simple little mechanism that renders a lethal weapon harmless with a flick of the finger. Presto! With no one seeing me, I had put the safety on. I raised the huge shotgun and pointed it at Chuck.

He laughed. "You better be careful," he said calmly. He wasn't worried because he knew he had put the safety on before he handed it to me.

"I know what I'm doing," I stated quite confidently, knowing full well that I had moved the safety switch securely in position. I wheeled around and aimed the shotgun directly at Steve. He began stuttering again and his face had gone sheet-white. I pulled gently on the trigger, thinking, "With the safety on, you can squeeze this thing 'til the cows come home and nothing will happen." I squeezed a little harder, shouting, "Hey, Steve. Bang! Bang! You're dead!"

Then I glanced up to see Steve, waving his hands wildly. His animated body was contorted as he attempted to get me to point the gun away from him. I was almost ready to laugh. He was stuttering incoherently and frantically signaling to point the gun the other way. And now the memory comes flooding back to me as clearly as if it were yesterday. Although it all happened in an instant, I still see it in slow motion in my memory. I swung the blunderbuss around just as Steve took a dive out of the entrance-way and onto the kitchen floor.

Immediately after I swung the shotgun away from Steve and towards the naugahyde curtains, it fired! No more than a split second from the time I was pointing it at Steve to the time it went off and there was a forty-inch hole blasted through the accordion curtain!

I dropped the gun and ran towards the curtain, accompanied by my shrieking, screaming sisters. I yanked the shredded material apart in the middle. The six-foot mirror on the wall was shattered above a long, white couch. There in the middle of the couch sat Stretch. He had just settled down with a big tuna fish sandwich sitting on a plate in his left hand and a glass of milk in his right. He was frozen in shock. A huge piece of mirror rested point down in the milk like an arrowhead, and he and his sandwich sparkled like a Christmas tree. There was shattered mirror all over the place. And there was a gaping hole at least two feet in diameter in the dry wall behind the couch.

Steve finally poked his head around the corner. Still petrified, he stared at me and screamed, "You almost killed me!" It was true. I almost did. It was stupid, and I know Steve didn't hold it against me, but I believe it was probably his closest call with the grim reaper. Of course, it's hard to say. He has worked and lived in Hollywood for a long time, and one meets all kinds of strange and dangerous characters there.

My heart was in my throat that day, and my head was up my ass. (In fact, I don't think they have ever been as close to one another since.) How careless and stupid I was! I loved Steve more than a brother, and the fact that I had almost blasted him into a thousand pieces left me stuttering. There was nothing humorous about it at the time. When Steve left my house that day, he was mumbling to himself, and he didn't talk to me for two weeks. I would see him in school and around town, but he still looked white and couldn't seem to talk directly to me.

The next time I saw Steve with a gun was in *Three Amigos*, when he thought the banditos were shooting blanks at him and he took a hit in the arm. He reassured Martin Short and Chevy Chase that it was just a blank, but the expression on his face when he touched the wound and saw the blood was priceless. It was as if the pain had not occurred until the realization of it was proven to him with the blood as evidence. Shock can cause amazing changes in our response patterns when our adrenaline goes goofy.

That day in our living room there must have been divine intervention, because it was so close. As Steve dove for the floor and I swung the shotgun around, it went off. The blast occurred a split second before Steve hit the ground. If he had died that day, it would have changed history. Everything would have happened differently. Who knows, maybe Pee Wee Herman would have been the comic genius of the century instead of just another jerk-off.

Now, I could tell you that Steve's hair turned white that day, but it didn't. The truth of the matter is that for as long as I've known Steve's family, his mother and father also had gray (now white) hair. It's just a Martin family trait. On the other hand, I remember one of Steve's girlfriends, Teri Garr, telling me about a rare night years later. Steve was quite freaked out while he was stoned on some rather potent pot, and she said he looked like he had seen a ghost. She thought his hair color changed to white more rapidly after that experience.

Steve has smoked very little pot in his life, and his experiences with alcohol are also quite limited. He tried the pot scene and others, but realized more quickly than most that it was okay for him to sample dope, but he didn't want to *be* a dope. He didn't mind being a "fool," but he never wanted to be a dope. That's why Mick Jagger and Steve—who are close to the same age—look so different. Jagger, despite all his charisma, looks like somebody did hit him with a shotgun–bull's-eye! Steve's complexion is as smooth as a newborn baby's butt. He has somehow managed to keep living a very straight life, despite all the pressures of fame. He was just born smart. This is another reason why success has not frazzled him to the core, as it's done to so many famous personalities.

Steve was the only one who sensed the incredible terror that day with the shotgun. He managed to make me turn—just before I realized I had taken the safety switch off! Chuck was sure I wouldn't get hurt because he had secured the safety, and I was so sure because I thought *I* had. Steve was only sure of one thing. I can still hear him gasping, "I wouldn't do that if I were you!" And you know what? He wouldn't have. He wouldn't have touched that gun. But me, I foolishly blasted the entire room to smithereens.

One time while my wife, Lynn, and I were touring in the South, Steve was on a concert tour nearby, and we managed to catch his show. We had coffee together afterwards and laughed about the near-death experience with the shotgun. Steve still looked a bit uncomfortable when recalling that incident. I suppose it's because he plans out everything so well—and death was not part of his plan at that time in his life. He still doesn't own a gun, and he's still the marvelous pacifist I grew up with. To understand the extremely sensitive side of Steve Martin, you need only see him with a puppy or a kitten. (And I don't mean in his cat-juggling act.) There is a great inner peace in this quiet man.

One night while we were still very young, before we began the seventh grade, Steve and I had just finished our daily duties at Disney's main gate. The night was California warm, and wisps of a coming santana wind breezed through the streets of the Park. I remember clearly that we had just left the Fantasyland Magic Shoppe and were standing on the bridge overlooking the moat. A large, bald-headed man walked by us with a woman we presumed to be his wife. They were evidently in the midst of a family altercation, and their two little boys (perhaps six and seven years old) stood beside them. The father stopped and turned to the mother, pushing his face close in and mumbling menacing words at her.

One of the kids pulled on his father's sleeve, and the man turned around and casually slapped the boy. Then the mother yelled at the man, and they grabbed the kids and marched on through the gate toward the Peter Pan ride.

Steve turned to me with a mature look beyond his years and said, "Life is too short for people to hurt people. I will never hurt anyone like that!" He looked very sad, as if he had been the one the man slapped. His compassion was running close to the surface, and from that moment on, I knew how Steve disdained violence.

But for a simple twist of fate, I could have splattered the future of American comedy on the inside of the front door of our little house on Eleanor Drive. But God had higher plans for Steve. He didn't let him get drafted and lose his life in President Johnson's miserably stupid war in Vietnam like many of our peers. And he didn't let him do thousands of shows, never to be discovered. God, in all His wisdom, allowed the phenomenal Steve Martin legend to grow to enormous proportions. But I swear that from the time I looked down the barrel of that old blunderbuss and foolishly pulled gently on the trigger, to the moment I turned and blasted the hell out of the curtain, was no more than a fraction of a second. The one singular memory that is indelibly burned into my brain is the vision of Steve's petrified, quivering body appearing in my sights.

The next time I saw Steve's body that contorted was in an all-white suit as the wild and crazy guy at the Dorothy Chandler Pavilion in L.A. Although *I* had missed, by that time it looked like he had definitely been shot in the head—by an Indian.

Chapter 10

BO BO SKEE
WATTEN DOTTEN

"Die, you gravy-sucking pigs!"

—Steve Martin

What do Sandra Bullock, Madonna, Susan Sarandon, Sally Field, Meryl Streep, Lily Tomlin, Kim Basinger, and Steve Martin have in common? Fame? Success? Money? Yes. But there is more. Do they all enjoy being in front of an audience? Yes. But still there is something else. All of these superstars shook their booties at bleachers full of high school peers as cheerleaders. The only difference (other than the obvious) was that Steve and I were there for only one reason. It provided us with a built-in audience for the Gopher Boys, and that was all the incentive we needed. And though Steve had a powerful physical ability and athletic inclinations, his heart was in comedy. And he preferred my company to the football crew of jocks.

Ultimately, Steve's primary reason for not playing football was that he didn't want to hurt his fingers, which would prohibit him from doing his sleight-of-hand magic tricks. It was also the fact that, although football was a form of entertainment, it wasn't up-front and personal. Steve loved the laughter. We reveled in working an audience into rounds of laughter. The challenge was to spark audiences. We had gained a reputation as "class crack-ups" in our freshman and sophomore years at Rancho Alamitos High. Everyone knew who we were and knew that comedy was our purpose for living. Now we had been transferred to Garden Grove High School, and for our stint as juniors, we spent the time letting everyone else in the school know who we were. Soon it would be summer, and Steve and I made the decision to run for the position of school cheerleaders.

As the big election came, we planned our campaign. Now, in order for you to really appreciate our format in this campaign, you must remember that this was the pre-hippie era. "Uptight" was a way of life. In those days, not many people rebelled by growing their hair long or by dressing in the latest new styles—or by doing much of anything else, especially in our quiet, conservative Garden Grove, California. Things were quite different from what they are now. The American space program hadn't done anything yet, and President John F. Kennedy was alive and well. The world has changed dramatically since 1962. In 1962, girls were cheerleaders and boys played football, and there was no room for questions. But that never occurred to Martin and Walker.

We were sincerely unconcerned about what people thought about us. I was recently reminded by another one of our friends from school, Greg Magedman, that Steve and I had a constant presence in and around the school's administrative offices. He said he thought we were practically running the school. When a secretary wasn't present, either Steve or I would sign hall passes and notes for other kids. I still don't know how we got away with that. Steve was generally more conservative than I, but when the idea surfaced to be cheerleaders, we looked at each other and the decision was made. A captive audience. This was a goal worthy of our efforts. We set forth on our campaign, bent on humor as the way to acquire those prestigious positions.

A wonderful thing I've noticed about true friends is when you're with your friends, you experience the ability to actually care more for their happiness than your own. I suppose it would have to be deemed a form of "love," a willingness to sacrifice for another person's happiness. In any event, we made a pact as we embarked on the campaign trail to become cheerleaders; that if one of us made it and the other one didn't, the winner would not accept the position. Our campaign was a joint one; we were known as partners. We felt that it would not be proper for us to endure all that time growing up together and then be separated by some meaningless popular vote. After all, it wouldn't have been any fun to win alone!

With cunning and comedy, we sat and calculated our campaign. We began the advertising by placing posters in locker rooms. For the men's, I made a cartoon poster of a man peeing in a urinal and looking over his shoulder saying, "Stand Up for Martin and Walker." In the girl's locker room, our poster read, "If you stripped for gym today, the least you can do is vote for Martin and Walker tomorrow." Along the entire length of the girl's gym, we stretched a roll of white paper about three feet wide with a campaign message on it. It read: "Martin and Walker are ninety-nine percent school spirit and one percent human."

By the way, since I mentioned peeing, I have to mention that after Steve had done the college tour in the early seventies, he returned to the Golden Bear club in Huntington Beach, California. It was a popular folk club, and Lynn and I were there to see him. The front three rows of people had arrows through their heads, and I knew then that his cult following was beginning to happen. The backdrop was that of a Grecian scene with painted fountains and urns. When they introduced Steve from offstage, he walked on, strolled directly to a water fountain in the mural, turned his back on the audience and pretended to unzip and pee in the fountain. There he stood pretending to be urinating in the fountain, and the audience was already in stitches. And he hadn't said a word. At the end of the show, he walked out the front door with no less than three hundred frenetic fans following like puppy dogs. He walked halfway out on the Huntington Beach pier as they followed and he talked. Then he walked back as they happily wandered behind him. He stuck his thumb out, a car stopped, and before climbing in and disappearing with a complete stranger, he simply said good night to everyone.

I apologize for deviating from my story about our campaign, but deviations became the norm while growing up with Steve. Steve was still working regularly at Disneyland at the main street Magic Shoppe when we started campaigning for the cheerleader positions, and he came up with a novel but simple way of promoting us for the election. He obtained several 8x10 glossy black-and-white shots of well-known film stars in screen roles. For instance, there was a shot of John Wayne with a comrade, gazing through binoculars at a distant object. The photo looked like it was a World War II army-type flick. Underneath the picture, in neat, black lettering, we placed a caption, as if it were coming from John Wayne's mouth: "See there, third floor down, fourth window over…she ain't got no top on." Steve had acquired several of these photos and conceived many effective lines to accompany the pictures. Then there would be a simple message at the bottom: "Vote for Martin and Walker."

How perfect! I must admit that ever since that point, I've considered comedy the most valuable type of advertising. We wanted to wow them, and we really went all out. Entertaining the masses seemed the sure way to win. Meanwhile, we found an old quilt that looked like a wild tie pattern. You know, colorful and repulsive at the same time. With the aid of a pair of scissors, we trimmed that quilt to look exactly like an 8-foot tie, and in large letters we printed, "Don't be tied down. Vote Martin and Walker." This monstrous tie hanging from the side of the roof near the art class area had an amazing effect. When we realized just how much the tie had dazzled them, we searched for more items of clothing in the king-size line. It didn't take long before we hit them with a loud pair of undershorts, ten feet long, hanging from the side of another building on campus. It said: "Don't be caught short— Vote Martin and Walker."

Our campaign intensified, and we joined forces with a clean-cut kid named Alan Langdon, who was vying for student body president. As the election day drew closer, we gained momentum with the voters, but how were we to win over our cute and bubbly female competitors? Steve always seemed to get elected for one thing or another. Our freshman year at Rancho, he was class vice president. Sophomore year, he was elected "Most Talented," and our senior year, he was elected "Most Talented" again. I would also win class elections sporadically. The same year that Steve received his title of "Most Talented," I won "Best Personality." As for becoming cheerleaders, I was sure Steve would win, but was not so sure of myself—although we had a pretty good indication of our standings. Then, at long last, the results came in. Alan had won the presidency, and we successfully bagged first and second choice as cheerleaders. Our abstract campaigning did the job. All our hard work had paid off, and we were two of the five official new Argonaut cheerleaders.

We wasted no time in letting the student body realize just how grateful we were. That night, we went to work preparing our thank-you note. Early the next morning, we arrived at school before any of the personnel and staff. With the aid of some rope and a little climbing, we were able to mount our banner across the main walkway, in between two large buildings on Golden Fleece Avenue. We were proud, and we wanted everyone to know it. To win was one thing, but to thank our constituents in a public manner was important to us. The banner was shaped like a huge bra which read: "THANKS FOR YOUR SUPPORT!—Martin and Walker."

That summer found us preparing for the task ahead—dreaming up cheers and routines that would inspire and entertain our entire school. By the way, in Steve's comedy act in the 70s, he told his audience a story about our cheerleading days, stating that one of our special cheers was: "Die, you gravy-sucking pigs!" This was not one of our cheers, but it's amazing how many people took him literally.

Red and white were our colors, and we were called the Garden Grove Argonauts. After due consideration, we agreed upon white sneakers, knee-high red socks with a garter on one leg, and white Bermuda shorts. To top off this shocking and wacky adornment, we wore red shirts and cardigan-type sweaters that came halfway down our thighs. We even had little red knit hats—but that was really going too far. On the pocket of these exceptionally long sweaters was a knitted insignia that we created of a little argonaut with his head stuck up a megaphone. I suggested the idea to Steve and, as always, he encouraged me to go ahead with the irreverent design—which won everybody's approval.

Our megaphone also had to be different. We found a teacher in another school who was quite good at caricatures, and for no charge, he painted the images of us on our megaphones. I recall that he smiled at Steve and told him that he had heart-shaped lips and that they were considered very sexy. Steve shrugged and discreetly told me, "This guy's a little off the beaten track."

As the school year approached, we were invited to participate in a cheerleader camp in Redlands. Steve didn't make it, and I always regretted that. We surely would have had a good time. There were three hundred girls and a few boys. As I've mentioned, Steve was a good tumbler and a quick study, and I didn't come back with any tricks that he couldn't already do better than me.

You can just imagine how effective Steve was as a cheerleader. Even if you couldn't hear the energetic screaming through his caricatured megaphone, you could see his cartoon-like gestures. If there was a routine to be done, Steve picked it up quickly. To be perfectly honest about it, we didn't really work hard on routines, at least cheerleader routines. We were obviously more concerned with comedy, and cheerleading was really just an excuse to perform in front of everybody. As you know, we had been at Rancho Alamitos for two years and, like all good freshmen, we'd committed the school alma mater to memory. When we finally arrived at Garden Grove High, we never really learned the school song. So when we stood in front of the student body raising our voices to the tune of "On Ye Argonauts," we were still singing the lyrics to the Rancho High School song. But nobody knew that. We would glance at one another and wink, knowing that nobody in the whole student body had any idea.

"Bo Bo Skee Watten Dotten," we would bellow, raising our arms to the sky and bringing them back down as we lifted one leg up like a dog anointing a hydrant. "Hmmmm dotten shhhhhh." Then we would repeat the dog move with the other leg as we shouted the gibberish. "Who can beat'em, we can beat'em, we're the ones that can defeat them. Bo bo skee watten dotten hmmmm, dotten shhhhh!" If there was ever a precursor to "happy feet" and "getting small" and using antics which exaggerated body movements, this was it.

As I flash back over the last four decades I've known Steve, and I talk about things like his stand-up comedy act, I assume most Boomers in America know what I'm referring to. I fully understand that there are millions who were born after all that, but I was a little surprised the night I met Steve's ex-wife (before she was ex-ed). Victoria Tennant evidently married Steve after meeting him on the set of *All of Me*, but she had no idea of his national fame as a stand-up comedian. She told me that she didn't even understand what people were talking about when there were references to "the ramblin' guy" or "getting small" routines. I just thought that was incredible.

Amazingly enough, our school had an outstanding season in 1963, which made it a memorable senior year at Garden Grove High. The Argonauts won the league and went to the CIF playoffs, where we promptly lost to a team that simply overpowered us. I ruined my voice for a couple of years and probably did permanent damage to some degree. I would come home after a game and be so hoarse that I had to whisper. Steve would also strain his vocal chords, but, as always, he was slightly more conservative and wiser than I. If his voice was hoarse, mine was gone.

Sometimes after the games, Steve and I would double date. He would take Ratty more often than not, and I was going with a lovely girl named Paulette Bricky. Our dates were fun and exciting, even (unfortunately) without "going all the way." High school was fast coming to an end. Graduation was upon us. As the year drew to a close, Steve and I faded apart just a little. Since I had introduced Steve to the banjo, he was hanging around with John McEuen, playing chess and picking up more banjo licks. This growing period was turning into occasional get-togethers instead of a daily habit for us. It was time to hang out with other people off and on. Steve never seemed daunted by peer pressure about who his friends should or shouldn't be. No matter who it was, if Steve liked them, they were instantly a friend. There was a particular fellow named Donald Dobmeir who was such a distinct individual that Steve really admired him. Despite social attitudes towards clothes and styles, Donald would wear a vested wool suit with a neat watch and chain draped carefully from one vest pocket to the other. He also sported spats occasionally. Generally, he was considered a "weirdo" or a "nerd" by all our friends, but not to Steve.

There were times when our cheerleader antics turned into genuine support for the struggling Argonauts on the gridiron. After our team had won the league and went to CIF finals, we all traveled in a bus to that memorable encounter. We were behind, and the small core group of Garden Grove fans huddled together as we screamed, helplessly watching the Argos get crushed by a bigger and better team. At that moment, I remembered Steve playing rugby at Rancho when we were sophomores, when he would literally drag three or four seniors across the field. He was determined to score and not give up until he scored or was simply overpowered by several gorilla-sized opponents. I looked at our exhausted team and knew that, had Steve been playing that night, we might have had a chance of winning. But consider the consequences. What if he broke one of his fingers or if his hand became paralyzed through some unimaginable twist of fate? He wouldn't have been able to do sleight-of-hand tricks or roll coins over his knuckles or pick the banjo. Being a great athlete has its limitations, but being Steve Martin has had none.

Nineteen sixty-three passed quickly, John F. Kennedy was assassinated, and we all cried in sorrow. The Dick Van Dyke show became a television classic, and a dragon named "Puff" ushered in a strange period in history. Our country was permeated with songs about dope and love and lovin' dope and hippies and war and making love and not war. The earth-shaking change in my life was that Martin and Walker were not together every day as they had been since the sixth grade. But we had left indelible marks on one another. Steve wrote a note across a photo and gave it to my sister Marsha. It said simply, "Marsha, I've known you for a long time. We have really had fun. I think knowing you and Morris and your mother has really changed my life. I hope we can always be together. Love, Steve."

We had lived inside each other's heads, and then time moved on. But he influenced my life more than any man alive until my son came along—that's when I traded my old best friend for my new best friend. And it was my son, Skye, as a baby, who inspired me to write this book. I was burping him one cold evening in a log cabin that we had settled in for a time in the snow-covered San Bernardino Mountains of Southern California. I held him up and lovingly gazed at his chubby little face, when he suddenly hurled a mass of baby puke at me. I dodged the first volley and then he upchucked again. There he was, my darling baby son, with mush smeared all over his chin and down the front of his little blue bib. I instantly remembered the time Steve was over for dinner and got my sister Lesley giggling so hard that she broke into laughter and spewed a mouthful of mashed potatoes and milk directly in Steve's face. At first, he was disgusted, but then we all started laughing hysterically. Steve's face was filled with innocence and beaming with laughter and mush that night.

And then the idea struck me. It was January 1979, Steve was the number one stand-up comedian in the country. I thought I'd better write down some of our exploits while they lingered. My buddy Steve was definitely going places. And then, I realized Steve could even be President someday! After all, Jerry Brown made a statement that sounded a lot like something Steve Martin would say if he ever ran for President. He said, "It doesn't matter what I say as long as I sound different from other politicians." I remember Steve being quoted in an article saying something like, "It doesn't matter if it's really funny as long as everybody laughs!" Sounds like a plausible platitude to me.

If Steve ever ran for President, it would be a hell of a campaign.

Chapter 11

ONCE A "FOOL,"
ALWAYS A "FOOL"

"Nothing is foolproof, to a talented fool."

—Masters

We were no fools. We were students of the art of humor. And we were no less serious than pre-med students who must delve into countless resources in order to someday be able to say "endoscopicesophegel gastroduodenotomy" without biting their tongue or spitting at their patients. Steve and I realized at an early age that the response to our comedic antics could be enormous, hysterical, sometimes indiscernible, periodically angry, and often nonexistent. It didn't matter. We determined that these were all good reasons to fulfill our apparent destinies in the humorous resource market of life. We were freshman in high school.

It was at about this time that we met the ultimate whacko, Doug Rowell, at Rancho High School during our freshman year. We were discovering that there was a humor beyond the obvious, something that the audience does not perceive at first but which, nevertheless, becomes quite funny in the end. Steve has said on many occasions that his humor was based on giving the audiences so much unfunny material that finally they couldn't handle the pressure, and it all became funny. To see Steve do his "nose on microphone" in his old stand-up act was proof of this theory. When he and I did an act together, he would do the magic, and I would be the comedy relief. And then, after college, we both began entertaining at coffee houses, where he would blend magic and comedy neatly together.

Doug had the same nature as Steve and I. Humor was his mainstay. But he was even more radical in many ways. He would do *anything* for a laugh—fall, eat something off the ground—anything to get attention! One night in a parking lot by a bowling alley, we were leaving a coffee shop when Doug called our attention to a raunchy, old piece of pie that had, evidently, been run over by a car. He reached down, picked it up and took a large bite. Chewing it up thoroughly (much to our dismay and amusement), he swallowed and then admitted candidly, "That was the worst cherry pie I ever ate. I'm never going to eat cherry pie here again." As much as Steve would do things out of the ordinary for the sake of humor, he would never take things that far. With Doug, anything was worth the laughs. The three of us together were a threat to sanity.

One of our favorite gags took place in the school hallway. Steve would stand at one side of the hallway in school, and I would stand at the other, while Doug would come walking briskly down the corridor. As he approached us, Steve and I would kneel on the floor. Just as Doug would pass between us, Steve and I would yank an imaginary cord, and Doug would sprawl on the hallway floor.

Now, we didn't expect to convince anybody that we were really pulling a cord—any idiot could see there was nothing there. Yet the crowds gathered and laughed outright. Why? Because it took guts? Because we were putting on a show? Because we were the three class clowns? Or because we were delving into a different type of humor—that which is so *unfunny* that it teeters between the ridiculous and the hilarious? Obviously, Steve refined this form of comedy to a fine art. When asked about the wild and crazy guy, he'll say, "I did that, it's over."

If people expect something funny, they sometimes react according to how they believe they should act. Little kids are a perfect example. If they think a cartoon is supposed to be funny, they will sometimes force their laughter…and don't we all, sometimes? But when something is intended to be funny, yet seems to have no point, we generally assume that it is not funny. In trying to understand why Steve was funny in his stage show, we should understand that he was funny because he was *not* funny! He has caused us to question, "Is that funny? And, if not, why?" Finally, Steve Martin shows us that the obvious is supposed to cause an expected reaction, but that the indirect approach to humor can tickle your funny bone and still be highly effective.

Audacity itself is funny. The fact that someone has the guts to do something with no guarantee of results is, in itself, exceedingly funny. Years ago, in his half-comedy, half-magic act, Steve would announce that he was going to perform his famous paper napkin trick. He would draw out a napkin and, with a flowery gesture, stretch it across his mouth. After a few seconds of earnest concentration, his large wet tongue would poke through the tissue. The cartoon effect was there, but also a large touch of the ridiculous. Well, I saw this routine knock 'em out in some places and get no reaction in others. But Steve thought it was funny and, therefore, it was. As much as Steve's overall humor (especially during his wild and crazy days) seemed to be so physical and abstract, the truth of the matter is that Steve demonstrated a highly intellectual, thought-provoking nature in his comedy. This is exactly why his ad-lib ability has been so profound.

Ed Wynn once said, "A comic tells funny stories, a comedian tells stories funny." Given a story to tell, Steve can make it funny. Given four square feet in which to carry off a humorous antic, he doesn't need more than his allotment to make it work. Surely, it was the mere body language above and beyond the plot in *All of Me* that absolutely destroyed audiences with laughter. It was as if you didn't need to know that Lily Tomlin's character had invaded Steve's body and he was being torn apart between his own mind's ideas and her invading presence.

Since Steve had been my best friend and was practically my sole companion for a long time, I observed our circle of friends expand in high school. Our group of friends included some unique people. For the two years that we attended Rancho Alamitos in Garden Grove, we, in conjunction with Doug Rowell, Doug

Rhodes, Rick Kendall and Richard Burger, formed "Fools Unlimited," a rather absurd organization of like-minded individuals bent on entertaining the masses, whether they were aware of our efforts to amuse them or not. This loose-knit group of "comedians" decided that there were at least ten thousand humorous episodes to be perpetrated—and we should try a few of them—which we did. We assumed that the title of our organization might indicate that we were fools, but we knew that, in fact, all who would fall for our pranks were the fools, not us!

One prank we used to play was when Steve and I would fake carrying a huge piece of glass. One of us would be holding the top and bottom at one end, while the other would be doing the same at the opposite end. We would walk by a classroom door, for instance, so that everybody could see that we were pretending to carry this large sheet of glass. They would giggle at our mime activities, and we would smile and pass beyond their vision. As soon as we were out of sight, one of us would withdraw several pieces of metal from his pocket. These thin pieces of sheet metal were hooked on a short string of wire. I would loudly holler, "Oops!" and Steve would throw the metal pieces on the floor. They actually sounded exactly like glass shattering (another Fantasyland trick). It was a great illusion. Everybody knew that we didn't really have any glass, so the crashing of the imaginary glass always had an astounding effect.

As I've mentioned, between our sophomore and junior years, we were transferred to Garden Grove High. But we always knew that we had made lasting friends with the other "fools."

Steve once wrote me a letter while he was filming *Parenthood*. In it, he told me he was vicariously feeling what I had been experiencing in raising a family. I was so moved by his letter that as soon as the movie came out I took my darling eight-year-old daughter to see it.

Whoops! The movie was a big success for Steve, but it was definitely not for children. My daughter cried when I took her out of the theater. And even though I told her why, she could not imagine at that point that "Uncle Steve" could do anything on the screen that I could not explain to her. That was because she wasn't watching the screen when Steve ran out waving a big dildo. Nowadays, of course, she has a better understanding of those bold, sexual innuendoes that were blatantly mixed into the final edit of that movie. But she still doesn't understand why Steve got to meet Keanu Reeves and she didn't.

Parenthood was a big success, bagging over a $100 million at the box office. Steve's performance was excellent. In the scene where he had to entertain the kids at his son's birthday party, he was absolutely priceless, playing with balloon animals and doing his schtick direct from the old stand-up Steve. Naturally, when watching the movie (the second time), I flashed back on the many hours Steve and I spent in the Golden Horseshoe Theater in Frontierland watching Wally Boag. Wally would do his vaudeville act almost the same everyday, but that didn't lessen our enthusiasm for the program. He was a master with balloon animals and other vaudeville craziness. Of course, his balloon animals actually looked like animals. Steve could also create adorable little balloon animals, but in his act in the late seventies, he preferred to create a large, obscene, balloon monstrosity and call it an interuterine device for an elephant. After Steve had perfected many magic tricks at the Magic Shoppe in Disneyland, Wally Boag featured Steve in a show at the Golden Horseshoe that was supposed to be called "YOUTH AND MAGIC." Fate must have grabbed the painter's brush, because when finished, the sign accidentally read: "MOUTH AND MAGIC."

My life has been woven into a patchwork of personal vicarious experiences with Steve's success. When he did well, I felt better, no matter what problems I was going through. I have dozens of letters from Steve reflecting moods and insights that have been very fascinating to me. There were times when he was struggling, and he told me about his financial woes, and other times when he talked about responsibilities to his parents, managers and agents. Occasionally, he would simply be responding to one of my missives and staying in touch.

The "Fools Unlimited" set us all off on the foolish journey of life, but Steve has been a beacon of success for the rest of us and, as Mark Twain so eloquently put it: "Let us be thankful for the fools. But for them the rest of us could not succeed."

Cheerleaders, Garden Grove, CA Morris, Diane, Troy, Trudi & Steve

Cheerleaders doing "The Snake Dance"

New GG Yell Leaders
View Comical Future

By SUE HAWLEY
GGHS Teenage Page Reporter

Pledged as "friends to the end," Morris Walker and Steve Martin of Garden Grove High School, the zaniest duo on campus, live a colorful life and have fun doing it.

The two juniors think life's biggest delight is humor. Both are playing lead roles in the upcoming comedy, "Ask Any Girl," at the Argo Theatre Thursday and Friday nights.

Spotted on campus, they could be putting "Out of Order" signs on restrooms, dressed in Arab towels to shield the rain, or just amusing classmates with their congeniality.

Both Morris and Steve have many unusual talents. Aside from doing clever comedy routines together, both are aspiring actors. Morris runs a small business, building tjkis, some to eight feet. Steve is a magacian at Merlin's Magic Shop in Disneyland.

Recently the two were elected yell leaders at Garden Grove. Before the election, they staged a unique and witty campaign. One banner covering a wall reported that "Martin and

MARTIN AND WALKER
... funloving duo

Walker Are 1 percent Human and 99 percent School Spirit." They made huge ticles of clothing that said, cloth posters depicting arr "Don't Be Tied Down— Vote . . ." and "Don't Be Caught Short—Vote . . ." Next year as yell leaders, they will add to Garden Grove's pep and spirit.

Steve and Morris transferred from Rancho Alamitos this year and are now permanent figures on the Argonaut campus. After graduation both hope to attend college and then become a comedy team.

In their spare time, Steve and Morris never have a dull moment. They can always think of some startlingly original scheme to a m u s e themselves and others.

At school, whether throwing a fancy line of double talk or just conversing with classmates, the active pair make things interesting for all

Martin & Walker, "Friends to the End"

Wild and crazy antics, cheerleaders

Cheerleaders Steve & Morris "Is This A Cheer?"

FOOL'S GOLD

Dedicated to Humor

By Fools Unlimited

Having just started our column, we would like first to present the constitution on which our writings will be based.

"Two years, one and a half months ago, there came first upon this campus a new club, conceived in wit and dedicated to the proposition that humor is the axis of a happy world. It is here in resolved that this column shall be be dedicated to wit and humor, and lots of other neat funny stuff."

So much for our constitution.

The object of our column is to present views and outlooks on up-to-date subjects such as "How can a girl be cool if she's allergic to ice-blue Secret?" and "How to be as popular as a surfer and still maintain your self-pride?" We will present revues on the latest issues such as Morris Walker's shocker "Surferella". The story of young surf-bunny whose fairy Homomy turns her board into a nine foot, two inch banana every evening at six o'clock. We will present items of Psychological interest such as "How to explore one's inner-self without getting all bloody."

We hope you appreciate our type of humor, but if you do—don't admit it. They might put you away somewhere.

Steve as Tarzan

Steve with the girls at Garden Grove High School, 1963

"Fools Unlimited" Morris, Steve, Doug Rowell, and Rick Kendall

Steve's first girlfriend Linda "Ratty" Rasmussen

Chapter 12

STRAPPING
YOUNG JOCK

*"I'm sorry, Coach Ambrose. If I play varsity football I'm afraid
I'll break my fingers and won't be able to do magic tricks."*
                                                    —Steve Martin 1961

I know that Steve enjoyed sports but never thought of himself as a great athlete. He never seemed to have visions of Super Bowls or the Olympics. Steve was, more than anything else, a serious candidate for a professional career as a magician, an actor or a comedian. With the study of magic and the coaching he received from Aldini, Steve was at the expert level long before he got out of high school. Sleight of hand was one of his specialties, and it was his great fortune to have hands that were the size of a mature man's while he was in the ninth grade. This fact, coupled with his amazing dexterity, provided Steve with the ability to captivate an audience of any age with his illusions.

When we were seniors in high school and well known by that time in both schools we had attended, we were asked to perform at an awards banquet. Steve had a fantastic routine worked out in which, among other things, he conjured a magic silver ball into floating around the room. It was the effective maneuvering of his quick hands and the long thin wire beneath the translucent scarf covering the ball that completely mystified the audience. I remember the tune "Poinciana" as the one Steve had picked for the background music. He seemed to prefer classical music for general listening purposes.

On this auspicious occasion, I was fondly introduced as "Babo of the Orient." "My lovely assistant..." Steve trailed off, pointing to the curtain where I appeared, adorned in black lace stockings, black bra, slip and wig—the works. Then, much like the silver ball, I floated around the room. I cuddled up to the Vice Principal, slapping him on the cheek and walking, strutting and talking my stuff like a sleazy can-can dancer. Steve produced a most effective magic show, and it was all categorized as another step into that obsession Steve still refers to as "show biz."

When we were in school, I must admit I was a bit jealous of Steve's many talents, and I constantly strived to keep up with him. After all, Steve was my best friend, and I was happy that he was so talented, but I too wanted to be just as funny, sharp, witty, and brilliant. But I knew I couldn't touch him when it came to sports. The nice part about Steve is that he is not "macho." He was not a tough guy. Being good in sports never went to his head. I doubt that Steve even realized how good he really was. I was always kind of pudgy and slow; Steve, on the other hand, was relatively lean, always agile, and quick on his feet. He also possessed a great deal of strength for his size, although I can't remember him ever lifting weights. We were going into our sophomore year at Rancho Alamitos High School. The first year had been good: shows, pranks, and new friends like Doug Rowell and Doug Rhodes, as well as the "The Fools Unlimited." I had illusions of going out for football and getting "tough"; Steve didn't really care about playing football because of his fractured-finger phobia. Nevertheless, both of us went out for the "B" football team anyhow, just for kicks, and they were plentiful.

Steve was by no means "chicken." He was a fearless opponent. We played rugby as a training aid for football, and believe me, rugby was rugged. All the baddest, macho, dimwitted, buffed-up, beer-drinking football players from the upper classes played at the same time. There was no equipment, and just tackling someone was considered not acceptable in that jolly old sport. The object was to stop the ball carrier's forward motion and hold him to the ground, applying all the brutal, inhuman actions at your disposal for teaching smaller boys these rights of passage.

I think our coach was a little unreasonable. His intention was to make the guys tough. For instance, one memorable day, some big lug's foot came up directly between my legs, catching me full-force in the family jewels. I had never felt searing pain and agony so abruptly before or since. As I lay writhing in pain on the ground, somewhere between death and ready to retch my guts out, the guys gathered around. As I looked up at those gorillas in the mist, it was as if everything was in slow motion. Pain was my reality as tears streamed down my cheeks. I moaned like a dog hit by a truck. But then the coach kneeled over, his compassion overflowing. "Don't worry 'bout them nuts, Walker. You won't be using 'em for a couple of years anyhow!" Then he immediately stood up and shouted, "Okay, guys, let's shower up! Now, hustle, hustle, hustle!" What a swell guy.

The mighty rugby team was gone from my vision. I was down for the count. I still couldn't move, but I was almost capable of focusing again as Steve appeared in my dim vision, leaning over with a concerned look on his face.

"What happened, Morris? I was in the locker room," he said.

"I got kicked in the nuts, Steve. It really hurts!" And I told him painfully about the coach's sarcastic and uncaring remark.

Steve's compassion was sincere, unlike the coach's, and I'll always remember how he helped me up and supported me as I limped across the football field. We sat outside the locker room until everyone else was gone. I really didn't want to see any of the inconsiderate jerks who had delighted in my agony, and I couldn't walk very well anyhow. He sat there with me, quietly sharing my pain. He didn't need to say anything, it was enough that he was there for me when I needed him.

Two of the worst senior giants we had to compete against were Phil Murphy and Fred Barg. Murphy was a monster. He was maybe six-foot-three, 210 pounds, and had incredible muscular definition. To top it off, he had the deepest voice I have ever heard.

He was mean and nasty and reveled in his reputation. Steve and I were both in awe of his voice and strength. His partner, Fred, was heavier, shorter, and stockier. Fred had developed his trapezius muscles beyond reason. I don't think he could lift his bulging arms above his shoulders. It was hard to tell where this cretin's neck ended and the arms began. In private, Steve and I called him "no neck."

On another warm, winter Southern California day, it seemed like everybody had shown up for rugby. It was an afternoon of ass kicking and more ass kicking. But it never made Steve angry—just more determined. I remember this day as clearly as yesterday. Steve and I were on the underdog team. All the biggest, baddest dudes were on the other side. I guess the coach thought this would make us tougher. So if you didn't get scared out of playing rugby, you got beat to a pulp and couldn't play.

The ball was rucked, Steve grabbed it and began dodging the adversaries right and left, quickly darting from the diving bodies of the bloodthirsty and larger upper classman. Finally, someone caught him. And then another. When I got there, I began trying to pull the opponents off him, but Steve still wasn't down. He continued grinding forward, his powerful legs seeming to drag the better part of both teams. Several guys had their hands on him, and we tried to pull them off. I jumped on the group again, trying to penetrate the mass of bodies—only to glance over the top and see Steve's shirt being violently ripped off him. Then he was finally down, only a few yards to go. The ball was fumbled, and a teammate snatched it. There was only one obvious thing left to do: give the ball back to Steve. Sure enough, he went right over the top of the mass of violent, stumbling opponents and scored!

Meanwhile, one of our team members, a junior, was down, apparently with an injured leg. He was lying there without a shirt, struggling to get up. Phil Murphy approached him, mumbling some profanity in his shockingly deep voice. Then, without rhyme nor reason, he held one nostril with his forefinger and snorted a glob of snot on the back of the fallen teammate. I don't know what I would have done. The guy Murphy slimed was half the size, and intimidated, to say the least. Nobody did anything. Steve stood there like the rest of us, looking disdainfully at the scene. Then we returned back to the game. I was standing nearby when big Phil

Murphy bumped into me, causing me to accidentally bang into Barg, hitting him with my elbow. I began to apologize and tried to convince them that I sincerely didn't mean to bang into him—which, God knows, I didn't. Next thing I knew, Murphy was standing over me. Now he seemed about eight feet tall. I was sure he was about to kick my ass for my indiscretion, but miraculously, nothing happened—yet.

In the ensuing plays, I somehow managed to commit another dangerous mistake. I accidentally banged my elbow in Barg's face. I didn't really notice what I had done, and he growled but didn't say anything. Again, I thought I would be pulverized, but again, nothing happened. Steve proceeded to be the main reason we won that game and many others. Anybody who played ball with Steve will remember what I'm talking about. After that Olympian effort to gain winning points that afternoon, we all went back to the locker room with a greater admiration for Steve's ability as an athlete.

I was in the locker room after most of the guys had left, slowly putting my socks on and recovering from the onslaught. Barg came around the corner of the lockers with no shirt on, trying to show off his massive chest, and Murphy appeared menacingly from the other side. I nervously stuttered, "Hi, fellas."

Barg didn't say anything, but they both moved closer, and Murphy muttered something about my hitting Barg with my elbow. I began to apologize and tried to convince them I didn't hit him intentionally. Murphy began walking slowly towards me. I could just visualize him snorting a glob of snot on me, but then he just started shoving me, which was even more scary.

Sitting on a bench in my jockstrap, I felt helpless and embarrassed, which certainly didn't offer me much leverage or allow me to muster up too much courage. However, I did my best to gracefully recover from his pushes. Then he started on a new obtuse tact. He attempted to intimidate me into tying his damn shoelace. While this goon was harassing me, Barg stood there on my other side. "You meant to hit me in the face with your elbow, you shit!" he sneered at me. I was intimidated and scared, but at the same time proud. I determined that I would never tie Murphy's shoelaces, no matter what the consequences were. They could kick my ass, they could slap me around and they could stomp me into jelly, but they wouldn't succeed in making me play their little game. It didn't matter what they did to me. I objected with yet another apology in the same breath.

They were the only guys in the locker room, and I just knew there was going to be a nasty incident involving either my blood or his snot or maybe both. My family jewels were still aching, recalling my recent introduction to genuine pain. Nevertheless, I was not going to tie his shoelace.

It seemed as if things were moving to a crescendo, and shortly, I was about to wind up as nothing more than a sophomore grease spot. Just then, Steve entered the room. Still, Murphy and Barg didn't stop their harassment. They knew they were getting to me as their Converse tennis shoes stared at me unlaced and demanding.

Steve observed the situation for a few seconds, realized there was a problem brewing and then, without hesitation, spoke up. "Come on, guys, leave him alone." The two ignored him and Steve moved closer, this time more loudly insisting that they lay off. I knew I had them a little unnerved, because I refused to capitulate and tie the laces. I stood up as tall as I could, no longer willing to be compromised. Now I was not alone. Steve was suddenly at my side. If only our old compadre "Ivan the Terrible" had been there, perhaps it would have been different. We were going to have a fight.

We would lose, but I wasn't alone. Just then, Steve disappeared behind the lockers. "My, God," I thought for a moment, "he deserted me." With him there, the bullies might have backed off, but now that Steve seemed to have walked away at the last minute, I was again in deep trouble.

Murphy looked at me, and his deep, evil laugh filled the locker room, echoing back and forth as he stared alternately at me and his sneaker's lace. I was in a cold sweat (a jock strap doesn't offer much warmth). And then, suddenly, the fire alarm went off. Good old Steve!

Murphy was the first one out of the building, and Barg was hot on his heels. Steve walked around the corner, showing up with an ear-to-ear grin. As the fire alarm blared its warning, the assistant coach ran in yelling, "Who did it?" I had a great idea on how to answer him. "I can't say, coach!" I stuttered, "He-he'll kill me!"

"Murphy!" he shouted, immediately laying the blame on him.

"Don't you worry about him, Walker."

He started out after the culprit, then spun around and shouted to me, "Walker, get some pants on! You'll freeze your nuts off in here!"

After he left, Steve smiled at me and said, "Don't worry about them nuts, Walker. You won't need them for a few years, anyhow." At that point, there was nothing to do but laugh at my predicament.

I thanked Steve, and I have never forgotten his act of bravery in standing up for me like he did. In later years, I lifted weights, pumped myself up and studied martial arts, finally learning how to properly defend myself. Then I got older, hurt my back, dislocated my shoulder, and hyper-extended my knee. So now when there's trouble, I just look for a fire alarm!

I knew that the last thing in the world Steve wanted to do was get into it with two gorillas like Murphy and Barg. I don't think Steve considered the consequences when he came upon the scene and courageously took the risk to stand up for me. He just did it. I never saw Steve get into a fight. To the best of my knowledge, he never did, but he would be an intrepid opponent if he ever had to be. He was actually too smart to ever have to prove it, but on this occasion, he was certainly willing to put it on the line for a friend.

A year later at Garden Grove High School, a few coaches saw Steve's potential and tried to get him to go out for the football team. He never did. He and I decided that being cheerleaders would put us out of danger (his hands and my nuts).

There are just a few more memories I'd like to share about Steve the Athlete. I could never figure out why, but Steve would swim differently than anybody I knew. He would breathe properly, make long, sweeping strokes with his well-defined arms, but, inevitably, he'd cross his legs and not kick with them! No motion from his legs at all! Yet, even with his legs firmly held together, he could swim as fast as the rest of the group.

I remember one time in our junior year when Steve told me quite candidly that he was disgusted with himself for getting fat. I laughed, of course. He was as thin as ever. But he was serious. I knew the difference. So, in a more concerned way, I gently questioned him.

"Look," he said, lifting his shirt and pointing to his stomach, which pushed out a little. "I'm getting fat." He pulled his shirt down, and I didn't really know what to say.

"Do you feel all right?" I asked.

"Yes," he said, "but I'm worried."

Later that day, I saw him and asked how he was feeling. "Great," he said.

"What about your...?" I asked, pointing to his belly.

"Promise you won't tell?" he questioned me.

"Sure," I said. (But I'm going to now.)

"The coach says it's a muscle!" He lifted his shirt again and this time pridefully pushed it out. Sure enough, Steve had developed quite an admirable abdominal muscle.

If you have ever seen *My Blue Heaven*, you will notice Steve's expertise in the handling of a basketball in one short scene. Or in *Roxanne*, you would see his acumen for movement in the well-choreographed opening scenes. When he moved to Aspen in the 1970s, Steve stopped drinking and smoking and regained his youthful vigor permanently. In fact, he became such a great skier that after a year of regular practice, he was able to defeat macho Clint Eastwood in the downhill competition at the John Denver Ski Classic. And at that time, Eastwood was still in his prime. Nevertheless, Clint didn't like being beat, and when he shook hands with Steve he said, "Good job, punk!"

To which Steve responded, "Well, Excuuuuuse me!" It was all in good fun. I know Steve has had a regular regime of calisthenics that he's done consistently ever since we were kids. In the movie *Dirty Rotten Scoundrels*, he is seen romping on the beach, his hairy chest bared and his obvious muscle definition exposed. He looked exactly the same as he did in high school—and white, forever white. I guess Steve doesn't like the sun. Maybe that's why his skin is in such good shape.

A couple of years after we graduated from high school, I was in a convenience store in Orange, California, when an enormous guy walked up behind me and tapped me on the shoulder. It was Phil Murphy. He was bigger than ever, and his voice was two octaves below reality. The bully was gone, yet his appearance, in fact his very presence, was still intimidating. Looking at me for a moment, he smiled and said, "Hey, Martin, how ya doin? Ya ever see Walker anymore?"

Early publicity photo

Chapter 13

DRAMA: A CLASS ACT

"We like meeting many girls and being next to their big American breasts!"
—Yortuk Festronk, 1977
(Saturday Night Live)

Steve and I had a drama class together in junior high and through all four years of high school. At Rancho, our drama teacher was Miss Singletary. She was an attractive woman, around thirty years old, with bright red hair and a slightly freckled complexion. Her claim to fame was that she had slept with Frank Sinatra. I can't remember her telling us that, but, supposedly, she privately told all the girls in her classes. She might as well have announced it on the school P.A. system. She was sensitive, vain, cool, and nervous—all at the same time. I think Steve and I were a little much for her to handle, though. And to top it off, she also had to cope with Doug Rowell.

We were doing a school play, and Steve and I volunteered to announce it over the P.A. system in the morning, right after students had gathered for their first-period classes. We had our routine practiced to perfection.

Steve started with, "Oh, Morris, how come Miss Singletary got such big hands?"

Morris: "Oh, Steve, that's 'cause she used to pat them hands around in the mud quite a bit."

Steve: "Hmmmmm. Well, how come she got such big feet?"

Morris: "Oh, that's 'cause she used to stomp around in the mud quite a bit."

Steve: "Hmmmmmm. Well, I 'spect she must have sat in the mud quite a bit then, too."

Miss Singletary did have a couple of saddle bags developing on her hips. Upon hearing the routine, she turned beet-red and stomped out of the room in a rage. She marched straight to the office to demand that Steve and I be expelled from school. We were reprimanded and suspended for a couple of days. That was the only time we ever really got into trouble for our antics in school.

But Miss Singletary was really quite a kind soul. I remember one afternoon when Steve and I were approaching one end of the football field, in plain view of the bleachers. I saw Miss Singletary sitting on the bottom row watching the junior varsity game. There was a chain strung across one end of the field about twenty feet from the end zone. We were cutting across the field towards the bleachers when we noticed the chain, which was perhaps two feet off the ground. It was on the edge of the parking lot. We could see that many people in the stands were observing us, so, without speaking a word, we glanced at each other, non-verbally communicating our plan.

We took two steps, skipped and jumped over the chain, purposely catching our trailing feet on the obstacle and falling flat on our faces, simultaneously. Everyone laughed. As we recovered, Singletary was the first one I noticed. She loved it. So did we. We had this innate ability to read each other verbally and non-verbally. We were especially pleased, because we had pulled this off with no prior planning. We had the good fortune to be able to skip together and trip together on the same foot.

Comedy, like any other occupation, becomes second nature to a degree, and if you work with someone long enough, you develop an uncanny sense of timing. I've had the pleasure of experiencing that kind of comedy rapport with four people in my life: my wife, Lynn; my son, Skye; my daughter, Amoris; and of course, my buddy, Steve Martin.

There was great similarity between our antics and those of Jorge and Yortuk Festronk. Do you remember those names? Those were two of the wonderfully creative characters that Steve Martin and Dan Akroyd created for *Saturday Night Live*. They were the personification of our madcap high school beginnings. The setup for the story is as follows: There were two former brain surgeons who escaped a communist uprising in their homeland and moved to America to start a business specializing in bathroom fixtures. America loved these guys. Those swinging Casanovas in plaid slacks and shirts that didn't match stole our hearts with kinky slang phrases like, "How about a swinging drink?" To which Jorge would reply, "No way," as he gyrated his arms up and down like pumps and helped himself to a drink. "We like meeting many girls and being next to their big American breasts!" shouted Jorge, as they continued to move across the stage in exaggerated contortions. Then Yortuk would see their black neighbor (Greg Morris) and say, "Slap my hand, soul man!" Then he would look at his hand to see if any of the pigmentation had rubbed off.

Steve adored those *Saturday Night Live* days where he had the opportunity to work with some of the greatest impromptu comedy stars of the century like Dan Akroyd, Gilda Radner, Eddie Murphy, Chevy Chase, and Bill Murray. He (Steve) holds the record for hosting more SNL shows then anyone else. When we were in high school, our exposure to comedians was limited to the few who lightened the load of the mostly astigmatic and boring black-and-white television fare of the day. Classic performers like George Gobel, Milton Berle, and Red Buttons. And all-time great sitcom stars like Lucille Ball, Amos and Andy, and Dick Van Dyke. In many ways, Steve was in tune with them, and in some ways, he was already light years ahead. Our situation was such that our greatest source for original comedy was whatever we came up with. It just wasn't possible to sit around for hours on end watching sitcoms like the kids do today. That would not have satisfied our comedic addiction, anyhow. We needed constant action, audiences and input. With those stimulating elements, we were always "live" and ready for anything.

Careful planning, in conjunction with destiny, karma, prayer, and masterful juggling of our schedules, dropped us in the same drama classes year after year. For our eighth-grade teacher, it was more like trauma class. So for six years, from seventh grade until graduation from high school, Steve and I were the Yortuk and Jorge of our drama class.

Our dignified and highly respected dramatic instructor for the last two years of high school was Robert Farrell. He was aloof and serious and resembled the actor, Richard Boone. Although I never saw him do anything to demonstrate his talent, I always felt he had a reservoir of acting ability perhaps equal to someone like Boone. I really never noticed him reacting to anything but our comedy. It was hard to make him laugh, but well worth the effort. A sly smile would adorn his rugged features, and we would know we had penetrated his cool facade. He had been surviving as a drama teacher for many years. Let's face it, a drama teacher is an actor or performer who got a degree and then, when fate found him or her not making it onstage, he or she simply picked up their second option. Mr. Farrell was doing his time. *Mr. Holland's Opus* was the fictional account of a similar scenario. Ours was Mr. Farrell's opus.

Drama class could have been painful, but fortunately, Mr. Farrell let us do our thing—in fact, anything we wanted to do. And so did Miss Lombard, a young replacement for Mr. Farrell in our senior year. When she unexpectedly had to pinch-hit for Mr. Farrell, who was something of an institution himself, she was unprepared for the challenge. Her first day in class, we greeted her, and then escorted her to her desk and sat her down. Then we instantly jumped into our rendition of an ongoing take-off of a soap opera. She didn't say another word until the bell rang. We simply waved and said, "See ya tomorrow," and she said, "Thank you."

Things weren't quite the same with Miss Lombard, because we had already developed an ongoing, genuine rapport with Mr. Farrell. We had come to an agreement with him at the beginning our junior year. It was simply this: We could burn up class time with ad-lib comedy and receive "extra credit" for what we did. This was perfect. We came in the class and "faked it" for forty-five minutes. Everybody laughed and loved it. But we loved it more than anybody. As it turned out, the class was either working on a play, or Martin and Walker were working on the class. Mr. Farrell would sit there, leaning back in his chair with his feet on the desk, and nod his approval as we boldly went where no drama student had gone before. I think what we really adored was the fact that we were getting away with doing what we loved for the better part of our entire dramatic curriculum. We were testing our comedic ammunition on the class.

An exciting aspect of these exercises was the risk factor. When you are "hoofing" it through a routine with no specific guidelines, there will be times when, naturally, you may fall. This gave us both the opportunity to pick ourselves up in mid-stream and turn things around. Over the years, that little bit of knowledge has helped both Steve and me through thousands of live concerts. After graduating school, an ad-lib would turn out to be, first of all, a spontaneous thing and then a part of the act. All of our clowning around and creativity met with class approval, as their grades were all high and all they had to do was sit back and enjoy. This resulted in straight A's in drama for us and one hell of a lot of practical experience. Of course, we did school plays, and Steve and I got the lead roles for both the junior and senior plays.

Our senior play, which I remember particularly well, was *Ten Little Indians* by the master of mystery, Agatha Christie. I played the great white hunter who was mysteriously invited to a lonely island resort with nine other guests. Steve was the aging judge, also one of the recipients of the mysterious invitation. As the guests were systematically murdered by an unknown assassin, the cast finally dwindled down to myself and the heroine. (Steve was a victim of the murderer in the second act.)

Lee, the heroine I was left with, was now terrified, believing that I was the murderer instead of the hero, and in her fear and stress, she shot me. This was where you heard Steve begin to laugh maniacally and then appear from behind a wall. *He* was the murderer and tricked everyone into believing he was dead! He was fantastic. Several girls in the audience were screaming their heads off as he approached Lee with a noose in his hand, cackling like a witch and explaining how and why he had conceived this whole plan.

At last, he began to tighten the rope (shades of Miss Stepp) around her quivering neck, like a Jack Nicholson lunatic, and prepared to choke the life out of the helpless, frightened woman.

Recovering from a flesh wound, I suddenly lifted myself off the floor, picked up the gun Lee had dropped in her fear, and shot Steve. It was a little scary pointing a gun at Steve again, but this time I was positive it was only loaded with blanks. (It was only on play night that he allowed me to point the gun anywhere near his direction.) He took a terrific fall over the couch and sprawled out on the floor with a thud and an agonizing grunt. The play was a classic and a far stretch from our daily comedy, but it came easily to us.

In general, it's easier for a comedian to do a dramatic role than it is for a serious actor to do comedy. For instance, it would be very difficult for the average actor to carry off a comedic role like Robin Williams does, but Williams has certainly demonstrated his ability to perform serious roles, as he did in *Awakenings*. Or for Tom Hanks to play a serious role such as his Oscar-winning performance in *Philadelphia*. Conversely, we rarely see a serious actor succeed in comedy roles as Leslie Nielson has done after years of deep drama. He is one of the few who was able to switch from being a dramatic actor to absolute craziness, as he demonstrated in the *Naked Gun* movies.

Steve told me about a year ago that he was going to retire. I don't believe this will happen, not yet. Even after all the movies Steve has done to date, he told me that he feels he hasn't reached his dramatic peak. It takes a long time to convince millions of people that comedy is only a part of your talent. He hoped to gain greater respect for his dramatic abilities early on with *Pennies From Heaven*, but the movie was such a flop that it shocked him back into the reality of his talent for comedy roles. In more recent times, Steve has produced movies demonstrating his dramatic abilities, such as *A Simple Twist of Fate*, *L.A. Story*, and *Grand Canyon*. Probably the best blend of comedic and dramatic interpretations came in his *Father of the Bride* movies. But he still loves a silly comedy. After all, he wrote *Bowfinger*.

Back in the critical days of training, we were under constant pressure to come up with new routines on a daily basis. It was indeed a good way for us to prepare for writing comedy under pressure. Steve would discover that reality shortly after his college stint, when he became an Emmy Award–winning comedy writer for the Smothers Brothers. But long before that, in class, Steve would be Captain Cook, and I would be Peter Pan. He would ad-lib a monologue to an imaginary Wendy, threatening her with his sword. "If you don't tell me where the gold is, my little wench…I will stab you in the…" At this point, I would jump in front of Wendy and he would aim his imaginary sword at my lower abdomen and exclaim, "Pan!"

There were two drama clubs on campus: "Thespians," of which I was president, and "Jason's Jesters," of which Steve was president. I recall one routine we worked out that I've never seen Steve use on any of his shows since then.

We were a couple of tin soldiers on a Swiss clock. It was all mime. For once we didn't talk. We came out mechanically marching towards the class and then towards each other where we would go through a routine of saluting and bowing. Then, somehow, our clock mechanism was failing, and the saluting began to be repeated erratically. We struggled to return to our appointed rounds. Finally, the clock went completely haywire, and our misguided springs sent our mechanical bodies into spasms. We finally wound up with our bodies contorted into non-operation as the clock completely failed. It may be difficult to imagine, but it was humorous and fun for the class. There we stood—immobile, two broken toy soldiers, with our classmates urging us on, because we were funny, because we were clever, because we were unique, and because they didn't have to do anything but sit and enjoy. They rewarded us with the applause and laughter we needed to keep our motors going—and Mr. Farrell gave us all good grades.

I remember how we also ad-libbed though variations of Cyrano de Bergerac, which I realize became the basis for Steve's movie *Roxanne*. I remember not only watching *Cyrano de Bergerac* with him, but acting out various comedy routines based on that movie in front of the class. But when the movie *Roxanne* came out and I wrote to Steve reminding him of those times, he wrote back telling me that our days in school had nothing to do with the creation of *Roxanne*. Steve indicated he had rewritten the script forty times before it became a movie, and he made it clear he believed our earlier improvisation of *Cyrano* had nothing to do with it and that I had no claims on the writing of the screenplay.

That response shocked me, because I wasn't suggesting that I had anything specific to do with the creation of the screenplay for that movie. I was just reminiscing. I must confess that, for the first time, I was hurt by something Steve said to me. After reviewing his letter a few times, I began to realize how much pressure someone in his position must be under when others try to lay claim to their creations, intellectual property or other assets. I wrote back and explained to him that I had only meant to remind him of our good old days together and that I'd not meant to imply I had anything to do with his movie. I had truly hoped to have a good laugh with Steve and to relive a few happy memories with him the next time we were able to speak. Steve responded with a nice apology, admitting that he was under a lot of pressure.

He could have simply told me to get lost. He certainly didn't need to apologize. I think a lot of stars of his magnitude would have ignored my letter and minimized the long friendship. Let's face it, I'm just a regular guy running a small business in a rural town in Oregon. There's not a lot I can offer to Hollywood superstars—except my friendship, goodwill, and great memories. And this was enough for a guy like Steve Martin!

Drama class and cheerleading had Steve and me working around the clock. We organized trips and participation for our school drama festivals at Orange Coast College and Long Beach State. As it turned out, Steve went to Long Beach State and I went to Orange Coast College after high school. We also orchestrated a field trip to the famous Pasadena Playhouse. On another occasion, Steve and I drove all the way into L.A. to see a production of *A Midsummer Night's Dream* starring Burt Lahr at the old Biltmore Theater. We were impressed with the production and sat there in that huge, old theater for some time after the play was finished, musing over our love of performing. Burt Lahr, you will remember, was the lion in the *Wizard of Oz*. Finally, the custodian came out to sweep up the isles and said, "You boys gonna stay around for the next performance? 'Cause it ain't till tomorrow."

"No," I said, "but we really enjoyed it."

As we walked out the back door and turned towards the parking lot, Burt Lahr emerged from the stage door. We were awestruck and drawn to him magnetically. He looked small and wrinkled, and we could see that his onstage Puck was just that: another stage character that he portrayed beautifully. But now he was an aging actor leaving the theater; after the applause, after the curtains dropped and the lights dimmed, just a quiet, lonely exit out the back door. He stopped and watched us approach, and Steve immediately commented, "Mr. Lahr, you were great!"

I felt that wasn't enough, so I elaborated, "Really great!"

He looked at us, glancing back and forth slowly, and a glow adorned his aging features. "You two young men must be actors." We nodded. How did he know? "It's a difficult life," he said slowly and with his stage voice—but not in a phony manner. "It can be very, very hard, but never give up on your dreams. You might become rich and famous." He pointed at Steve. "And you might just have the privilege of entertaining your audiences and be poor your whole life," he said, and he pointed at me (oh shit!). "But no matter what," he continued as if to predict with more fervor, "don't give up!"

With that, Lahr shook our hands, buttoned his overcoat, threw his scarf over his shoulder, and strolled away looking larger than life, like the grand old performer we knew him to be. It was inspirational.

We hardly talked as we drove back, until we got about halfway home, and then we couldn't stop talking for days. That experience was a moment in time that neither of us would forget.

Steve was by no means the only talented or intelligent kid in that Class of 1963 G.G.H.S. Even now as I glance back at the school yearbook and see who was in Jason's Jesters, I see John McEuen of The Nitty Gritty Dirt Band fame and Bill (now "Basil") Poledouris, who has written the musical scores for dozens of major motion pictures. And of course, Kathy Westmoreland, who sang with the Metropolitan Opera at twenty-one and became Elvis Presley's lead singer and part-time lover.

The Garden Grove High School class of 1963 received more scholarships than any other school in the whole state of California that year. Interestingly enough, Steve, John, Kathy, and Basil received none of those scholarships. Lest you think Steve ever had it easy...at one time he was renting the maid's quarters in a Beverly Hills home for twelve dollars a week. Barely making it, Steve decided back then that he would never rest at whatever success he might attain in his bid for stardom; he would drive himself relentlessly beyond all expectations, including his own.

Chapter 14

THE AIRPLANE SCAM

"Eagles may soar, but weasels don't get sucked into jet engines."

—Hobbs

By 1972, drama for Steve was no longer a profitless flight of fancy in a high school class or school hallway. His intense and relentless pursuit of success in "show biz" had paid off in dividends. Steve had written comedy for everyone from the Smothers Brothers to Dick Van Dyke, performed hundreds of live concerts from coast to coast, and appeared on the *Tonight Show* two dozen times. The kid I knew in "the good old days" (as Steve lovingly calls them) was becoming a ubiquitous phenomenon, and the boob tube seemed the most logical step to his future world stardom.

By this time, my wife and I had stopped touring and were living in Big Bear Lake, California, with our son, Skye, who was still a baby. While visiting with Steve in Hollywood, we reminisced over veggie burgers in a local eatery. Steve has always enjoyed talking about the past more than the present when I have been with him. He relished discussing the smallest details of incidents that are now so distant. I'm grateful that we've had the chance to talk about so many of our happy past activities from time to time over the years. The particular story I am about to relate, like most of these early recollections, would never have made it to print otherwise. And for whatever they're worth, these evolutionary episodes are clips from a time in history that was critical to the development of Steve Martin as we know him today.

During high school, the only hobbies I had, besides my constant pursuit of pranks with Steve, were music, artistic endeavors— from painting to carving—and occasionally building model airplanes. I indulged myself by constructing balsa airplanes with tightly stretched tissue over their fragile but effective frames. I remember when I worked methodically for two weeks to put together the most complicated model airplane I had ever worked on. The plane was no particular technological achievement. In fact, it was a rubber band powered model. But the difference between this model and other similarly powered models was the size. Most rubber band powered planes had a wing span of ten to fifteen inches. This inexpensive, yet difficult to assemble, plane was a replica of a piper cub with a wing span of over three feet.

I diligently glued the fragile pieces together: the fuselage, wings, tail piece, etc. Then, there was the papering—gently measuring, cutting, stretching, and sealing it and finally, painting the exterior. In the back of my mind, I thought, " there must be a better use for this plane than just winding up the rubber band powered prop and tossing it ten feet into the air, only to see it completely obliterated by way of a head-on collision with Planet Earth." I decided not to fly my plane into obscurity with one frivolous thrust. (I had much the same attitude about that plane that young adults should have about sex these days. Are the consequences worth the risk, even with a rubber?) In the end, I had a much more reasonable use for that useless toy plane.

Not far from where we lived in Garden Grove is the world famous Los Alamitos Race Track. In the early sixties, between racing seasons, the monstrous parking lot was empty most of the time. I knew that many model plane enthusiasts frequented the area to take advantage of the massive lot when manipulating their radio controlled models. With nothing more than a small control box, these men flew a large variety of extremely valuable airships, ranging in price from hundreds of dollars to thousands. It was, and still is, quite an expensive hobby.

I was returning home from Long Beach, anxious to finish up my model, when I decided it was time to stop at the track and observe the fanatics. I was amazed and watched them for half an hour before I realized that this was the perfect testing ground for my recently constructed ship. I could go out there, wind up the rubber band, hold the plane high above my head, and watch it quickly smash into the parking lot! Not exactly. But, surely you don't believe that I was going to wind it up and throw it for one exciting thirty-second thrill. On the contrary, I figured my plane wouldn't fly properly anyway, so we (Steve and I) might as well have some fun.

I saw Steve that evening, and he was equally thrilled with the prospect of a new game involving the airplane. The "Fools" were now quite proficient at scams, pranks, and fakes—the more elaborate the schemes, the more appealing they became. Without delay, we contacted our buddy, Doug Rowell. Doug, as usual, was ready, willing and able to perform whatever devious plot we had conceived.

"You know what we really need, Doug?" I asked.

"No," said Doug. "No, but please don't ask me to eat cherry pie in that parking lot. I hear it is horrible!"

"Well, everybody down there at the race track has a little remote control box to control their models. We've got a model, but no control box." Doug smiled broadly and confidently announced that the box would be his end of the gag.

That night, Doug and I approached his father, Ed Rowell. After explaining our plan in detail, Doug looked at his father intently. Ed, a very personable and loving father, looked back at Doug and, after hearing the whole story, eloquently asked, "Uh?"

"Well, Dad, you can build most anything…and, well, would you make us a good-looking control box for our race track fake?" Doug's parents were wonderful folks. Ed looked down his cigar at Doug and calmly announced, "We'll do it together." And so they did.

The same day I finished my long, tedious work on the detailed painting of the airplane, Doug arrived with the newly constructed, imitation control unit. We called Steve, and he was there in a few minutes to observe our progress.

The little box that Doug and his father created was about fourteen inches long, ten inches wide and four or five inches deep. It was made out of polished metal and looked extremely professional. The top of the box was adorned with five knobs of various sizes, a meter, an antenna, and a plug for earphones. Above each of the little knobs, we clearly printed *arbigan, rebuff meter, feetle-forncaster* and more of our favorite gibberish. There were also several little, colored lights close to the knobs and a few toggle switches just for good measure. It was beautiful, completely ridiculous, and about six or eight times the size of a real remote control box. "All the better," Steve said. It even sported a huge six-foot antenna. It looked a little bit like a something created for *Star Trek*, but no one could totally dismiss the possibility of it seriously functioning. This added to the potential effectiveness of our scam.

I explained to Steve and Doug my ideas on what we could tell inquisitive guys who would, naturally, be skeptical about our plane's ability to fly. I kept in mind that we had to convince some real genuine model plane buffs of a line of malarkey, and that we had best be prepared with some technically and verbally confusing bullshit. The plane was all white with some intricate pin striping. Both of my comrades agreed wholeheartedly that we should have a pretty juicy story for the curious onlookers who would certainly be gathered around.

I had fogged the inside of the see-through windows of the cockpit with spray paint before I glued the plastic to the fuselage. This was to prevent any would-be inspectors from seeing the tightly wound rubber band, which would give away our little secret. On top of the wings and right over the cockpit, I installed a complex-looking, square mirror on which I had inscribed little black lines in a tiled style. I was so proud of my slick-looking model.

"You see, we tell them it's solar powered," I told my pals, "because nobody has a solar powered model, and they won't have anything to compare it with. We tell them that the mirror absorbs energy from the sun and, thereby, stores enough power in the non-existent batteries to fly the plane a great distance without refueling." The understanding smiles on their faces told me they liked the whole idea. Actually, this was a really progressive concept, and we were surprisingly ahead of our times.

"What do we tell them about the controls?" Steve asked.

"I don't know," I said.

We deliberated on this critical element long enough to come

up with the idea that it would have to be controlled by sonar high frequency sound waves. Sounded good to us! It was the perfect plan. We didn't know squat about solar-sonar anything. You have to remember this was years before microwave ovens and solar-powered cars. It just sounded like high-tech mumbo jumbo, and we were relatively sure that nobody at the Los Alamitos raceway could be sure that we just made it all up.

As soon as I got my driver's license, I was entitled to drive the family Oldsmobile almost anytime I wanted. It was a fifty-six Olds Ninety-Eight. A real tank. Our plan had been in the making for weeks now, and our enthusiasm was exceeded only by our cunning.

Early on Saturday morning, Steve showed up at my house. He usually walked over. He used to walk everywhere in those days. He hitchhiked to work at Disneyland for years, and when there were no rides, he would walk the entire distance—perhaps five miles. For a modern day kid, that was a real accomplishment. Most kids in those days would complain if they had to walk a block to the bus. I was expecting Steve, and my mother cooked a turkey for the occasion. My mom was always so supportive. She cooked a turkey for almost any occasion. (She even cooked us a turkey on the first day I had a paper route. I ate so much I could hardly pedal my bike.) Anyhow, Steve was early and anxious as always. On that particular day, he showed up on a unicycle. He said he borrowed it to try it out. Nobody else could get two feet on it. But his balance was so good that he mastered the thing in a matter of minutes.

While we waited for Doug, Steve took advantage of a few minutes of attention from my sister. They really loved one another back then. We were all pretty close at that time. On the other hand, I very rarely saw Steve's sister, Melinda, and never got to know her very well. Finally, Doug arrived and we prepared for one of the greatest pranks we ever concocted.

After careful scrutiny, we decided the airplane would be safest in the immense trunk of that classic 1956 Oldsmobile. We covered it carefully with white sheets and tucked them in and around it as we secured the plane in the trunk. The control box sat in Doug's lap, and a folding chair, card table, and other less important bits of gear fitted neatly in the back seat. We all departed at about nine-thirty and arrived at the parking lot of the race track shortly after ten.

The enthusiasts were out by the dozens. Most of the models in the area were a lot smaller than mine. The real difference, obviously, was the cost. I must admit, however, that from a few feet away my ship was quite impressive. It was the only all-white plane accented with neatly pinstriped red trim. We knew these people weren't stupid, but we hoped they were gullible. It was decided, as we approached the grounds, that we would have to keep the crowd away from the plane in order to preserve its secret power source—rubber power.

We pulled up to a wide, open area a hundred feet from the nearest model airplane buff. It was our careful theatrics that purposely attracted their attention. Steve began sweeping off the ground on which we were about to set the plane. Leave it to Steve to attract attention. Nobody swept the ground as meticulously as Steve. Nobody swept the ground at all! Then we set up the card table and chair, and finally lifted out the control box, which looked like a portable, intercontinental, ballistic missile control center. Now we had their undivided attention. We were delightfully committed to the hoax and slipped into our roles like seasoned professionals. Our audience slowly began to gather around in a large circle. Steve walked the perimeter of the circle asking them to please back up, mumbling double talk about "solar-*arbigan*, control *rebuff*, sonar *stagmas*." We executed our devious plans with the utmost efficiency. Already, we had the most gullible of the hobbyists in the palms of our hands.

As soon as we were able to get the crowd to back up and Doug was seated at the table with his absurd earphones plugged into the extraordinary fake box, we unloaded the plane from the trunk. With extreme care, Steve and I lifted it out of the trunk (still covered by a sheet), pretending it was heavy, and then set it on the ground right behind the car. In a very professional manner, Steve again widened the circumference of the circle, which by then had about forty onlookers dying of curiosity. They obligingly stepped back at Steve's polite request and, young and old alike, waited patiently for the unveiling. They mumbled as their interest level increasingly rose.

Steve returned, and we bent down over the plane to remove the sheet. "They're eating it up," Steve whispered to me. I looked over the top of my glasses at the spectators and then back at Steve.

It was murder to keep from smiling, but that would have botched the whole plan. We continued with our serious facade. As we lifted the covering from the shiny, snow-white aircraft, there was an audible gasp from the surrounding group. I just couldn't believe they were biting the hook we were tossing them! The crowd again started moving closer to get a better look at our plane, and again both Steve and I had to widen the circle. Meanwhile, Doug was sitting at the control box with several onlookers watching the flashing lights and his deft handling of the knobs and toggle switches. If anybody had perceived at that point that the box or the plane was phony, they didn't venture an opinion. Doug held up his hand and shouted, "Ready for testing!"

Steve responded with a loud, "Check *rebuff*!" Doug's hand quickly went to the *"rebuff"* knob and wiggled it enough to cause lights to flicker and a gauge to pulsate.

"Rebuff checked!"

Steve walked away from the plane and moved some extremely interested onlookers farther back.

"Please step back, folks. This is a dow for a *rebuff frazen*; please, just step back."

I shouted, "Check *arbigan*!"

Again, Doug leaned over the box and twisted the *"arbigan"* button.

Steve had returned and leaned down, telling me, "They are getting really anxious." Many of the enthusiasts had landed their planes, and, whether they believed it or not, they looked seriously interested in our bogus experiment.

Finally, Doug yelled, "Ready for the prop test?"

I leaned down over the model prop and said, "Okay, Steve, tell him ready for prop check."

Steve shouted back, "All ready!"

"3-2-1!" Doug shouted his countdown to blast-off prop test. At that precise moment, I pulled the sewing needle that was holding the rubber-band-powered prop in place. The propeller spun around, and our plane silently scooted five feet forward. There was another audible gasp from the onlookers. Little did they know at that point that they had witnessed the entire flight.

"Everything checks!" Steve shouted back at Doug. He tapped my shoulder and asked, "What's happening with Doug?"

I looked up to see a man in his late forties raising his fist and shouting angrily at Doug. "Keep everyone away from the plane," I told Steve, and hustled over to Doug's position at the box. I ran up and questioned Doug. "What's up?"

"This guy doesn't want us to fly," Doug said in mock disappointment.

"What's the matter?" I asked, as I looked at the bald-headed, red-faced objector.

"What frequency are you on?" he growled at me.

"Huh? We're not on a frequency," I replied, as if I knew what the hell I was talking about.

"What kind of horse shit is that?" he barked again.

"It's...uh...completely sonar controlled. It's a sonar unit specifically for hyper-sonar distance control. We intend on flying it to uh...Downey today." I stopped as he interrupted.

"I smashed up a thousand-dollar plane two weeks ago just because of some assholes like you who didn't know what the hell frequency they were on!"

He was vehement! We weren't used to such angry attacks, as none of our parents had ever used that kind of language with us, so it sounded scary. But I had a great idea on how to turn the whole situation around and how to make this guy look like a fool in front of the curious crowd. "Excuse me sir," I responded loudly, "I'm a member of Youth for Christ, and your language is very offensive to me!" He got embarrassed and grunted like an old bull, but it wasn't exactly an apology.

I think he thought we were a bunch of smart-ass, rich teenagers trying to impress the other plane hobbyists with our expensive, new, state-of-the-art toy. So in a way, he was taking the bait.

The crowd pressed in, angered by this fellow who was so taken in by our scam that he was actually trying to stop us ruin our experimental flight.

"I promise, honest, it can't interfere with your frequency!" I insisted, knowing full well that the thing couldn't even fly, except for a few feet on rubber band power. I said solemnly, "I swear to God!"

"Bullshit!" he blurted, almost screaming. I gulped. After all, he was a big, angry son-of-a-bitch, and we were only halfway between puberty and adulthood. I was having flashbacks to the bully Phil Murphy. I could just see him blowing a glob of snot on

Doug. And God only knows what Doug would have done with it.

"What is this shit?" he yelled as he slapped Doug's earphones lightly.

"Hey, knock it off!" another man in the back of the group shouted at him.

"All I know is you little bastards," he took a breath and his red face puffed like a blow fish, "may damage my plane with your fancy toy, and I'm going to fly my plane first. Then you can do what you want with that piece of shit." Steve was far enough away that he was only catching bits and pieces of the skirmish. This incident was actually a blessing, as we needed an exit option at this point, and we really weren't quite sure what we were going to do to keep the show going (we never wrote a second act to this scam).

"Okay," I said, as I threw my hands up in the air, pretending as if I was disappointed at having to give in, "go ahead and fly yours!"

Several people from the crowd booed him loudly. We had now become the underdogs and everybody loved us.

"We want to see them fly the good one!" a boy shouted at the man. "Yeah!" exclaimed another.

"Sorry, folks," Steve said as he turned to the group, holding up his big hands and turning to convey his information to the entire crowd concisely. "We'll let the expert fly his first, folks, and then we'll be back later."

Another volley of boos found the disgruntled intruder walking back toward his plane. I noticed, even from a distance, that he had an extremely sleek-looking model with a glossy black paint job. I assumed this was probably the most expensive rig there, and deep down I understood why he didn't want to take any chances. Nevertheless, he was foul mouthed and rude, and I was happy to hear the crowd renounce him. I jogged back over to Steve, and we were lucky enough to get the cover over the plane and quickly tuck it away in the trunk of the car without anyone getting close enough to discover our ruse. Then we drove over to where Doug was putting the equipment together. The crowd had thinned out, but we had acquired several fans and they shot questions from all around.

"When will you fly it?" a boy queried.

"Later today," Steve answered. "Where will you fly it to?" another questioned me.

"Downey," I replied as I folded the table.

"Are you guys for real?" a dubious onlooker ventured to inquire.

"Do you know what a *dow* for a *booberday* is?" Steve sternly asked the man who had doubted our credibility.

"Uh?" said the man. "A what?"

We packed the goods in the back seat and, even as we crawled into the Oldsmobile, we could hear our new fans yelling out things like, "What makes it work?" "

Solar batteries!" Doug shouted back.

"It's a completely solar-sonar powered unit," I announced from the driver's seat as I started up the Olds.

"We'll be back in a while," Steve waved to them victoriously from the passenger side as we departed. Off in the distance, I could see our red-faced blow fish checking his plane for his carefully planned first flight of the day.

A few blocks away, we stopped at a Frosty Freeze for lunch—three hamburgers and three malts—Steve was not a vegetarian then. As a matter of fact, nobody was a vegetarian then. As far as we knew, everyone in the world ate meat. We were overjoyed with the magnificent success of our plan. Originally, we considered going to claiming a malfunction and quietly fading from the scene, but our blustering buddy had opened up a whole new chapter. Because of his irate attitude, we left not only successful with our plans, but victors! Champions of the people! After lunch, we couldn't resist the chance to return to the scene of the crime and visit our supporters.

The clouds were gathering, and it was almost four o'clock when we returned. As our big, two-tone, green-and-white Olds moved slowly towards the area of activity, a few fans waved and smiled broadly. We stopped and climbed out of the front seat to welcome our followers.

The first guy to reach us announced happily, "The smart ass cracked up. Looks like you can fly yours now." We looked at one another curiously. The next arrival slapped me on the back and said, "Orville Wright wiped out. Why don't you get your plane out and do your stuff?"

There on the other side of the field I spotted our angry adversary. He sat there like a small boy over a broken toy, bent sideways on his bended knees, staring at the remains of his sleek black plane.

It looked like it had splattered like a water balloon. Someone said it took a nose dive from about two-hundred feet. Evidently, he had lost control and could only watch his virgin machine collide with the pavement at a devastating speed, disintegrating without any hope of ever being repaired.

A boy ran up to my side and bumped me. "Hey, mister, you gonna fly your plane now?"

"Well, uh...I, uh...." I glanced up at the sky, which was filled with large cumulus clouds. "Sorry, fella," I replied. "I can't fly a solar plane without the sun." I smiled sympathetically. "But we'll call Downey and check." Doug went to the phone booth, made believe he was making a call, and then returned with the sad news. The flight plans had been postponed.

A few more people approached us before we returned to the car, inquiring about our plane and its functions. "Do you know what a *dow* for a *booberday* is?" Steve asked.

"A what?" someone asked. We threw in a few more lines of gibberish to respond to their questions and then slowly drove off. We all felt sorry for our pompous antagonist—but not for long. We had entertained dozens of people, and they all enjoyed it, all but one guy who crashed his plane. We had a great time, as always, and we often reminisced about that incident, laughing at how *comedy isn't pretty*.

The plane, while being stored on a shelf in the clothes closet, met with a tragic end one night under a bag of laundry tossed unknowingly above the hangers. An unfortunate, quick crunch and it was history.

Here's some related Steve Martin airplane trivia. Steve has flown millions of miles since that fateful day. In fact, he even caused problems with the airline industry's 800 lines one day in the late seventies. When his comedy album *Let's Get Small* was released, he advertised an 800 line where people could hear him talking. It was another of those clever promotional scams that worked like, you guessed it, magic. When someone would call the 800 number, the caller would hear this message. "Hi, this is Steve. Why don't you go on down to your record store and buy my new album? I'll meet you there. Bring a friend, and they can buy one too."

It was brilliant. So brilliant, in fact, that, although they expected hundreds of calls a day, they got thousands an hour, which totally screwed up 800 lines all over the country, including United Airlines and Hertz.

One afternoon in 1981, I was talking with Steve, and I told him that I hadn't had a performing gig in a while because of our new baby. He said he was producing a television special called *Comedy Isn't Pretty*, and said that a casting director would call us, as they were hiring actors to fill various roles. Sure enough, we received the call a week or two later and met the cast at the L.A. Arboretum to shoot some scenes for the special. Although we didn't have speaking roles, we seemed to appear on camera a lot. It was terrific to see Steve in action at the helm of the production. Unfortunately, when the show was finally aired, most of the scenes we were in were left on the cutting room floor. The most amazing part of the situation to me was the fact that, although our appearances were not more than a few seconds long, we received $600 for the first airing and two more checks for $600 for the two times it ran after that. That kind of money was big stuff for us, and we really appreciated it, particularly at that time.

Just before we left the set at the L.A. Arboretum, we waved to Steve, and he stopped what he was doing to call us over. He asked how we were, and we talked for several minutes before departing. That was a valuable conversation. As we drove up the treacherous, winding, icy road through the San Bernadino Mountains to our home an hour southeast of L.A., we came around a bend to find the remnants of an accident that had occurred only minutes before we arrived. We helped one driver out of his inverted truck and tried to talk with him, but he was a slobbering drunk. We couldn't move the other driver, so we just comforted him the best we could. We waited until the police and the ambulances arrived, and then we continued on our way. We didn't need to discuss the series of events, but we both knew that the last few minutes we had spent with Steve had kept us from being the vehicle that idiot collided with. The driver of the other vehicle was not as lucky as the drunk.

Photograph from cover—early magic show, circa 1965

Chapter 15

THE GREAT OIL PAINTING CAPER

"The world today makes no sense, so why should I paint pictures that do?"
—Pablo Picasso

Steve could do most anything he set his mind to. He was capable beyond any of our peers in most things he aspired to achieve. He has scored music and written television shows, plays, screenplays, and books. In almost every case, he has won national, highly-coveted awards from Emmy's to Grammy's. But there was one thing Steve could never do; Steve couldn't draw. Maybe this explains why he is a passionate collector of fine art (primarily nineteenth-century American art). Steve currently has millions of dollars' worth of paintings he started collecting over twenty years ago.

In his most reclusive moments, he is known to sequester himself in a room with one of his highly prized paintings and look at it for hours like a kid watching *Barney*. He emerges from his solitude refreshed and revitalized. But whatever his personal admiration for drawing or painting is, he himself is not an artist. Fortunately for Steve, if he could not create something himself, he could go out and buy it. During our childhood, neither one of us had any money. We were just young men blasting off from high school into an unknown arena I called "the Matterhorn of life."

Steve would have surely had a showing of his art if he had been able to paint, but he wasn't so inclined. This reminds me of a story about something Steve did relative to art. In his early Hollywood days, while I was honorably performing my involuntary duties for the United States Armed Forces, Steve actually rented the Molly Brown Art Museum and presented to the media something called the "Steve Martin Invisible Art Show." Can you imagine? He figured out how to make something funny and profitable out of nothing at all. Steve proved that he really could make something of nothing! And this particular venture was the kind of creative caper that tickled the former "Fools" to no end.

The walls and easels at Steve's art opening sported magnificent empty frames, and all kinds of people came to view this inconceivable and, more precisely, invisible spectacle. Vacant pedestals with little brass plates identified the nonexistent pieces of art, which were so apparently not apparent. Only Steve could have carried off such a hoax. I was so impressed with his Invisible Art Show because it was a throwback to our former prankster days. When Steve wrote me about the event, I was stationed in Germany and immediately remembered the invisible-glass tricks we pulled in the hollowed halls of Rancho and Garden Grove high schools. I wanted to be at his art debut so badly. I told my first sergeant about it and asked if he could help me get some leave time, because Steve was a close friend, and this was going to be a turning point in his career. Let's just say that the U.S. Army didn't exactly see the beneficial effects of Steve's art show on the Vietnam War effort. I told the sergeant, "At least nobody dies!"

Five years before the memorable showing of that forgettable art, Steve and I still saw each other regularly, but it was no longer a daily habit. In 1963, we graduated from high school, but not from our fraternity of fools.

The Fools Unlimited and our mission of mirth still had a grip on us, and there were a few more pranks that we would pull off together. I was living in Fountain Valley, California in an unfinished room above a garage. I had an easel on which I'd created many magnificent blunders in oil paints, water paints, and general goop. The easel was set up next to a window that had become a haven for local birds. Beneath the easel was a piece of particleboard to catch the droppings of the various birds that had flown in the open window. One day I noticed that the particleboard was covered with droppings, dust, and ashes, and it was unmistakably disgusting. I carefully picked it up and put it on the easel. Something was missing. I studied my "creation" for a few minutes and realized what it needed. I proceeded to paint a solid black circle in one corner and a solid line from top left to bottom right. I stood back and looked at it and knew it was a terrific hoax in the making. I immediately called my partner in crime. Once again, our minds began brainstorming on a plot more detailed than anything we had ever conceived or pulled off to date. (Steve Martin was a hard habit to break. It wasn't until I fell in love with Lynn that I found a soul mate as close as Steve had been.)

It was a time in our lives when we were all facing the future with a keen curiosity. High school was completed. We were no longer little boys with nothing more to do than play games. But we were convinced that the painting caper would be our "Fool's" gold. We met and formulated our mission. For this event, Steve and I dressed in ties and sport coats, while Doug was more casual. We then drove to the Los Angeles County Art Museum, our artwork mounted in a slick metal frame and looking very professional. The Modern Art exhibit was upstairs on the third floor. We began to case the joint for a place to plant our painting. But finding the right location for this historic piece of art wasn't as hard as we thought it would be. There was a large room filled with the confusing and colorful art they called "modern."

On one wall was a large oil painting, maybe five feet by five feet. It had a plain background with three huge, orange balls changing slightly chromatically from light to dark. We studied this work and concluded that, although it might not have taken a lot of skill to paint that canvas, it did indeed take balls! Lo and behold, there was a vacant space on the wall right next to the orange balls painting! On the other side of the vacant space was a famous oil painting of a can of Spam by Ed Ruscha. We couldn't have created a more perfect location. So this was destined to be the final resting place of our magnificent, multi-media concoction.

After titling our painting "La Crapola De La Flambay," the purpose of our little Mission Impossible became more simple and the execution of it more complex. Now we knew where the painting would go, but how to get it there and on the wall was a problem. Fortunately, it was just the kind of problem we anticipated, and we swung into action. We met back at the Oldsmobile and proceeded with our dastardly scheme. Doug worked at a theater as a prop man, so it had been no problem for him to rig a nice professional frame for the "La Crapola" (that's what we called it for short, just short of calling it crap; bird crap would have been exactly correct). Steve volunteered to discreetly place a stick-on wall hook in the appropriate position while Doug and I tenaciously guarded the two entrances, looking out for guards and gallery personnel. At the L.A. County Museum, they obviously do not like people walking in and out with paintings unless they know who they are and exactly what is going on with the painting. Too bad they weren't ready for the likes of our little Mission Impossible group.

Circumstances considered, it became necessary for us to deceive those people entrusted with guarding the main entrance. Doug was well adapted to the art of tripping. Just like the old-time, professional stunt people, he would take a calculated risk with a fall or a trip to achieve laughs or get the job done. We all enjoyed tripping and stumbling in public. Rick Kendall even purposely and graciously fell off a dock at Balboa Island on one occasion as part of his initiation to the Fools Unlimited. Steve was an excellent tripper, more agile than the rest of us in general. Nevertheless, despite the fact that Steve was better qualified, Doug was chosen for the necessary tripping scene. Doug tripped with abandon. He also didn't care if he got hurt. When he was drafted, they rejected him because he apparently had fragile bones. The military doctors had determined this based on the fact that he had inexplicably broken his ankles a total of 13 times. He failed to explain to them that he had jumped off thirteen buildings for one reason or another. (Or for no reason at all.) Years later, Doug would take a final big leap off a four-story building in downtown L.A. He didn't really mean to fall this time, but he was drunk, slightly stoned, and experimenting with Quaaludes and with someone else's wife.

We had to get the security guard's attention off the main doorway, and Doug was the main distraction. There was also a young lady in an information booth by the two huge entrance doors looking through an inside window. Apparently, her job was to watch and give out information to the visitors. There she sat, just inside the entrance, with a clear view of the large hallway through which all visitors had to pass. It was my job to talk to her and block her vision while Steve casually walked in and placed our "La Crapola De La Flambay" behind a wooden bench just out of her vision. This part of the plan was quite slick. Doug, in his own inimitable style, strolled quickly by the young lady, smiled, and proceeded to fall down four marble stairs landing neatly on his face. As he lay there writhing in pain, gasping for breath and twisting his face in agony, I approached the lady behind the window. She was a bit disturbed, and her attention was drawn to the security guard and Doug. It worked just as we planned.

I placed myself in her line of vision the opposite side of the hall. Between Doug's antics and my positioning, neither the security guard nor the gal at the counter could see Steve walk swiftly from the entrance to the bottom of the staircase where he quickly stashed the "La Crapola" behind the wooden bench we'd selected. Doug recovered, thanked the guard for his help, and in a few minutes was with us again.

Phase One was completed. We all sat silently on the bench gazing around the room, hoping our six legs and feet would cover up our contribution to modern art that was resting on the floor behind us. Now the security guard was talking to the girl at the counter and his back was towards us. His rather pudgy body was blocking out the girl completely. Now was the time. We grabbed the painting and proceeded to the second floor. As I reached the top step and glanced down the hallway, I noticed two men walking in our direction, so I signaled Doug and Steve to halt. Steve, who had the painting in hand, didn't hesitate to slide it behind the door at the top of the stairs—and there we all stood innocently.

Finally, after what seemed an eternity of waiting and hustling from hiding place to hiding place, we reached the third floor of the colossal building. There were a few tourists drifting through, but not much traffic to speak of. Soon the room was clear of people. We could see that the hook Steve had stuck to the wall was still there, and we hoped it was stuck firmly enough to hold the painting.

We rolled into action, with Doug guarding the north entrance to the room and me at the other. Steve quickly apprehended the masterpiece, and then dashed in. He looked both ways, then jumped over the low-hanging rope that separates these valuable paintings from the public's hands. I peaked around the corner on my end of the room in time to see a man and woman ascending the staircase. I signaled Doug at the other end of the hallway, but Steve was still busy hanging and straightening the fraudulent "Crapola." I looked again as they approached the top of the stairs on our floor, and Steve was still adjusting the painting. Needless to say, it would not have been good for Steve if anyone in authority had caught him behind the rope messing with paintings.

Right next to me at the top of the stairs was a statue of rather immense dimensions. It looked like it was made of plaster. I had a small goatee and was dressed fairly well, so I stepped in front of the couple, blocking their way, greeting them with a smile. I began explaining the abstract statue to them in an effort to keep them from catching Steve behind the rope. "This statue, believe it or not, is made of plaster."

"Is that so?" the man said. "Do you work here?"

"No," I countered, "I'm...er...the artist who created this particular piece and an assistant professor of abstract sculpture at UCLA."

"You look awfully young to be an assistant professor," the woman said softly.

"Nevertheless, I am, and this particular work of art is my most successful piece to date."

The man was still sizing me up as he glanced at the plaque and said, "It says here that this is Franz Klouber's statue." I could see Steve down the aisle behind him, still behind the rope, straightening "La Crapola."

I could see Doug at the other end of the hall, not able to get Steve's attention and gesturing to me with a wave of his hands his inability to do anything. The man started to turn, so I purposely stumbled and then grabbed his shoulder for stability. He looked at me again, and I said, "I, er, uh, sold it to Franz after the revolution!"

"Revolution?" he said. "What revolution?"

Why the hell did I say revolution? He just stood there with a big, blank, confused look on his face. Steve heard me stalling for time, and by the time these tourists looked around, he was casually standing appraising the artwork from the proper side of the rope.

I faked a pain in my leg and said, "Excuse me, just talking about this hurts my, uh, wound."

I then limped to a nearby bench and sat there as if in pain, motioning them on. After the couple walked thorough the room and gazed at the various paintings, including ours, they walked briskly out of the building. The three of us gathered together by a bench across the room from our contribution to modern art, and there we sat, overjoyed with the success of our seemingly pointless venture. Quite frankly, there was a point to be made. Several museum-goers, all ages, wandered by our painting. They glanced and then walked on. Not one hesitated or said anything about this horrible mess we lovingly called "Crapola." We were entertained beyond words, but our paranoia over our illicit activity was still resting in our throats.

All of a sudden, from behind the bench we were sitting on, a huge security guard appeared and grabbed Doug by the shoulder. We all snapped around, our faces white and our bodies limp. Doug looked up at this massive man like a puppy, expecting to get busted and arrested.

"No smoking," the guard stated in a stern voice.

A relieved Doug put his cigarette out in the palm of his hand. There were no ashtrays, as usual, and Doug didn't want to miss a chance to entertain. Then, it was time for us trendsetters to head home. We had made our artistic statement, and the job was done.

As we were leaving the museum, the girl behind the window asked Doug if he was all right from his fall earlier. "I'm okay, thank you," he said, faking another clumsy trip down the steps he'd been approaching.

Just then a man in his forties, dressed in a plaid suit, quickly strolled by us with a large oil painting under his arm. "That guy is walking out with one of your paintings!" Steve exclaimed to the young lady and pointed to the man escaping with the canvas.

"Oh, don't worry, he came in with a painting," she responded sarcastically.

"Does that mean if you come in with one, you can leave with one?" I inquired.

"Yes," she said matter-of-factly. Apparently, we could have walked right into this heavily guarded facility with the painting right under our arm!

"Well, good-bye." We waved to her and walked out, our mugs shimmering with success.

Two weeks later, on November 22, 1963, Doug and I were returning to the Museum of Modern Art to see if our "La Crapola" was still on the wall. It was a surreal experience when the radio announcer began repeatedly announcing that President Kennedy had been shot in Dallas. "He's been shot, the President has been shot, he's been shot, President Kennedy has been shot..." We couldn't believe it was happening, as we had never experienced a political assassination before, and we didn't know how to react. Did anyone? Nevertheless, we were close to our destination, so we proceeded to the main door of the museum of Modern Art. However, it was closed for remodeling.

To this day, we don't know what happened to the original "Crapola," but I'm sure that whoever found that masterpiece still has it and enjoys telling the story of how they found it mysteriously hanging on the museum's wall. We also still wonder if they ever found out what the painting was made of.

This episode was nearly one of the last of the Fools' golden years of pranks, but, no doubt, a genuine precursor of some of the truly classic Steve Martin routines that manifested themselves while he was playing clubs around the country as a stand-up comedian. One time, years after the painting caper, Steve was playing a club in the Midwest. While the lines were forming outside, a van drove back and forth with a loudspeaker hooked up and Steve inside saying to the crowd, "I wouldn't pay good money to see Steve Martin!" Guess who!

He had countless, silly routines where the audience would be included in his pranks. At a small club in Florida, he took the entire audience outside and told them to hide. He then put his thumb out, and when a car stopped, he asked if they could give his friends a ride, too.

The following were two of the most memorable Steve Martin club pranks. He was performing at a small club near Vanderbilt University in Nashville. The club had seating for about 200 folks. There was no dressing room and nowhere to go after the show. So he invited the audience to go with him to a local joint. Like a modern day Piped Piper, everyone followed. When he got to a local hamburger stand, he shouted out an order for three hundred hamburgers. A few minutes after the laughter died down, he changed his order to an order of french fries.

Another time, Steve was performing at a college in Columbia, South Carolina. There was an empty swimming pool located directly in front of the theater. He conned the entire audience to get into the pool; whereupon, he dove in on top of the crowd and, with their helpful hands, swam to the other side. It was 1976, and he was racking up a reputation that landed him his first network variety show. On October 23, Steve hosted *Saturday Night Live* for the first time, with Bill Murray, Jane Curtin, Dan Akroyd and the late John Belushi.

It was about that time when Steve started seriously collecting artwork. It was a genuine *déjà vu* for me when I saw Steve's movie *L.A. Story*. There he was, probably one of the museum's most ardent fans, a major contributor to the institution, and he was sneaking around until he could fold little wheels out of his customized shoes and start roller-skating around the galleries. He had the same look on his face as the day we planted "La Crapola" on those hallowed walls.

Chapter 16

STUDLY STEVE

"Sex is the most fun you can have without laughing."
—Leo Rosten

Barbara Walters is famous for interviewing the hottest celebrities of the moment. Her forte is visiting them in their homes and exposing their opinions and lifestyle to the world in a way that no one else can. Her reputation depends on acquiring only the most eccentric, most powerful, or wealthiest personalities that no one else can get. Steve Martin was quickly becoming an international phenomenon when he was asked to appear on the *Barbara Walters Show*.

The couch-potato Babs fans were waiting with baited breath as the show began. You can imagine that it was an unusual opening. Once introduced, Steve asked her if he could blindfold her while they drove to his chalet. It was a great surprise when they arrived at the house and it turned out to be just an old shack. This is where the interview took place. Steve was affable and, as usual, very funny. Steve makes his money by entertaining folks, and you can always rely on the fact that he will come up with rewarding and novel material no matter what. But Barbara didn't seem amused.

I remember one year at the Golden Globe awards. Steve appeared on stage on a huge screen where he was holding a microphone and standing in front of the Eiffel Tower in Paris. He began talking about how his busy schedule hadn't afforded him enough time to make it back for the Golden Globes, but during his little speech, he kept looking off camera and repeating emphatically, "Don't touch that button." He continued to carry on about his incredible trip abroad and every once in a while telling the person off camera, "Don't touch that button." Finally, he looked startled and shouted, "No, don't touch the button!" as if the person had done just that.

At that moment, the whole stage at the award ceremony began rotating around, displaying what was on the other side of the screen. Suddenly, the audience could see Steve standing in front of a camera holding a mike with a small screen behind him displaying a view of the Paris scene. This ruse was priceless. The Golden Globes and Academy Awards shows, for all the pomp and circumstance, all too often demonstrate just how hopelessly lost the stars are in an ad-lib or live situation. The planning of this nationally televised hoax was, no doubt, the brainchild of Steve Martin himself. It had Steve's signature written across the routine as indelibly as the memory it rekindled in this old "Fool."

Tricks and games for the sake of a great, surprised response was a way of life for the Gopher Boys. Steve lived on Brookside, and I lived on Eleanor Drive in Garden Grove, California. It was a quick, three-minute walk to get to each other's house. Most of the homes in the area looked alike, static stucco. It was beginning to be an Orange County tradition—housing tracts. Five or six houses up the street from Steve's place there lived another boy who attended school with us. His name was Frank Ford, and he was our age. Frank had an older sister, who was perhaps sixteen when Steve and I were twelve. She was actually a very attractive girl, but, unfortunately, she had psychological problems. Although her appearance was unaffected, she had the wandering, curious mind of a three-year-old. As we walked by her house, she would stand in her yard, one toe pointed awkwardly in, and coyly say to one of us, "Hi, boy." We would smile back at her and say,

"Hi," feeling sorry for her but unavoidably attracted to her protruding womanhood.

While strolling home from the store one day, we walked by her house as usual, but this day there was something a little unusual. She was standing there in translucent panties too tight for her and no top on at all, her budding breasts larger than life itself. We gawked at her as she tilted her pretty head downward and then looked up at us with her big brown eyes and said, "Hi, boy." Her pert nipples seemed to stand at attention, each one in its own way repeating, "Hi, boy. Hi, boy."

We said, "Hi," back, giggled and stared, and then walked on by. Steve tripped over the curb, and I ran into a tree, but we both looked back at her slim, sensual-looking body as she waved and mouthed the words, "Bye, boy." We then looked at one another with bulging eyes. Her mother finally came out and grabbed her by the arm, yanking her back into the seclusion of their stucco abode.

This brings to mind a movie Steve produced with Carl Reiner. If you saw Steve's *Dead Men Don't Wear Plaid*, you will no doubt remember the leading lady, Rachel Ward. She was, without a doubt, one of the best-looking leading ladies Steve ever worked with. In the opening scene, she fainted into his arms. He shook her a little to make sure she was out, and then kissed her passionately. She didn't respond, so he shook her again like she was a big, rubber sex doll. Then he looked around to make sure nobody was observing, and carried her to the couch. When she woke up, he had his large hands gently massaging and exploring her breasts. She asked, "What are you doing?"

With a very matter-of-fact attitude, he responded, "You fainted, and your breasts were all out of whack—I was adjusting them!"

She smiled curiously and said, "Thank you." There is no doubt in my mind that Steve wrote that part into the show.

My next-door neighbor was a heavy-set real estate broker named Norm Abrams. One afternoon, he conned Steve and me into doing some advertising work for him. We needed the bucks, and he needed our youthful enthusiasm to disperse leaflets regarding his business.

So here we were, working for Norm. He would pay us fifty cents an hour. This seemed to be a fair wage, until we realized that he would be coaching us like we were training for the Olympics while we were performing our duties. Steve would go door-to-door on one side of the street, and I on the other. Norm would drive slowly down the middle of the residential avenue shouting, "Hup, hup, run, run, run. It's good exercise. Double time! Come on, let's move. Chop, chop!" Not until I was drafted and my drill sergeant started barking at me did I hear that kind of prodding again.

Gasping for air, we would catch a glimpse of each other jumping hedges and flower beds, always punctuated by his frequent "Chop, chop! Remember, it's good exercise!" As we puffed and pushed our aching legs to promote Norm's business, I looked at Steve's face and felt intuitively that Steve would never find his fate or fortune in manual labor.

I was reminded of this event by Norm's daughter, Sue, at our ten-year high school reunion. Lynn and I were on the road performing in British Columbia when I heard about the reunion. Tom Carter, a good friend and vice president of our class, tracked me down. I returned for the occasion, hoping to see old friends and especially Steve.

I decided that I had to wear something unusual to the reunion. I found a rare, seventy-year-old set of tails and spats that fit perfectly. As Lynn and I arrived at the hotel near Orange Country Airport (now known as the John Wayne Airport), we began to recognize old friends. At the ten-year reunion, they hadn't changed too much—at the thirty-year reunion, we all looked like Muppets.

Very casual California attire was the order of the day, but I was enjoying my outlandish regalia. When we finally finished the ritual of signing in, I glanced across the banquet room to see my old friend, Steve Martin. There was a comfortable, warm chill that came over both of us when we saw one another. I hadn't talked to Steve for about a year. Ironically, he was the only other person in the whole assemblage dressed in an old tuxedo with tails! I felt the same kind of satisfaction as when we tripped on the chain together, without a word spoken prior to the action. We shook hands, sharing a smile that made the whole reunion worthwhile.

That night, I spoke with a girl named Jean Mann, a tall, short-haired, athletic girl I had taken out in high school. She had also been one of Ratty's best friends. Jean said, "Morris, I'm still pissed off at you!"

"Why?" I asked curiously.

She looked at me with a stoic expression and questioned me further. "Do you remember the night Ratty and Steve and you and I double-dated at the Warner Drive-in theater?"

No, actually I did not, but I surely remembered the Warner Drive-in in Huntington Beach and every other drive-in theater within fifty miles of Garden Grove. Drive-ins were the cheapest and best places to take a date. There was always the promise of cheap thrills, primary passion, and, sometimes, accidental procreation. We were either pulling pranks or exploring regions of the opposite sex that were becoming more interesting to us than comedy. At the Warner Drive-in theater, you could get a whole car of people in for a flat rate of a buck-fifty. You didn't need to smuggle five people in the trunk of the car to save money. You could have as many as you wanted in the car. Even though there was no need to be deceptive, the "Fools" used to smuggle in three or four people in the trunk, just for kicks.

I couldn't remember a thing about the incident until she began to relate it to me. When I finally heard her recollection, it made me laugh out loud. I didn't remember it as well as she did, but I certainly did remember what happened—including the prelude to the incident itself.

Jean reminded me that this is what we did: Steve and I always thought it would be extremely entertaining if two seniors in high school went to the drive-in dressed in pajamas like little children. The girls were tickled with the idea, so, sure enough, we wore our kiddy pajamas to the drive-in. We knew the girls wouldn't come with us to the snack bar to see the public's response, so we devised phase two of the plan expressly for them.

We went gleefully to the line forming by the candy section and stood there looking at the ceiling like innocent, little children. The people who hesitated and stared at our "jammies" could not resist a smile when they noticed Steve's little teddy bear clutched tightly in his huge hairy hand. Some snickered softly, and some laughed out loud. Amazingly enough, the little kids didn't notice at all. They thought it looked like the appropriate attire for the occasion.

Meanwhile, back at the Chevy (we were in Steve's parents' car), Ratty and Jean discussed their feelings about us. Little things like what we had already tried, how far they would go, if they enjoyed being felt-up or making-out? You know, teeny-boppers love to talk and compare those types of important issues. It's only natural. What wasn't natural, and what I had forgotten about completely, was that we had stashed a small, battery-powered, reel-to-reel tape recorder under the seat that captured all their discussions. I don't know how that tape got out of our hands, but, evidently, it offered quite a bit of entertainment to a lot of other Garden Grove classmates and cronies. After all these years, Jean was still rightfully mad at Steve and me.

I've already mentioned Basil Poledouris as another genius who came from old Garden Grove High School. You have heard his music in many movies over the years: *The Blue Lagoon, Big Wednesday*, all the *Conan* movies, *The Hunt for Red October*, and the list goes on and on. The last credit I noticed was *Under Siege II* with Steven Segal, and *Les Misérables*. Basil was very popular in school, and he looked older than the other guys. He had a heavier shadow of beard and, luckily for him, he started his sexual escapades earlier than the rest of us. Basil, who back then was known as Bill Poledouris, was a kind and keenly sensitive musician whom both Steve and I admired in school. He played guitar and piano long before we ever tried to play instruments. The result for Basil was a career in composing music for over one hundred flicks.

Sometime after graduation from high school, when Steve had stopped working at Knott's Berry Farm and was starting his college career, Basil and Steve went to Catalina Island. On a clear day, you can see Catalina from the Southern California mountains. It's a wonderful, year-round resort, with ships from all over the world sailing in to visit the well-known casino and bay in the protected harbor. The small town of Avalon bristles with tourist activity in the summer and slows to a crawl in the long winter months.

On that particular adventure, Basil had invited Steve to perform for the Long Beach Yacht Club in Avalon. Although Basil had played guitar and sung with a group called the Southlanders in high school, his job there was simply to play the piano. Steve was to perform his magic act. The older Steve got, the more his comedy permeated his magic act. A portion of his show was comedy even back then. It was more a combination of dialogue associated with his deft hands performing effective illusions. This improvisation had been a long, transitional metamorphosis from his ten-year-old magic act, where he would simply memorize the standard lines that came with the tricks in the little magic kits he would buy.

So Basil and Steve hopped on board Basil's cousin's yacht, and off they went to Catalina with visions of bikini-clad beauties running around in their heads. Steve's heart had taken a long time to heal since his romance with Stormie Sherke. The relationship had left him with many scars.

Shortly after they docked, Steve told Basil that he was going to take a look around. Steve has always been a curious traveler. Even as a young man, nothing escaped his sense of wonderment about the world around him. Although women were, of course, a part of his curiosity, they did not totally dictate his basic approach to life. Nevertheless, a couple of hours later Steve returned—with a gorgeous lady clinging tightly to his arm. High school had concluded several months earlier, and Steve already looked the part of the established, college campus stud. Basil said that he and the other guys were a little dumbfounded, because Steve had acquired a real gem and they had nothing to show for their time and hunting efforts on the island. Steve introduced the young lady to his friends and announced that he would be back at seven, knowing that the show started at seven-thirty.

At seven-thirty, Basil glanced at his watch and thought, "Steve must be getting laid." He looked up, and there stood a slyly-smiling Steve—the lost virgin. And our hero was no longer a boy. He couldn't wipe the grin off his face all evening. Basil told me that when he asked him, "How was it?" Steve had only one word to describe his entry into the world of sex.

"It was *great!*"

Chapter 17

WHAT'S MONEY GOT TO DO WITH IT?

"His money is twice tainted; tain't your's and tain't mine!"
—Mark Twain

Before Jim Carrey or Jay Leno, there was Steve Martin. And before there was Steve Martin, there was Martin and Lewis, Abbott and Costello, George Burns (God Bless his soul) and his best friend, Jack Benny.

Steve was never an impersonator. That's a different kind of talent. Steve has always been Steve doing another version of Steve. He could never do accents, they always came off sounding strange. But whether he was trying to do a French accent or a Spanish accent, it was always his own concoction with a different twist. In *My Blue Heaven*, his impression of an Italian accent was more like Steve doing Joe Pesci. But that's what people love about Steve, his individuality in all of his artistic endeavors. Impersonating is just one aspect of comedy that Steve never really pursued. It would not have enhanced his brand of humor. In fact, it would have detract-

ed from it. I doubt that you will ever see Steve cast in a role portraying another famous person, as Anthony Hopkins did in *Nixon*.
Of course, he does willingly play roles like *Sergeant Bilko* (for several million bucks). But that kind of acting was left entirely up to
Steve's own impressions of what this fictional cartoon character
would be like, based on the comic strip and the old TV show with
Phil Silvers.

Of all the old-time comedians, Steve truly loved Jack Benny
the most, and was able to gather the poise and sophistication to
master that classic Benny look. With just a few words, all who witnessed this impersonation by the young Steve Martin knew instantly that he was the great Jack Benny incarnate. Steve picked up tid-
bits from all the great comics who were, in fact, part-time mentors
to the young genius who was absorbing information, skills, and
techniques like a sponge. There was only one other time I saw
Steve mimic one of the comedians he had watched as a kid. In
Dirty Rotten Scoundrels, as Steve played the dumb brother of his
co-star, Michael Caine, he actually did a spectacular impersonation
of Jerry Lewis playing a slobbering, incoherent, crazy person. I'm
not sure he was trying to impersonate Jerry Lewis. He was definitely a Martin and Lewis fan when he was a kid.

There was a lot more to Steve's adoration of Jack Benny than
most observers might think. He adored Benny's cheapskate routines. He identified with the desperation of needing money on a
daily basis and squeezing every penny. This made Benny's material all the more humorous to Steve personally. Although Steve's
parents were financially secure, Steve had to earn every cent for
everything he needed or wanted, including lunch money or transportation to Disneyland. You see, Glenn and Mary Lee Martin
loved Steve and Melinda dearly, but, for whatever reason, it was
not within their nature to dole out money to them. This was an
early and profound directive for Steve's unmistakable "Pure
Drive" to become rich...very rich.

Unlike Steve's family, my mother would provide me with
small amounts of money. She was certainly not in any better financial position than the Martins, but she just couldn't resist. When we
needed things, she would buy them. When we wanted to go places,
she would take us and pay for it. There was a gaping ravine
between Marjorie Walker's approach and the Martins' approach to

money for kids. It's very simple—we got it, Steve earned it. I would borrow a nickel from Steve for milk, and he would bug me about it for days. I thought he was a cheapskate. It was years later before I realized how we had both been conditioned about money.

Our ideas were a product of what we had been forced to understand. I understood that if I wanted something, I simply asked Mom for it. Steve, on the other hand, was not exposed to such a liberal situation. His parents did not shower him with gifts or clothes. For the most part, it seemed like whatever money he did get his hands on, he had to earn, and therefore, it had to be carefully budgeted. He learned his lesson very well. When Steve was with my family, my mother would pay for Steve, no matter what it was that required money. Steve was witness to a different type of priority in our family. My belief now is that there is a wonderful middle-of-the-road parental philosophy in which kids are neither spoiled nor deprived. Although Steve's attitude towards money seemed to change when he got out of college, he still had a solid "budget minded" self-confidence.

I do maintain, and history will bear out the fact, that Steve is a self-made man. There was no Hollywood nepotism that smoothed his way into the entertainment field. This is a rare scenario in this world where rich or connected relatives and friends are so often used as stepping stones.

You've probably heard about how Elvis would give his friends and fellow performers gifts of Lincolns and Cadillacs. But did you know that Steve Martin gave his agent, Marty Klein, a new Rolls Royce? He didn't do if for the publicity; he did it because he wanted to. To Steve, this was an act of gratitude. Steve always believed in paying his debts. As soon as he was hired by Mason Williams to be one of the writers for the *Smothers Brothers' Show*, he was granted a salary of $500 a week. This was a lot of money in those days. For a twenty-one-year-old kid in 1967, $2,000 a month was a lot of money. And the first thing Steve did was buy a color television set for his parents. Steve has done a lot of generous things for his parents over the years.

I'd like to share a revealing incident that took place when we were still seniors in high school. Doug Rowell, Rick Kendall, Steve, and I attended a magic show at the Anaheim Bowl on Lincoln Avenue. Steve drove us in his parents' '57 Chevy that he bought from them in his senior year. (Of course, my mother gave me my car. Who do you think appreciated the value of having a car the most?) We were all spruced up that night and trying very hard to look mature. Rick was the soft-spoken one with a very clever mind. He was not always seeking attention, but it turned out that he would attract it by virtue of the fact that he would always say something witty. Like young gentlemen, we arrived at the dinner show area of the bowling alley. Considering it was a bowling alley, it was fairly ornate, decorated with red velvet and such. We were allowed to enter the dinner show area and partake of the cuisine, but we were, of course, under age and not allowed to drink. The dinner was nominal, but the setting was pleasing to these four young men assuming an older, executive look.

Finally, the curtain rose, and we were amused by the magician who was really no better than Steve. But Steve, even in those early years, was ever so gracious towards other performers. In all the time I've known him, I have never heard him bad-mouth another performer. (Except on one occasion, when he was doing a college concert near Houston, Texas. I kept bugging him, asking him who was the biggest jerk he ever worked with. At long last he confided that it was Mac Davis.)

Meanwhile, back at the bowling alley, as the departure time neared, Doug and I excused ourselves and went to the men's room. Inside the restroom, I noticed another exit. We decided this time we would play a joke on our own friends by slipping out the back door and leaving Rick and Steve to pay the bill. We agreed we would wait outside and pay them when they finally realized what we were doing.

It was a rainy night and unusually cold for California at that time of year. We shivered and laughed about what extreme contortions Steve must be going through when he realized he was going to be stuck paying. We did talk about the fact that he might be mad, but assumed that in the end we would all just laugh about it.

Finally, after what seemed like an hour or more, we saw Rick and Steve dashing from the main door to the car. We shouted, and Steve looked at us quickly from over his shoulder. We started jogging across the puddle-filled parking lot and were about halfway there when Steve pulled out, waving at us. Then he drove off, leaving us standing there in the freezing rain. We stopped and looked at each other, and agreed that he might be a little angry. He must have been really pissed off, because after standing there in the rain for another half-hour, we knew he was not coming back. I learned a very important lesson about the young Steve Martin on that rainy night in Anaheim. When it comes to money matters, don't play games with Steve. Few things were as serious to Steve as his money.

My mom eventually rescued us, and we kidded ourselves into thinking that it had been worth it to get a free dinner from Steve. But I felt really bad about it for a long time because I knew I hurt Steve, and never before or since had I seen him so cold or angry at me. We never talked about this incident again. By the next time I saw him, it was forgotten, maybe.

Getting back to the point I was making, eventually money came to Steve, like metal to a magnet. It didn't come easily. It was a roller-coaster ride of unparalleled proportions, but a quick one lasting only a few years. In the great scheme of things, a few years of struggling is an exceptionally short time compared with other talented entertainers who struggle for a lifetime and never reach the top, or even get successful sustenance in their chosen field.

For a while after college, it looked like Steve was on his way up financially, writing for the Smothers Brothers and then a short stint with a show starring Ray Stevens. Then he wrote for Sonny and Cher, John Denver, and Glenn Campbell, and was knocking down a hefty $1,500 a week. Money was important, but the performing side of Steve was gripping him. He thought, "Am I going to grow old spending my life writing jokes for other people?" He just wanted to be in front of audiences. He could have kept on grinding out the gag-writing jobs for the rest of his life. At twenty-three he was an Emmy Award-winning writer in Hollywood, a town that traditionally wastes youth away. But he broke away and began performing at small clubs again.

He went through a period when he drank and smoked a little dope, but cautiously, ever so cautiously, unlike many of his peers. When Steve started having a drink before he went on stage, he thought he was becoming an alcoholic. At that time, he had long, brown hair with streaks of gray and a full beard. His act consisted of juggling and magic, as well as comedy lines. He worked coffee-houses and clubs from L.A. to San Francisco. However, it got to the point where he was making only a couple hundred dollars a night and not really entertaining the audience the way he wanted to.

When his long-time friend and manager, Bill McEuen (John's older brother), booked him on the road as the opening act for the Nitty Gritty Dirt Band, he had many a miserable night when he couldn't get a rise out of the audience. They were stoned, drunk, and spaced out, basically enduring his act about as well as he was enduring their disorientation and apathy.

One night, in 1970, he was performing as an opening act for The Dirt Band, The Birds and The Animals. His response from that audience was so bad that he called the experience "humiliating." I myself have also done thousands of shows on the road to audiences—good, bad, and indifferent, and believe me, indifferent is the worst. At least Steve was able to pull out of the nose dive. He made a big change in his life by uprooting himself and leaving Hollywood. He had a girlfriend at the time named Iris. I never met her, but he must have thought a lot of her because they moved to Santa Fe together. For a year they lived there, which was a long time for Steve to be with one woman in those days. Steve had made a sincere promise to himself never to go in front of the rock 'n' roll type of audience again. It was too demoralizing for him. It's demoralizing for any comedian.

I've seen audiences sometimes forget that the performers on stage are human. They are treated as targets for the restless audience's mood swings. I've played in clubs where a jukebox got more attention. In fact, I've played in honky-tonks where someone would drop money in the jukebox in the middle of the show. Now that's a tough crowd. But nobody in the business of working their way up through clubs has successful nights without their share of the dismal nights of rejection and frustration, including even "The King," Elvis Presley. All of us on the road have scores of these kinds of trials and tribulations. I've been in this business as long as Steve has, and I will never watch an act, no matter how bad, without offering a round of applause for the performer. I have on many occasions been the only person in the audience who was clapping. Believe me, when you are up there, that one person can make all the difference in the world. I know it's hard to imagine that Steve could do a show with no response, but you can surely believe that in the beginning there were some rough times. Those were lonely years for him, full of disappointments.

Steve began to doubt his potential for a successful career as a comedian during these difficult times. Being on the road and trying to maintain a relationship with his main squeeze, Iris, was too difficult, and finally, he parted company with her. He also had the need to be alone, periodically, and I don't think Iris could accept a part-time lover. Steve is generally warm and personable. I've never known him to be other than that in my relationship with him, but there is that loner inside of him. He has a distant, private side that sets him apart from most people who are just as gregarious as he.

He wore crazy outfits in those days of the early seventies and his act fluctuated. Money was really tight for him again, and from time to time, he wondered why he had left the security of writing comedy in Hollywood. Before long, he was asked to perform as an opening act for Ann Margaret, another upswing in his lagging career. Although this was a good thing, Steve was generally put off with Las Vegas audiences. They were a lot like the rock 'n' roll audience: enthusiastically apathetic and overly concerned with alcohol, gambling, and sex.

There were other bumpy times, too, like when Steve was hired to do the Playboy Club circuit and he thought he was back on track. He actually called it his "big break." However, the audiences turned out to be even more dismal than Las Vegas in general. A busboy even stole one of his suits from his dressing room. Nobody responded to his humor, and he learned what it was really like to "die" on stage. He called these days "blow-your-brains-out times." He was further quoted as saying they were "absolutely the worst audiences in the world."

Steve returned to Hollywood defeated and began working as a writer again on a show called the *Ken Berry WOW Show*. Berry had been one of the stars on the timeless, TV favorite *Mayberry RFD*. The show had mild comedy glimpses of different periods in history—the thirties and forties and so forth. Unfortunately, it didn't wow the audiences. Steve did develop friendships with Cheryl Ladd (at the time Cheryl Stopplemore) and Teri Garr. Despite his career ups and downs, Steve still had an ample amount of money saved from budgeting and careful financial planning. He appeared as guest host on the *Tonight Show* periodically, which gave him a nice financial and career boost.

In 1974, Steve discovered the charms of Aspen, Colorado. A lot of people had done that, thanks to John Denver's song "Rocky Mountain High," and of course, Steve and John were friends. In fact, so many people had come into Colorado over those years from a smoggy California that there were bumper stickers that said, "Don't Californicate Colorado." Nevertheless, Steve loved it and bought a solar-heated home in the mountains near Aspen.

Moving to Aspen was good for Steve. He made some life-time decisions that were, without a doubt, directly responsible for helping him become a superstar. Steve gave up drinking and smoking pot, and became a practicing vegetarian. People can ruin their health, waste money, and destroy their initiative with one or more of these habits. This was not Steve's destiny. Instead, he got into top shape and became an avid skier.

We were on tour in Colorado one particularly nasty winter, and I called Steve in Aspen to see if he was home. He had his friend, Teri Garr, with him at the time. When we visited, she was pretty depressed about her career but was warm and friendly to us. She has done quite well over the years since that freezing night in Aspen, with leading roles in many major movies. It was fun for us to visit with them that evening and to share some of their vegetarian cuisine. The time passed quickly, and soon we thought we should be leaving. It seemed near blizzard conditions when we left Steve's spacious house that night, but we had a little wooden camper with a wood-burning stove on the back of our pickup truck.

That night, we found a place in a state park to set up camp. We were young and in love and warm despite the weather; however, it got so cold that night that my anti-freeze actually froze. That's how I can still remember how cold it was. But I need nothing to remind me of the warmth of my wife Lynn's love on countless nights on the road. As much as I have tried to extricate myself from these memoirs, I think it's important to mention, from time to time, my Middle American status while Steve rose to his mind-boggling success. Yet, I could no more give up my life with my family for Steve's success than Steve could think about sacrificing all that he has for something that perhaps some would feel is as easy to acquire as a wife and children.

Years later, when I was living in the mountains in Big Bear, I invited Steve to come skiing. His response was not exactly sneering, but it was a careful and definite rejection, suggesting that he would not ski in anywhere less than the best areas. I didn't hold this against Steve; I guess I was only a little surprised at his response. Before moving to Aspen, Steve had been wearing loud pink shirts and band uniform coats when he first hit the road performing. Soon, it was transition time, and he began reorganizing and changing his act. At that point in time, it had not produced the results he wanted.

There was another Playboy gig that was disappointing; however, it made a credible difference in Steve's future. He had to perform for a group of Japanese businessmen who were not the least interested in anything but Playboy Bunnies and booze. The day after the show, he purchased a white suit he saw in the window of a thrift store. He paid $25 for the old suit, which was quite a bit for a thrift store suit at that time. But there was a little bit of magic in that suit. Before he eventually hung up his white suit routine, he would be paying thousands for finely tailored suits and haberdashers to fit him properly. And yet, they were always just a bit too tight. He wanted them to look that way. It gave him the smooth look when he needed it and the gawky look when he would do highly animated routines like "Let's Get Small."

Performers live for an audience. It's the rush one receives from the applause and acceptance that gives a performer life. Any entertainer who has toured on the road and done countless gigs, like Steve or John McEuen, can tell you about a very strange phenomenon. You can be sick with the flu, for instance; deathly sick with a fever and aching muscles that scream to be soaked in something hot enough to burn—those nights when the money is shorter than short, and the motel rooms are frigid and dirty. When you are sharing your deepest thoughts with a cockroach the size of a '38 Packard and wondering why you ever wanted to be an entertainer. You have to fight the blizzard and go to the club to do your show barely able to stand up. You just can't cancel...and it's not only the money. It's those people you've never met whom you owe something to, and this is what drives you. Then, if God is good to you that night, the metamorphosis of a miracle begins. You are introduced to the audience, and whether they applaud or not, you mount that mighty steed, the stage. You do your best, you put out all you have. Slowly you get a grip on the sort of crowd it is as your clothes cling to you with an icy sweat. The material starts working, the audience begins to respond. They clap, they giggle, they laugh. You begin to roll at first with the punches and then with the punch lines. You ad-lib a line or two. It works, you feel a motion within you that takes hold of your performance and you know that the audience is with you. Now you are flying high on the wings of a thunderous applause and the cheers of those who have, hopefully, come to love you. They are giving you an energy in return for what you have given them. Time is up, the show is over, you finish your last line and bow—only to look up and see them leap to their feet, beating their hands together wildly and screaming their approval. You do an encore, and they respond adoringly again. You leave the stage. You are healed.

This is what can happen to an entertainer. This happened to Steve. It happened to me. It's the juice that keeps you going, because no matter how long it has been between the standing ovations and the encores, you never forget. The endorphins are the same as the endorphins that drive world-class athletes to break all records. It's no different. You sweat, you suffer, you strain, you don't give up, and you win. It's an electrical exchange of energy that transpires between an audience and performer, and it's the manna an entertainer lives for. It was nights like that in Steve's struggling years which drove him to the phenomenal heights he has achieved in his career. Steve has performed at the MGM Grand in Las Vegas and made an incredible $160,000 for one show. There were days when people would stand in line and wait from five in the morning until show time in the evening, just to see him perform his comedy.

It's also interesting to note that when Steve made a movie a while back called *Mixed Nuts*, he was paid seven million dollars! That was his salary. When he is the executive producer of a movie, he makes even more. My point is that all of Steve's hard work and talent resulted in an amazing ongoing payday for him. Money has had a lot to do with Steve's success, and success has a lot to do with Steve's money. He collects paintings worth millions, he has property worth millions, and he donates large amounts of money to good causes. He has made millions on his records, tapes, and an odd little book called *Cruel Shoes*. I can't tell you how much money Steve has. He would never be so crude as to discuss this subject with anyone except his accountant. To a very close friend, Steve might bare his soul, but not his bank account. You can kid with Steve and share priceless moments and laugh until you cry and be closer than a brother. But don't stick him with the bill, like I did once, because he doesn't think that's funny.

When it comes to love, Steve is as guarded as he is about money. I thought for a long time in the late seventies that Steve had found his permanent love interest in Bernadette Peters. She was young and vivacious, and knowing Steve as I did, I would have picked her out of a hundred girls as the one he would choose to stay with. The late Marty Klein (Steve's agent at the time) introduced them in 1977. Shortly thereafter, they both became members of the Kenny Rogers celebrity softball team. He—the six-foot-one-inch hunk from Southern Cal, and she—the well-endowed, five-foot-two-inch, perky sex pistol from Queens, New York with the all-too-kissable lips and curly, reddish-brown hair. Months later, when they were both guests on *Hollywood Squares*, Steve kept throwing little things at her, and he finally asked her out. He was definitely affected by the multi-talented charmer—and vice versa. How perfect could it be? The East and the West met. Both were vegetarians, they had both been performing since they were kids, they both liked old movies and both respected each other's privacy. Steve purposely wrote the part for her in *The Jerk*. David Picker, who was a Paramount executive and the co-producer for *The Jerk*, said, "The fact that they knew and loved each other made the scenes in the movie work even better." This was very true—as the scenes were absolutely charming. They walked on the beach and sang in harmony as Steve strummed a campy little ukulele.

There was talk then of Bernadette moving into Steve's new Beverly Hills home with him. He admitted that he wanted to get married someday, but had never trusted anybody enough. Of course, at the time, he was living with Mary and Betty and Dr. Forbes. Now you are probably asking yourself if Dr. Forbes was a woman, too. No, Doctor Forbes wasn't even a doctor. In fact, Dr. Forbes wasn't even human; he was a cat. So were Betty and Mary. Steve is a felineophile. He loves cats. The time soon came when Steve took Bernadette home to the folks and introduced her to Glenn and Mary Lee. They thought she was perfect for Steve. I can't imagine what went wrong. But something ended it. Anyone who professes to understand someone else's love life is guessing at best. I've been married for 30 years, and I still don't understand our love life. It appeared that Steve had made the biggest romantic mistake of his life—until he met Victoria Tennant on the set of *All of Me*.

Victoria was blond and sophisticated, the goddaughter of Lawrence Olivier. Victoria and Bernadette were as different as night and day. Bernadette was bright and perky and would light up a room when she walked in. Victoria was as cool as a cucumber, and although attractive, she could not hold a candle to so many of Steve's gorgeous leading ladies like Darryl Hannah, Rachel Ward, or Goldie Hawn. When I met her, she sent up a flag that said, "DON'T GET CLOSE AND PERSONAL!" God, she was testy. She shot arrows through his heart and his pocket book when the divorce became final. When Steve got married, I believe he felt it was for life. He thought he had found his soulmate. The way he talked about Victoria was the same way he talked about Linda Rasmussen at Garden Grove High, kinda goofy and gooey. And as careful as Steve has been with his money, I seriously doubt there was any prenuptial agreement between them. But I must admit that I don't know the details. I wouldn't even consider asking Steve. So, you won't hear how much he lost, or how much money he has now, or anything about Steve's personal financial situation. That's the way he likes it.

Time marches on, and money is not the most important thing in Steve's life now. It never really was; although, there was a time when I thought it was his only god. If anything above and beyond a friend or a family member is of critical importance to Steve, it's life. Humans first and cats running a close second. And of course, art. It's the one thing you can enjoy without remorse. If you would like a barometer on Steve's wealth, consider these things: By the time Steve's first major motion picture came out, he already had a number-one, best-selling book, *Cruel Shoes* (a collection of short stories). He had won an Emmy with his first job as a writer for the Smothers Brothers (1967–1969) and became the number one comedian in the country. In 1977, he released an album called *Let's Get Small*, and it went gold almost immediately and eventually went platinum. He also won a Grammy Award for the best comedy recording in 1977. He had signed a contract with Warner

Brothers to make six albums for a cool half million dollars. By September 6, 1977, *Let's Get Small* had become a gold record. Now, he could regularly fill ten-thousand-seat arenas with fans.

Steve never stopped promoting his stuff. He appeared on the *Tonight Show* extolling the virtues of his new LP. He pulled out the record and showed it to Ed McMahon, demanding closeups of the album jacket and acting serious when discussing the "beautifully crafted spine and jacket." Then in 1978, he produced another platinum album, *A Wild and Crazy Guy*. His albums were so big, they provided a boost to the whole record industry.

Soon, Steve topped these phenomenal accomplishments with a song that commemorated the Treasure of Tutankhamen exhibit, which was touring the U.S. at the time. Steve introduced his unexpected hit, "King Tut," at a surprise appearance with the Nitty Gritty Dirt Band at the Dorothy Chandler Pavilion. Before long, he appeared on *Saturday Night Live* and told the audience that King Tut had come to him in a dream and told him to write the song. Then he danced around wearing an elaborate Egyptian headdress in a palace setting with dancing girls and bebop pharaohs. He sold a million records in a very short time. An old classmate named Randi McGill told me that the song and the whole routine reminded her of Steve and me putting on Egyptian headdresses when we were high school cheerleaders and doing a cheer we called the "Egyptian." I had forgotten.

Everything he touched turned to gold. It wasn't necessary for him to sell, sell, sell. But still he never stopped promoting. He had telephone hotlines people could call to hear a comedy recording so he could sell more records and tapes. He was a marketing magician. Unflappable and focused, Steve was on a roll. Other comedians let their agent and manager handle their business, but not Steve. He has his deft fingers carefully placed in the pulse of his businesses. His hands touched every aspect of every single deal that came his way, from concept to completion.

There were friends and there was business. Steve Martin has always been a businessman. He is almost a better businessman than he is a comedian. How else could he outsell every other guidebook salesman at the main gate of Disneyland every day he worked there?

On the cutting edge of promoting his creative products,

Steve's timing is exquisite. The day before *Father of the Bride II* hit theaters, he went on a national media tour to promote the film. I happened to catch him as he appeared on *Regis and Kathy Lee*. I didn't see the whole show, but he mentioned Stormie, which I thought was interesting, and he did a couple of things that took me instantly back to our youth. Regis made a remark that caused Steve to strike a traditional Jack Benny pose, one arm across his stomach supporting the other arm and his chin resting safely in his palm. And then for the clincher, he started talking about the movie. They showed a clip of the movie, and then he proceeded to explain that not only does his daughter get pregnant in the movie, but after making love to Diane Keaton (on the kitchen floor), she, too, becomes pregnant. This is, of course, the hook that makes the movie so cute. But at that point, Steve said, "It's kind of a…" and then he paused. I was sitting in the comfort of my home with my wife and kids, and I spoke out: "Kind of a double whammy." And then seconds later, Steve said, "Kind of a double whammy." Not earth-shattering, but nevertheless, kind of ironic. You had to be there. Once a Gopher Boy, always a Gopher Boy.

Getting back to Steve's wisdom when it comes to business, I probably admire him as much for his sagacity in business matters as I enjoy his wit. Billionaire investor, Warren Buffett, once said, "It's not that I want to make money, it's the fun of making money and watching it grow." Steve learned that lesson early on, and it has been a standard bearer for the success reflected by his fame and fortune.

In case you didn't know, Steve made over a half a million dollars for writing and starring in *The Jerk* in 1979! But consider the whole deal with Universal at that time. No actor had ever managed to negotiate anything like this. Steve was to receive half of the profits from the movie. It cost six million to produce and netted that much in the first two days. When Jim Carrey signed a contract in 1995, for $20 million to star in *The Cable Guy*, people everywhere were amazed that a goofy comedian could bag that kind of money for a stupid, mediocre flick. Flashback: *The Jerk* grossed $40 million in its first month of release. That was in 1978. Since then, *The Jerk* has grossed more than that in video sales. *Roxanne* grossed $39 million at the box office. *Parenthood* grossed over a $100 million. Most of these facts are available for public review, but you will never see Steve's spreadsheet mentioned anywhere. His financial situation is his own private, personal business and will never be publicized, but it's safe to say Jack Benny would be proud.

In all fairness, and for those of us who have not amassed fortunes of any size, I must mention the extraordinary accumulation of expenses Steve encounters on a daily basis. His living expenses for one year currently amount to more than a million-and-a-half dollars. It's easy for one of us on the lower end of the financial scale to claim that Steve has enough money to survive for a lifetime. However, it costs money to make money, and expenses rise to meet income. My point is that Steve and others like him have managed to balance the delicate scales of income and output in such a way as to find themselves in the black. Permanently. Other great stars have amassed similar fortunes and lost or dissipated their resources more quickly than they acquired them. Accumulating great wealth is one thing; keeping it and building it is another.

All things being equal (which they rarely are), it's quite obvious that Steve's Martin's success is not unlike that of so many American entrepreneurs who had to work hard as youths to get what they wanted out of life. Those lessons were the foundation for their financial success. Young Steve was never poverty-stricken, and his parents never had to let him "go without," as did the parents of some other great financial wizards of the past. But the results were the same. He was made acutely aware of the need to respect money at a sensitive time in his youth. If I have learned anything about Steve at all, it's that once the point is made, the lesson is learned.

Chapter 18

"I SCHELPT WITH STEVE"

"The love game is never called off on account of darkness."
—Anonymous

Steve is not a womanizer. His sexual appetite is not compulsive. Steve finds himself comfortably above those temptations that could obviously wreak havoc on a rich superstar. With his good looks, fame and fortune, and a legendary sense of humor, Steve could have stumbled down the primrose lane into oblivion many years ago. If he has one addiction, however, it's work. It's like this Steve Martin tunnel vision that sees his goals first and foremost. He accomplishes the goals, bringing all the financial rewards anyone could dream of, and along this tunnel of visionary accomplishments, he treats himself with the accumulation of fine art. Nice, non-intrusive habits.

One night in a blur of performances, when we were on the road somewhere in Texas, Steve was performing at a college and his opening act was a mime called Toad. Her real name is Antoinette Attell. She was also a good friend of ours, and we decided to detour to catch the concert. Toad always had a crush on

Steve and told us that she always dreamed of making love with
him, but felt that he never knew she existed. After Steve's concert,
there were a few reporters that came into his room. Steve, Lynn
and I were visiting, but they needed photos, etc. They shot questions at him, and he was keenly on top of every response. There
was one, however, that gave him pause, which surprised us.
Someone asked, "Were you always so funny when you were
younger, Steve?" He stopped and pointed at me. I was busy being
a bump on a log.

"No," he said. "When I was in high school, Morris was the
funny one!" Everybody glanced at me for a moment as if they
cared and then started shooting questions at Steve again. I wondered why he did that. I never thought I was funnier than Steve. It
just seemed that he was always funny to me. But Steve, at any
point in his life, seems prepared to give credit where he feels it's
due, a trait that is an attribute uncommon in most stars' egos. That
night after the show, Lynn and Toad went to have coffee somewhere, and I went back to Steve's room with him to gab a while.
Although he was the star of the show that night, he had still not
risen to his peak and had many more lonely nights on the concert
road before he would find his white suit of success. I was still surprised when his road manager insisted he carry Steve's banjo for
him. To me, it was a sign of imminent stardom. Back in the room,
we talked and laughed.

Someone knocked on the door, and Steve opened it, cautiously peeking out. There was a student from the college and a beautiful red-headed co-ed with him. The kid told Steve he had organized the concert and asked if he could come in, because he had a
girl that was dying to meet Steve. Steve declined, saying he was
tired, and besides, he was visiting with an old friend.

"Do you turn down a lot of beautiful, young girls like that,
Steve?"

"Well..." he said, hesitating, as if to carefully phrase what he
was about to say. "You know they're not really serious. They're
just here because I was on stage. I don't want to take advantage of
anybody."

Pretty admirable, I thought. For the vast numbers of stage performers, that little red head would have been another notch on the
guitar neck. I had a constant, loving companion, and I didn't have

to deal with loneliness. But Steve was, basically, one who traveled alone on the road when confronted with amorous opportunities. I'm not suggesting Steve didn't have some happy horizontal highlights during those years of touring, but caution and potential liability were never thrown to the wind.

I had the opportunity of appearing on *The Dating Game* at one time, and my sister, Marsha, and Steve worked it into a genuine reunion. Steve had already appeared on *The Dating Game* a few times and at one point suggested to the producers that they consider interviewing my sister, Marsha, and me. He was a successful comedy writer at the time, and had a bit more clout than the usual bachelors they dealt with on the show. As a result of Steve's intervention, we were both chosen to appear on separate occasions.

Marsha was forewarned of the interview by none other than Steve, who thought it would be a great idea if they could somehow arrange things so they would wind up with each other.

They were still pretty close, but not like brother and sister. This seemed an ideal trick, fun and rewarding. Steve informed Marsha that he was to be on the show on a certain date, and he would arrange to have her on at the same time. Of course, the audience would be told that they were old friends, but Marsha was not supposed to know in advance that it was Steve Martin. Marsha's part was simple. All she had to do was say that she liked number three's comment on how sweet mothers are. This was the tip-off, although that was hardly necessary. Marsha would have recognized Steve's voice anywhere.

This was a great opportunity for a professional TV comedy writer like Steve to write some great material. Steve and Marsha got together and came up with some hilarious questions and answers. I wish I could remember them all.

I do recall that Marsha asked, "Bachelor number three, if life were a holiday, what holiday would it be, and how would we celebrate it?"

Without hesitation, Steve quipped, "Arbor Day, and we'd get potted."

After the prepared questions were asked, low and behold, the audience was elated to see the reunion of these two old friends. They hugged and kissed as if they would never see each other again. The prize for a couple of California kids who were reunited, happy to see one another, was about to be announced. The executive producers could have gone all out on this one. Paris? Tahiti? Nope, try a trip to sunny downtown Tijuana. Whoopee! A few hours drive from my sister's home in California. They were in for a less-than-glamorous afternoon at the bullfights.

It didn't matter to them, as Marsha was anticipating sharing old times with Steve. They made the best of it, but the couple that won after them received an all-expense-paid five-day trip to the Chicago Centennial (it was 1968 at the time). Their spirits were not dampened, and they both excitedly anticipated their upcoming date.

For the sake of publicity, *The Dating Game* always sent a photographer along to capture the wonderful and exciting moments the couples would have at the exotic destinations they visit. (Tijuana?) A little stoned and really ready for the occasion, these *three amigos* boarded the plane and flew to San Diego, where they were actually chauffeured to the bull ring across the border. This particular ring is right near a hotel called La Sierra. At the hotel, they met the famous young matador who was to fight for the first time north of Mexico City. Steve absorbed the surroundings like a sponge, the pomp and glory of old Mexico, the nachos and tacos of a time long gone. This was at a time in history when, if you wanted Mexican food, you had to go to a Mexican restaurant. There were no Taco Bells. The *matadors'* and *picadores'* regalia made indelible impressions on Steve because nothing gets by Steve. Perhaps somewhere in the back of his mind he was already generating ideas for a movie, which he would someday make. This is speculation, but I've seen how Steve's mind works. Steve can instantly bring up a memory from thirty years ago and explain it to you in detail. I believe Steve's movie, *The Three Amigos*, was inspired by this very trip.

The honored guests, Steve and Marsha, were treated like royalty. They met the handsome and brave young matador who had recently been hailed as one of the best in Mexico City. And they were set up with front row seats and the works. Neither Steve nor Marsha had ever been to a bullfight before. The crowd cheered, and the stadium was packed to full capacity. Vibrant with the fervor of anticipation, the spectators immediately calmed after cheering for the proud and handsome matador. Marsha and Steve sat on the edge of their seats. The bull was on the loose. He charged the matador. The bull got him with the first horn, goring him severely, and the bloody mess revolted poor Marsha and Steve. The bull won. That's not how the spectators wanted it. They sought more action, and they wanted the bull to suffer (which it did eventually). But from the animal's side of this archaic spectacle, it was a good fight. From the unfortunate matador's, it was bullshit.

Appalled and astounded for their new friend, the matador, Steve turned to Marsha and suggested, "Let's go see a dirty movie." The lecherous photographer eagerly agreed, but Marsha was a little apprehensive, although curious, as she had never seen one. At that point in time in the U.S., pornography was kept carefully hidden and was not readily available to the public at large. The chauffeur drove them through the dismal back streets of the red light district. Still having second thoughts, and yet trying to flow with the tide, Marsha accompanied Steve and the photographer to the show. In those dark alleys of Tijuana, there were a number of prostitutes who propositioned the clientele between, and sometimes during, the poorly made "blue movies." It offered an interesting perspective for two clean-cut, conservative Orange County kids. All during the dubious performance, Marsha was also aware that the photographer never took his eyes off her. She was nervous and accidentally dumped a bowl of salsa on Steve's shirt and pants. Steve realized how upset she was and allowed her to dip her chips on his clothing and lap for the balance of the movie. Marsha recalled that incident as "romantic." I'm not sure, but I think Marsha said the movie was called something like "El Crapola," but I might be thinking of something else.

Needless to say, such an exciting cinematic experience can really stimulate the appetite, and after the show it was back across the border to La Mesa for dinner and the flight back to L.A. The photographer finally departed and left the two of them alone; although he did jokingly offer to go with them and photograph them making love. They acted insulted at the idea and assured him that no such thing could possibly happen. They were just old friends, and they didn't need his services any further. Steve tipped him a buck, and they drove to Steve's apartment where Marsha scratched Steve's back for old time's sake. They did make love. It was inevitable. After all, these two had known each other for more than ten years. That much back scratching is a lot of foreplay.

Marsha called me the next day. I asked how the trip to TJ turned out, and she simply shocked me by saying, "I slept with Steve." And then she began to elaborate. Marsha said she wished it hadn't happened, because Steve was more like a brother, and being lovers was something she had never really anticipated or desired. I think she felt it caused too much confusion in, what had been, a beautiful, platonic relationship.

Well, I guess after all those years of Steve and me going around pulling gags and tricks on people, my sister can say she slept with him, but quite honestly, I can say I *"schlept"* with him. Oh, by the way, for the uninitiated, *"Schlepping"* is another term we heard from old Aldini at the Fantasyland Magic Shoppe. As I understand it from my friend Herb Shapiro, it's a Yiddish term for hauling things around in a sloppy fashion. We hauled everything from phony paintings to invisible glass. We even carried each other from time to time.

Marsha confided to me that Flydini's performance between the sheets was as entertaining and fulfilling as his wild and crazy performances in front of the curtain, only without the white suit.

Steve reminded me a few years ago of another *Dating Game* experience and a date he won with the late, great Dean Martin's daughter. I remembered that show. She asked him, "Bachelor number two, if I could see you right now, what would you say?" And Steve's response from the other side of the curtain was, "I'm completely naked!" They won a week in Italy. He said he had to call her time after time to confirm the date. After not being able to reach her, he called the folks at the *Dating Game*, and they had to get involved to put it together. Steve said it was miserable. She stayed in her hotel room with the door locked the entire week.

Early publicity photo, circa 1970

Chapter 19

A SIMPLE TWIST OF FOOT

*"Steve Martin is the best vaudeville performer since Gracie,
but he'll never be as pretty!"*

—George Burns

Rarely has there been a Steve Martin movie in which tripping has not been an integral part of the appeal. There is a good reason for that. Tripping was a critical part of our approach to life. We tripped all the time. We tripped over everything, anything, nothing. We tripped at Disneyland, at school, at home, in the yard, at the bus stop, in class, in the hallway, and in the bathroom. Next to walking, we never had so much fun as when we were tripping, and this was before LSD.

We realized very early on that it is quite easy to trip and still be in complete control. You merely hit the heel of your left foot with the toe of your right foot and you have completed an apparent trip. Reverse this process if you are left handed. Observers, in general, are rarely watching your feet. The ensuing body language is all that it takes to convince someone that you have tripped. The body language Steve has developed over the years is both wonderful and undeniable.

It was our great pleasure to periodically stumble, trip or fall at a moment's notice for the amusement of each other. Steve would look at me and wink or smile, and I would watch as he would take a stumble and fall in front of an unsuspecting tourist at D-land. Sometimes it was my turn. It would depend on the situation. Inevitably, depending on how bad the fall was, the bystander would almost always come to our aid. To watch the reactions was priceless. There was an instant, sudden shock, however subtle, that changed their expressions: first, surprise and pity, then sometimes laughter quickly suppressed. The bystander would then feel obliged to help Steve get up and see if he was okay. We entertained each other time after time with simple trips. It was a wonderful pastime. There were no victims. We left the scene of the *trip* with a richer understanding of how to successfully fall on our faces. The bystander left with the feeling that they had assisted some poor klutz. It was a lesson in compassion. Just as in major emergencies, people love to help people, even neighbors they have never even talked with. It's human nature, the nuts and bolts of our most beautiful human intention, to help and to love one another. Tripping backwards was not part of our repertoire. You could lose control falling backwards, and being in control was the great part of these antics.

Falling into girls was always fun. For the most part, they would help catch you and get you back on your feet. Every once in a while, they would react with a startled and insulted look. The response was usually something like, "Jerk!" (little did they know that someday he would be the most famous "Jerk" of all), or "Yuk, get your hands off me, you geek!" But for the most part, they were just wonderful, empathetic *femme fatales*. Steve and I would not go overboard when falling into girls, it was usually a gentle trip and a fall which required a little bit of readjusting to regain vertical composure. This was a nice way to meet girls, but it never really worked as far as generating meaningful relationships. We just never seemed to successfully fall into that sort of thing.

Doug Rowell always seemed to take these antics one step further. He would walk with us along the sidewalk or in a public place and see a girl or two coming towards us and begin preparing for his assault. He would act as if he was telling us a story, stretching his arms wide with his hands open as if to demonstrate a point. When we were a few steps away from the oncoming "*Aardvarks*," Doug would look at us, pretending to be conveying some significant point, and then he would trip forward, with his outstretched hand reaching desperately for something to stabilize his fall. His accuracy was astounding. It seemed inevitable that his hands would grab one of the girls' breasts and squeeze quickly, sometimes clinging, as if desperately seeking stability before sprawling out on the sidewalk. Some girls were terribly embarrassed. Others were concerned about his well being as he lay moaning on the ground clenching his elbow or knee. It was a gross, macho, cheap shot, and neither Steve nor I would think of doing such a thing. Although we did watch Doug do these things periodically, we only observed, because it added to our knowledge of the tripping, entertainment phenomenon, and we couldn't have stopped him if we had tried. Sometimes he would manage a two-breast grab, either two different girls or one poor victim. It looked so intentional that we thought for sure he would get busted. He certainly deserved to be caught, but he instead always managed to get away with murder. I'm sure he pulled these sexist antics even when he was alone. Sometimes I thought he had ulterior motives, as if he were doing it for more than just the thrill of falling.

We all loved slapstick, and tripping is no small contribution to any slapstick approach to comedy. Subtle slapstick was more of our thing than the Three Stooges' stuff. Steve was especially good with the ol' fun-filled "foot-to-nose door-bash." This simple routine was a delightful addition to our daily repertoire of schtick.

Steve would walk up to a door (almost any door with a handle or knob) and pull it quickly towards his face. Just before the door smashed into his nose, it would hit his pre-positioned and ready foot. The illusion was marvelous. Anyone watching would hear the thud of the door hitting his foot. But instantly they would also hear the anguished sound of pain as he would clench his nose with both hands. Once again, nobody was looking at the foot, if they were looking at all. The instant impression was that some poor slob had opened the door and smacked it right into his own nose. It was a harmless routine and one that we have done so many times that the distance between the nose and the door at the moment of impact was, seriously, a fraction of an inch. And yet, knowing the foot was strategically placed, we could pull the door open very quickly, making the whole situation work magically.

Steve had taken so many falls in the movies that it would be hard to itemize them all. For instance, in *Planes, Trains and Automobiles* he took four beautiful falls. In the beginning of the movie, he fell while chasing a cab. Later he fell down a snowbank while trying to get to a car rental facility. He also got knocked down in front of another car as John Candy was driving. A classic tripping scene then happened when John Candy and Steve were sitting on Candy's trunk on the soft shoulder of the Interstate after their near death experience of being scrunched between two oncoming semi trucks. They noticed their car was on fire, and Steve stood up, turned, and fell over the trunk. Granted, there are times when stunt doubles take Steve's falls. But that was actually Steve. I can spot a Steve fall a mile away, cause nobody falls like Steve. The arms don't move the same, and the body is not animated in just the right way. Steve's body language is just one of his indelible signatures. If he had been born in 1900, Steve would have been a star of the silent silver screen. He is an extraordinary mime.

Another extremely important trip was the stair stumble. Here again, the technique was a *simple twist of foot.* As you ascended the steps, one merely needed to place the ball of the leading foot on the edge of the intended step and let it slip off, stomping down on the ground or the step below it. It worked well, a swell little piece of "slap-step" comedy.

One warm summer evening, Steve and I wound up in Palmdale, California. I can't even remember why we were there now but I distinctly recall Steve's unparalleled enthusiasm for carnival people. Therefore, it was only right and proper that we should go to the local carnival. It wasn't Disneyland, but by that time we knew Disneyland inside and out. It was different, funky, and cheap, but exciting.

We met one carny who was barking out his routine to draw people into his domain. In his booth, you had to try to pop a balloon for a quarter and take a chance on winning a trinket worth a nickel. We talked with him for a while about his occupation. He was more than willing to give us some advice. He told us that he could sell anything to anybody. We laughed accordingly, and he smiled a patronizing smile. "Okay, fellas, watch this. I'm going to sell this empty box." He proceeded to show us a small, empty, white cardboard, jewelry box. He motioned us aside, and we watched. He snagged some passerby, and in less than two minutes, he sold the box. He even told the victim that the box was empty! To this day, Steve and I couldn't figure out how he did it.

We wandered around, took a few falls, and followed a few "*Aardvarks.*" Steve would spot one and loudly respond with a comment to me. "Hey, Morris, the *aardvark* in the *fedelforinstaf* has a graduation of regal proportions, and it tookas a long time to see the *dow* for a *booberday* since we have a special purpose for being here…" He would trail off, as if he had just eloquently recited the "Gettysburg Address." What he really said was, "The girls with the large, well-developed chests also seem to have attractive asses and beautiful legs, and it seems that there are a couple of *special purposes* for following them until there is a significantly important reason for doing something else." The phrase also most likely contained an in-between-the-lines reference regarding Steve's ultimate idea of the perfect girl—"peddle-pushers and pony tails." As time moved on, we got their attention, and the girls would watch us as much as we would watch them.

It's not possible to become proficient with tripping, stumbling, and falling without gaining some expertise in fake punching and slapping. We had a simple routine which, once again, we practiced at a distance in front of strangers or in drama (comedy) class. As Steve would stand there innocently with his face hanging out, I would swing hard at his face with an open hand. Timing was key. Just as my hand swished by his face, he would turn his head and clap his hands. What a great party gag! Fake fighting was a real attention-getter, and it was easy to fake a punch. Just punch with one hand, pulling your other hand in quickly to your body causing a muffled thunk. By the time we were going into our senior year, we were quite proficient at fake punching, slapping, tripping, stumbling, falling, and generally all elements of mimicking chaos.

I mentioned this story very briefly, but let me tell you the gory details. It was another balmy summer night, and the brisk, warm breezes found us in short sleeves. Steve almost always wore short-sleeved shirts. They were plaid ivy-league shirts, for the most part. He was always dressed conservatively, but then again, every one was, except the surfers. The party started after the sun had set and many of the kids from both Garden Grove and Rancho were there—I imagine about thirty-some kids. The mood was right for a gag, and Steve and Doug and I were primed. Some of the group had been drinking beer, which was not uncommon for most kids then. But not Steve—I *never* saw Steve drink in high school. Everyone knew us as class clowns, and we were almost always expected to pull something off. That was fine with us, so we began our plotting away from the main group. As we approached the group after our planning session, Doug got everyone's attention. "Hey, everybody, come here and watch this. It'll blow yer mind." The giggling, curious crowd gathered closer as Doug continued. "You won't believe this, but Steve Martin has the toughest face in the world!" We had their attention now.

"Really!" I said, confirming Doug's statement. "Watch this. I'm going to slap Steve in the face as hard as I can, and it won't hurt him in the least!"

Steve stood next to me, nodding his approval of this proclamation. "Yes," he said confidently. "My epidermis is impervious to pain!" We all nodded, looking at one another while the crowd mumbled trying to figure out what was coming next. We had pulled this prank enough that we felt like professional stunt men. The group formed a semicircle around us as I squared off, facing Steve. Most everyone was on my side of the ring, but a couple of classmates were standing behind them with Alan, our class president, being one of them.

"Okay now," I said, pausing and pulling my arm back, exposing my open hand. I spoke slowly and deliberately, showing my hand to everyone as if it were a tool. "I'm going to slap Steve in the face as hard as I possibly can, and he will not feel a thing. Are you ready, Steve?" Bracing himself as if I was really going to hit him, he confirmed his readiness.

"I'm ready, Morris." We knew the audience was closer than most folks that had inadvertently witnessed this prank before, so we were prepared to make our moves swift and tight to carry off the illusion.

I lowered my hand, took a deep breath and gathered my energy. Steve leaned forward, his hands hanging in front of him (preparing to clap them), holding his jaw out like a ripe apple ready for the picking. He smiled a Stan Laurel smile and waited confidently. Then I pulled my arm back, carefully aiming to come within no less than an inch of his turned face. At the precise moment, he would snap his head to the right and clap his hands. Moments before we actually proceeded with the stunt, Alan, who was a little drunk, decided he wanted to be part of the act. Just as I was swinging my hand towards Steve, and he was preparing to clap and dodge, Alan suddenly reached up and pushed Steve's head forward, placing his face directly in the path of my power packed slap. When I hit Steve, I hit him hard. I knocked him to the ground, and I instantly fell to my knees in front of him apologizing, not fully realizing what had happened. Steve's first expression showed that he was hurt and offended. Doug, who clearly witnessed what Alan had done, quickly explained the whole incident to Steve, who was, no doubt, in some kind of shock. It was all so quick. I wasn't watching Alan's hand; I was just trying to be careful with my own. I helped Steve up and felt like I had deeply wounded my friend. I was irate with Alan for his part in causing me to smack the hell out of my best friend. He apologized, and things slowly mellowed out.

As I look back now, it could have been worse. Steve was very forgiving, and everybody was apparently sympathetic to the painful blunder. As I helped Steve up, he raised his voice in anger, "Very funny, Morrrrisssss. What do you think about this..." He pulled his right fist back, preparing to punch me in the stomach. I saw it coming, and when he faked his punch, thumping his left hand on his own stomach, I hardened my stomach and bent forward just as he delivered the punch. I groaned and rolled sideways on the ground as the crowd stood by believing for a few minutes that our friendship was over. But it wasn't.

I don't know whether Steve ever took any martial arts classes, but he performed some pretty impressive moves in *Roxanne,* both in the beginning and in the famous barroom scene closer to the middle of the movie. He executed a beautiful, nonchalant back-fist to the antagonist, who, after being cleverly assaulted and demolished by Steve's wit, was then instantly knuckled to the ground. What a guy. People ask me, "What was it like growing up with Steve Martin?" I try to sum it up logically in a few words. "It was a trip!"

Steve Walters '16

Chapter 20

THE SOUND EXPLOSION

"Chaos in the midst of chaos is not funny, but chaos in the midst of order is funny!"
—Steve Martin

By 1970, Steve had maxed-out writing comedy in Hollywood. He had earned as much as $2,000 a week and won his Emmy (starting what was to be an enormous collection of awards). He weathered the controversial disagreements with CBS over material on the *Smothers Brothers' Show* and moved on. What they did on that show nowadays is like pabulum compared to the average talk show. But Steve had a constant battle on his hands over the smallest creative things he wanted to try. In order to capitalize on the overzealous censors in those days, Steve and the other writers created a routine where they all appeared on screen with the Smothers Brothers, acting as if *they* were the network censors. There was Bob Einstein (who also had been Steve's roommate when he first moved to Hollywood), Murray Roman, and Carl Gottlieb, who would later pen *The Jerk* with Steve. In the scene, each one of them would appear to read a little bit of the proposed script and then laugh loudly and tear the section out, passing it on to the next guy. Finally when it reached Steve, he would laugh outrageously, ripping out the last pages and handing what was left of the script to Tommy and Dick Smothers saying, "There's nothing funny here!" The Smothers Brothers would just stand there looking dumb. It was a funny routine to most people, but also one of the satirical stabs at the CBS brass that eventually caused the show to be dropped in 1969. Smothers Brothers...exit stage right. They had a fling at the top and then passed into history.

From there, Steve hustled around and easily found writing jobs for other well known programs of the day such as *The Glen Campbell Show*, *The Sonny and Cher Show*, and *Pat Paulsen's Half A Comedy Hour*. The late Pat Paulsen was a bare-faced, deadpan comic who used to come into coffee houses when I performed with my group, the *Settlers*, and do his Smoky the Bear routines for free. He always seemed like a nice guy, and I was glad he had bagged a show. But it didn't last long. By April of that year, Pat lost his show due to low Nielson ratings. Steve wrote for *The Ray Stevens Show* and other trendy shows that passed in the night, but he was quickly deciding to hit the road again performing comedy and magic. With that in mind, he contacted Bill McEuen (John McEuen's older brother) and asked him to manage his career for a while. Not too long after that, Steve became the opening act for the Nitty Gritty Dirt Band. As I've mentioned, that was a long, dismal ride for him. Performing for rock audiences on the road that were definitely not ready to accept his brand of humor was the ultimate let down for Steve.

Before he began touring with the Dirt Band, he still had fool's blood in him, which prompted him to come up with a wonderful idea. At that time, in 1970, Lynn and I were recovering from losing our Silverado Canyon cabin to a hundred-year flood. We moved to Modjeska Canyon, also in the rustic recesses of a now over-populated Orange County. El Toro, which is no less than a small metropolis between Orange County and San Diego, was beginning to bulge at the seams even then. Lynn and I would drive down from our canyon home, and I would flash back on the time when Steve and I passed west of that area on a train in 1962, on our way to San Diego to our first (and last) Full Gospel Revival Church Sunday experience.

Times were different; Lynn and I were young and in love and picking up gigs at clubs in Orange County. Steve was still living in Hollywood, as was Doug Rowell. One inspirational afternoon, Steve had a good idea for a "fake," but he needed some friends to help him pull it off. So, he gave Doug a call. He had tried to call me, but we were in the desert at the time. This idea was a direct hangover from the pranks we pulled in our high school heyday.

Needless to say, in time Steve would become "funny for money" and no longer would we enjoy his ability to entertain purely for the sake of entertaining (like the artist who is too busy to ever paint for the joy of painting again.) It was the end of a period in which Steve had nurtured the need to perform with appearances that were uncompensated with traditional remuneration. But his idea on this occasion was still based on the philosophy of funny for fun.

The plans came together quickly. A couple more phone calls were made and the four mischievous entertainers began plans to dupe an unsuspecting audience at the Troubadour, a well-known Hollywood club. Steve was more outlandish in his attire in those days, sporting long hair and a huge conglomeration of turquoise and silver hanging off his custom Levi outfits. This was Steve's "hip" look. But Steve was never a very good hippie. Real hippies couldn't afford turquoise and silver. And Steve was not very good at doing drugs or swilling booze. He was ahead of his time, and not long after this event, when living in Aspen, he swore off those debilitating activities so that he could seriously pursue his dreams. But even at his worst, he was no more than a casual pot smoker or drinker. I've seen Doug Rowell do more drugs, whiskey, cocaine, and LSD in one night than Steve did in his life. Steve was always too smart to delve into true hallucinogens like LSD—or one of Doug's favorites, hog tranquilizers.

It always looks inappropriate and difficult for Steve to smoke a cigarette in a movie or suck down some kind of hard liquor. It is really so unlike him in reality. He has a hard time faking it, as he was supposed to do in *Leap of Faith* or *Simple Twist of Fate*. In fact, if you ever saw Steve in concert, live or on tape, what he drank out of the glass on the stool beside him was always water. Doug

Rhodes, Doug Rowell, Don Giles and Steve prepared to perform at the Monday night "hoot" at the Troubadour. Don played drums, and Doug Rhodes played bass. Steve and Doug were to be the guitar players. Steve played guitar, although not as well as he played banjo. Not that it mattered for this particular "fake."

Doug Rowell finally reached me on Saturday and told me to be at the Troubadour on Monday. Folk music at the Troubadour had given way to rock, and groups like Canned Heat, Buffalo Springfield and the Association were standard fare at the "Troub." The place was packed to the brim, as usual. The audience swayed between being drunk, stoned drunk, or drunk and stoned or in other states of freaky disillusionment. About halfway through the evening's activities, the announcer requested the attention of the audience for the introduction of a new group. Frequently, such introductions are followed by a long, laborious delivery and set up of sound equipment, but not this one.

It's always been of prime importance for rock groups to blast their audiences beyond the sound barrier in decibels only recognized by rocket scientists. In this way, the audience will remember the group's name and appreciate the colorful Peter Max hallucinogenic artwork on old album covers when they join the ranks of the hearing impaired. On this particular occasion, there was no long waiting period. Doug was the first one on stage, his long, teased hair and beard complemented by his freaky-frenzied hippie attire befitting the role. For Doug it was no acting job to look like a stoned-out hippie. With an uncommonly serious expression, his countenance alone quieted the audience.

"Hi, my name is Doug and my group, The Sound Explosion, will be here in a minute. But first of all, I have to make an apology. We come from Seattle, and I guess we are pretty well known there, but this is our first shot at Hollywood. Anyhow, we arrived about an hour ago and hurried over, only to find out that not only did our manager get hung up on a layover in Portland, but so did all our equipment." At this juncture, he began to list the most incredible conglomeration of equipment you could imagine. "Super synchro fuzz phase reverb." But it wasn't fabricated double talk; Doug knew equipment. And if anybody in the audience was a sincere musician, they had to be impressed with the list of missing speakers, amps, and associated necessities.

"Soooo…" said Doug, still maintaining his serious approach, "what it amounts to is that all the fucking equipment," his anger peaking, "is hung up in Portland, and we won't have another chance to try and book this gig." He looked near tears as he went on slowly. "So we've decided to just go for it." There were a few "right ons" and a little applause from those who were sympathetic to this poor rocker's plight. Most of the audience was buying into this story, but a few of them immediately recognized Steve, who was a regular at the club. He was wearing a tie-dyed tank top and ten pounds of silver and turquoise jewelry, including his huge squash-blossom pendant. Don Gyles, Doug Rhodes, and Doug Rowell were also decked out in appropriate hipster apparel. There was a general giddiness throughout the entire club now. Something was going to happen, and the crowd was buzzing. Rhodes hung over his electric bass, as if tuning. Steve, appeared to be bringing his guitar up to pitch also, but of course, you couldn't hear any-thing—there were no amps and they were all solid body electric guitars. Doug Rowell pulled his guitar strap over his shoulder and strummed once or twice. Then he took a deep breath and looked back at the other guys, asking, "Okay, you guys, are you ready?"

They nodded, and Steve raised his hand and said, "Hold it!" He tuned a little bit more and then shouted, "Let's get it on!"

Doug counted, "One, two, three and…" With that, they all leaped into the air and struck their instruments simultaneously. The room was dead quiet except for the sound of flat picks streaking across unamplified strings and Don's sticks spanking his practice pads rhythmically. But there was a guttural laughter resting in the throats of most of the stoned-out audience. They were getting off on this show. Doug began to scream his rock song.

"Told ya one time, baby" and everybody in the group leapt into the air again.
"I'm a one time man." They all jumped again.
"Ya know I love ya, baby." Jump.
"But ya gotta understand." Jump.
Then they burst into harmony and a series of choreographed moves.
"I gotta have some peace, baby, gotta, gotta, gotta."
"I gotta have some peace, baby, gotta, gotta, gotta."
"I'm down on my knees, beggin' ya, please, my axle

needs grease."

"Gimme some peace, peace, peace."

The audience was mesmerized by the antics.

At this point, the two Doug's stepped to the rear of the stage. They continued to strum their strings to the clicking of Don's pads, as Steve stepped up for his lead guitar solo. While his face displayed a twisted comedic imitation of a serious guitarist, his big cartoony hands flew up and down the neck of the Fender Stratocaster guitar like Jimi Hendrix. Of course, he wasn't playing anything, but it looked like he would be if you could only hear the music. He quickly worked the audience into a frenzy. Then he stepped back, as the group repeated the chorus and closed with one of those acid-rock, soul-extravaganza, bebop dance ditties.

The house came down around them. The Sound Explosion gratefully nodded and straightened up as Steve took center stage by the microphone. Doug, Don and Doug played their silent instruments in the background and chanted a neo mystical bullshit chorus softly.

"Navyet nauyem, Navyet nauyem,"

"Navyet nauyem, Navyet nauyem,"

Over the chanting, Steve invented narratives and sang ridiculous lyrics of jungle natives and swamp dwellers in search of cosmic truths. These stories were punctuated by a swinging, animated calypso chorus singing and dancing to the back-up trio. The images and the effects were astounding.

"See ya latuh (bum de bum de bum bum) Alligate ah (bum de bum de bum bum)."

"Aftta a while, uh (bum de bum de bum bum) Crocodile uh (bum de bum de bum bum)."

They continued the jive boogie in a chorus line as Steve led them in a conga-style parade off the stage. They filed back on stage to a huge ovation, then they bowed and disappeared into oblivion. The Sound Explosion imploded into obscurity. The group was destined to do a show that worked only once. It was a little bit like that first man to ever try to swallow a sword. Everybody loved it the first time, but there was no reason to do it again. Any rock group that ever performed at that well-known club would have envied the response. I was the most delighted spectator in the audience. Of course, it hurt that I hadn't been able to be part of The Sound

Explosion, and afterwards we had coffee with the group and laughed our heads off at their success. These were the last of the youthful roots that would drive Steve into a comic career based on the indirect, the obtuse, the oblique. This is what Steve later called "the funny that's not funny until it builds so much pressure that it makes people laugh, and not even know why they are laughing."

Steve went through a lot of changes after that period. He lost the pseudo hippie image and eventually acquired the tightly tailored white suit. But beneath it all was a happy-go-lucky, Orange County kid who loved to make people laugh.

As I mentioned, Steve hit the road as the opening act for the Dirt Band. He attempted to entertain them with routines like his "canine comedy," where five dogs accompanied him on stage. He played "Melancholy Baby" to them on a dog whistle. It was very funny to me, but he bombed again and again with humor that was too far out. I don't think Steve ever did another show for rock audiences that went as well as the little known Sound Explosion.

He got occasional bookings on TV shows such as *The Virginia Graham Show*. He tried the dog act and a lot of off-the-wall humor, but the audiences just were not in tune with Steve's idea of what was funny then. He had hit some tough times—like when he had to perform at a club with no manager and had to work the lights himself with a foot pedal. There was another time when he had to perform his show standing by a salad bar. And in those days, he had to pay his own expenses, even when he was only making $200 or $300 a night. But before long, Steve started getting some breaks that would change his downward spiral. God must have loved Steve because soon his career began to go ballistic.

When his alter ego, the "Wild and Crazy Guy," in the tight white suit finally emerged from the flurry of endless one-nighters, he had a small cult following that grew like wildfire. When Steve began shooting to the top, with his loyal followers traveling anywhere to see him, some Americans were saying, "There's nothing funny about that guy." But the hardcore Steve Martin fans didn't just like him, they adored him. He didn't have to do anything funny. All he had to do was make a nonsensical comment or movement, and the audience would go wild.

Listening to the variety of comments about Steve has been an ongoing subject of interest with me for over thirty years. I've heard people say they love him, they hate him, he's handsome, he's a loser, a geek, a genius and so on. But that's to be expected with stardom. What nobody ever suspected was that he would have staying power. That's because they don't know Steve like I do. For years after his first movie, *The Jerk*, I would run into the same thing. Some people would say, "He is hilarious, I love his stuff." Others would say just the opposite. But as I have witnessed this phenomenon, I have noticed that the longer Steve makes movies, the more fans he acquires. It used to be that the public would only have one or two movies to refer to when they were making their judgments as to whether or not they liked him. Now that Steve has such a library of films he's been involved with, it seems that most people actually say, "I never liked him until he did *Roxanne!*" or "He wasn't any good until he did *Parenthood.*" Slowly but surely, they are conquered. Before Steve ever made his second movie, he told me that he was going to make forty more movies before he quit. I reminded him of that a few years ago and he said, "Oh, I don't know. I might retire pretty soon." To date, he has made in the neighborhood of twenty-eight movies. It seems to me that there is a subconscious power inside Steve, as there is with all of us. But that inner power in Steve, once set in motion, might have more control than even he realizes. Of course he will retire, someday, but I just wonder if his inner control center will make sure he finishes the forty movies before he is allowed to follow through with his determination to retire. One thing seems quite evident, though, as I sit in the peanut gallery and watch his progress. Steve is destined to be as well-loved and respected as the great mentors he holds in high esteem, such as Jack Benny and George Burns. When all is said and done, Steve Martin will truly deserve such legendary adoration.

The world, in general, will remember Steve from his movies, but movies are his vocation. Steve has admitted that he finds making movies "very very hard, even when working with friends like Goldie Hawn" (referring to *The Out of Towners*).

He considers writing his "luxury." Steve has written many short essays for *The New Yorker* and other leading magazines, and he published another short book of essays called *Pure Drivel* in September of 1998.

In the August 30, 1998, issue of *Parade Magazine*, Steve was quoted as saying, "The reward for writing is discovering something about myself I never knew before. And it's feedback. People say they laughed out loud or they faxed it to their friends. I'll tell you a secret which may be the key to me: When people compliment my movie work, I say, 'Oh thanks, but it's not very good!' But when they compliment on my writing work, I say, 'Really? What else did you think? Tell me more...' "

What amazes me more than any particular aspect of Steve's career is the incredible volume of work he has created in his life. It is really interesting to note that in his complicated and logical mind, he mainly focuses on his writing at this stage in his life. I believe Steve has taken this path because it will enable him to do what he loves when he finishes his career and does not want to be seen on the screen any more.

For his world of fans, it's nice to know that he will keep on creating. I was talking to John McEuen about Steve many years ago, and John told me how he missed playing music with Steve. And then he said, "I think Steve gave up his banjo for his word processor."

Chapter 21

A WILD AND CRAZY KID

"This certifies that you have had a personal encounter with me,
and that you found me warm, polite, intelligent, and funny."
—Steve Martin's business card

S teve's transition from wild and crazy kid to wild and crazy guy was a metamorphosis in which I reveled. The growing up process for Steve was a logical and rational maturing, in all ways, and also a retreat to an incredibly conservative, private personality, far more representative of his parents, Glenn and Mary Lee Martin, than that of the youthful Steve. I really enjoyed *Planes, Trains and Automobiles*, but I talked to a Steve Martin fan recently who told me that it was his least favorite movie. His feeling was that it made Steve look too stodgy, too businesslike, and much too conservative. In truth, the character was a lot like Steve in many ways. But not in a negative sense. We are talking about a very successful businessman who has made cutting edge history in the no-nonsense corporate world of entertainment. It's fine to admire the brainless characters in Steve's *Jerk* and his *Man With Two Brains*, but these days, the real Steve Martin is hardly wild and crazy; and no matter what anybody thinks about his goofy characters, he was never a jerk.

Fifteen years to the date after Steve and Doug and I planted the phony painting in the L.A. Art Museum, the first Steve Martin special, *A Wild and Crazy Guy*, aired on television. It was 1978. I've realized now that there are people everywhere who know Steve Martin by his movies, but they were either too young or just not aware of Steve when he began producing his television specials. With that in mind, let's go back to a period in time when voice mail was the postman saying, "You got mail in your box today," and only television stations had video cameras.

Steve's approach to promoting his upcoming movie, *The Jerk*, in the late seventies made the idea of a television special all the more viable. He created a many-faceted promotional concept, using one as a stepping stone for the other. After hit records, concerts, and everything else Steve had produced to that point, he was more keenly aware of the power of synergistic cross-promotions than a lot of marketing experts of the day.

If someone had not seen Steve before, it was hard to miss him on the occasion of his first TV special. Very seldom did anyone appear on three pages in a row in the *TV Guide*. Two advertisements told of the skits, antics, and guest stars to appear on his program, and one ad very cleverly suggested that you could dial a given number and receive a message from him personally. As I've mentioned, he used this trick very effectively with his records and cassette tapes. Also, there was an application for membership in the *Official Steve Martin Fan Club*, and last, but not least, a solid plug for Steve's new album, *A Wild and Crazy Guy*.

The TV special began with a terrified and disgruntled Steve Martin in a shabby, white suit being practically dragged down the hall to the stage. He stopped briefly for a little girl to whom he granted an autograph. Then he spun and bolted in the opposite direction, seemingly scared to death. Steve and Bill McEuen gathered a stellar cast for the special. They knew that this first major TV special should be spectacular, therefore they got Bob Hope, Milton Berle, George Burns, and Johnny Cash for guests. I know Steve must have been greatly honored to have these paragons of stage and screen there that night.

His biggest idol, however, was Jack Benny. Had the great

Jack Benny been alive, he would have been at the top of the guest list. Steve used to tell me how funny he thought Benny's blank expressions were. I suppose we all love slapstick comedy, and, if it's done well, it will crack up even the most reserved audience. Benny's slapstick was of the most gentle kind, not the extremely obvious Three Stooges type. Steve has managed to combine the two extremes.

Portions of this show were pre-recorded at a huge concert hall. Between prepared television routines, they would flash back to the concert. Steve would step briskly to the microphone and bang his nose directly on the head of the microphone, step back, and grab his nose as if to say, "What happened?" Short, cute, and extremely effective. I think Steve had been using that routine since the first time he stood in front of a microphone. It was funny. He was acting like a pro and telling people they were getting "professional entertainment;" and then, he'd bang his nose on the mike. It always worked. Of course, throughout the show the fans were delighted to see Steve with his bunny ears, arrow through the head, plastic nose and glasses, and animal balloons.

This wasn't slapstick—this was absurdity. It's something Steve and I thought was funny when we were punk kids. Everybody else thought it was absurd, naturally, but as we've learned, there is a fine line between absurdity and hilarity. Steve in his career has illustrated to the public that we are all subject to leaning either way. This couldn't have happened in years past. Comedy had to be traditionally funny, or, as censorship eased up, it had to be dirty. Even innuendo, which had been a reliable comedy ply in the early coffee-house days and before, was not effective anymore because comics could say almost anything they wanted. With the realization that absurdity is, or can be, very funny, the public, in general, acts accordingly. Sometimes they laughed at Steve, and then they would ask, "Why am I laughing?" It doesn't matter. In humor, the end justifies the means, and if they are laughing, whether they understand why or not doesn't matter—they are still laughing.

So much of that evening with Steve's TV special took me back in time. For instance, the arrow through the head routine. When we were thirteen years old and working at Disneyland, we would spend much of our free time in the Golden Horseshoe Saloon in Frontierland, drinking sarsaparilla and watching the Golden

Horseshoe Revue. There were can-can girls and singers all pumping out the *Pecos Bill Show* three or four times a day. But the star of the show was Wally Boag, a slapstick comedian of the old-school vaudeville period, whom we adored. It seemed that no matter how many times Wally Boag would do that ridiculous phony arrow-through-his-head, Steve would break up. Wally Boag was a funny man. There was one part of the show, in particular, that was my favorite. Boag would stop after fifteen minutes of performing and say, "Whew, it's hot in here," lift up his toupee, exposing his bald head, wipe it dry with his other hand, and quickly return the hairpiece, backwards. Each group of unsuspecting tourists would be caught off guard with a sudden burst of laughter that rolled through the audience. It was a real advantage for Wally to have a new audience with each show, but it didn't matter how many times we saw the show, it always tickled us.

Skiles and Henderson, a couple of very funny men, were also at the Horseshoe Revue. They performed sound effects and great comedy. To us at that ripe young age, looking forward to a future in comedy, we were filled with admiration.

Another sequence in his television special that smacked of slapstick was Steve as a ski instructor named Gurn. Steve was standing in fresh powder with snow falling all around, wearing a huge cowboy hat. He proceeded to give the worst advice you can give to anyone learning how to ski. Then, he tried to illustrate the effectiveness of his methods, failing and falling miserably, finally crawling into his front door. It was pure slapstick and the end result of so much practice doing amateur tripping as a young performer.

Most people will admit that Steve has unique body language. His gestures are cartoonish, and his facial features can become almost rubbery at will. His full smile almost makes his eyes disappear in a squint. And then came the ultimate flashback. There was a routine where Steve stated he was a cheerleader. Imagine that. In the skit, he was watching some vivacious, young cheerleaders rehearse, and, realizing they couldn't see him, he decides he is invisible. The routine was punctuated by the police dragging Steve out of the girls' locker room.

One of the last routines was a flash forward to Steve in the future. He was a washed-up bum in a bathtub, unshaven, covered with newspapers, and clenching a bottle of cheap wine. The narrator talked to him like a cartoon character from an old Walt Disney flick, saying, "What has happened to you, Steve?" The narrator then questioned him about what happened to his wine collection of ten thousand bottles? Steve admitted he drank them. The narrator analyzed that he would have had to drink five a day for five years to consume that much, and Steve excitedly announced (still drunk), "No, I drank fifty a day for three months!" The routine ended with the narrator telling Steve about the success of his big new movie and Steve, unbelieving, smiling and sinking back in his drunken stupor. The audience roared.

When I attended the premier for *The Jerk* not long after that and saw the opening scenes, it all made sense. *The Jerk* starts with that same scene: he is unshaven, covered with newspapers, and clenching a bottle of cheap wine. A hopeless bum.

I've often thought that, given the sorry choice of presidential candidates in our country, maybe Steve should run for the office of President of the United States one day. Consider this: He has all the qualifications. He is well educated, sophisticated, and mature. He has a proven track record as a successful businessman and a public speaker. He can double talk like a pro. He is kind to animals, small children, senior citizens, and biographers. Although he has been wild and crazy in the past, he has never been irresponsible or decadent. He is the perfect combination of a liberal and a conservative. We could call him a Republicrat or put him on the vegetarian ticket. He is the perfect candidate. I know, because I campaigned with him in his last election (in high school). He would never resort to pandering or pathetic platitudes. He wouldn't lie because his nose might grow. He has military experience as *Sergeant Bilko*. He's been a perfect parent in *Parenthood*, setting a precedent for all families. He's not married but one of the few men with *Two Brains*. He is used to traveling on *Planes, Trains and Automobiles*. He's familiar with cities and their problems, like the *L.A. Story*, and yet he understands nature, like the *Grand Canyon*. He knows how to say he's sorry and "Excuuuuuuse me!" Having worked with *Mixed Nuts* and *Dirty Rotten Scoundrels*, he should be comfortable with politicians. He should work well in the White House because he has been a *Lonely Guy* and a *Housesitter*, and yet he has international connections with at least *Three Amigos*. Sure, he's been a *Jerk*, but what President hasn't? With *A Simple*

Twist of Fate, he could actually win. His campaign slogan could be "If elected, I'm not going to give you just a part of me, I'm going to give you *All Of Me*!" And if all else failed, he could offer the public something no other President has been able to do since Abraham Lincoln...a really good show!

Steve's "Early Beatles" look, 1965

Morris in the Army, 1966-68

Early publicity photo

Steve's 1st publicity photo—The photo Steve sent to put in my locker

Stormie Sherke, Steve's first true love

Steve & my twin sister, Marsha, on their trip to Mexico after winning
The Dating Game

Steve, Morris, & friends, Modjeska Canyon, CA, 1970

Wild and handsome

Melinda Martin, Steve's sister

Steve clowning around with his father, Glenn

Steve & Kathy Westmoreland, 1965

Kathy Westmoreland with Elvis on tour in Hawaii

Kathy Westmoreland & Morris beside the Lincoln Elvis gave her, 1979

*Glenn, Skye (2 months), Mary Lee, Fawn (Marsha's daughter), Lynn, &
Morris at Big Bear Lake, CA, 1978*

Diane Sawyer with Morris for a 60 minutes show all about Steve

Steve with then-girlfriend Bernadette Peters, 1979

Glenn, Bernadette Peters, Steve, & Mary Lee, 1979

Steve Martin "Look Alike Sound Alike Contest" The Comedy Store, Hollywood, 1979

Steve, Morris, & Victoria Tennant at The Magic Castle, Hollywqood, CA 1986—No more "flydini" for her.

Morris & Steve—It's a deal!

Steve with his nephew, Rusty, & niece, Julie, 1977

Morris, Steve, & my son Skye Walker, 1979

Steve with Mickey Mouse—where it all began: The Magic Kingdom, mid 1980's

Steve, with my wife, Lynn, Hollywood, 1979

Morris & Lynn

The Earthwalkers

Chapter 22

GLENN, MARY LEE, AND MELINDA

"God could not be everywhere, so he invented mothers."
—Jewish proverb

Not until almost 1980, did I have the privilege of gaining a better rapport with Steve's parents, Glenn and Mary Lee Martin. I was not very close to them when Steve and I were growing up. There were so many questions I wanted to ask them. Finally, I had my chance when they invited Lynn and me over for a fine, home-cooked meal. They enlightened me about many things, and I felt they were very candid about Steve.

The coast of California is dotted with beach towns from the northern-most city of Eureka all the way to San Diego. After several years in the real estate business, Glenn Martin chose to settle in one of these beautiful, Southern California coastal towns in Orange County.

Just as the sun was setting, Lynn and I arrived for dinner at their modest but pleasant home with our son. As soon as we got within the gates, it became obvious that someone in the family had a green thumb. Actually, we had visited them several years earlier, after they had just moved in, but it takes living in a place to make a house a comfortable home, and now we could see the results of those last few years. There were potted trees and shrubs all over the concrete yard, which resembled a small botanical garden. As always, everything was immaculate. In all the time I've known the Martins, they have been as clean and neat as those well-tailored suits their son used to wear.

Glenn and Mary Lee were warm and wonderful hosts and made us feel instantly welcome and comfortable in their lovely home. The living room was separated from the den by a large fireplace with artificial logs and gas flames flickering. There were several original oil paintings that Steve had given to them. What really attracted my attention, of course, were the items associated with Steve. Although the wall in the den was neatly organized with an assortment of plaques, Steve's gold records, and family pictures, my curiosity was aroused by a small, gold-plated plaque that hung beneath the gold *Getting Small* album. This particular item was given to Glenn at a special banquet held in his behalf. Glenn had given much of his time to help with the Realtor's Education Committee. This committee, evidently, was responsible for helping many youngsters in achieving their educational goals. Glenn told me that the award itself was for his participation in the project. He chuckled as he read the inscription:

"PRESENTED TO GLENN MARTIN...IN SINCERE APPRECIATION FROM ALL THE CALIFORNIA REALTORS FOR BEING RESPONSIBLE FOR BRINGING STEVE MARTIN INTO OUR LIVES."

Lynn asked Glenn, "Do you think that you and Steve are closer now than you were when Steve was growing up?"

Without hesitation and quite frankly, he stated, "We were never really close while Steve was growing up. And we really aren't any closer now. We've always kind of been antagonists to one another. For instance," he said, "I remember having a confrontation with Steve about mowing the lawn when he was little. I insisted that he mow the lawn, and he just flat refused." He paused. "No matter what I said or did, he just wouldn't do it."

Another similar incident happened when Glenn insisted that Steve retrieve the newspaper for him one evening. He could not make Steve do it, even by insisting. Steve never did get the paper. There was resentment between them, and I knew it when we were kids. Whenever Steve came to our house, he would do anything my mother asked of him. But even with the resentment of his father, it caused no apparent aberration in Steve's character. He is a model individual in almost every imaginable way. Moreover, I think it demonstrates once again that indomitable attitude that has made him what he is. It was then, when he was a mere child, that Steve's determination became one of his character traits.

It's important to know that Glenn was also in the entertainment business. As if to suggest Steve was born to be an entertainer, his mother told me that he was conceived in Hollywood, California. Mary Lee returned to Waco, Texas shortly thereafter because Glenn had to leave on a USO tour to England. (He was performing in the play, *Our Town*, a classic with Raymond Massey.) Glenn told me of the early days on the road before then. He was a dramatist, a professional thespian. He really loved the theater, and probably would have stayed in the business had it not been for the necessity of providing for his growing family. God knows, there are countless great entertainers that have eventually bailed out on their dreams and aspirations in order to feed the family and pay the bills.

Glenn recalls that "on the road" in those days meant the only money he received was a small remuneration given him for the candy he sold. Sure he sold candy. In those days, you did it all— you acted, sang, swept stages, sold candy, etc., etc. I couldn't help thinking of Steve at the Bird Cage Theater in Knott's. His jobs included anything that needed to be done. Kathy told me that at times Steve would be in charge of raising and lowering the curtain. Unable to get his attention one time, Kathy and Stormie had to crawl under the front curtain. George Burns, the King of Vaudeville, endured years of petty jobs in order to be able to climb up on the stage with Gracie and perform.

Glenn had always been a talented man and surely would have

done well in entertainment, had chance or fate or karma been so disposed. Glenn was a handsome young man, standing over six feet two inches with strong masculine features and broad shoulders.

Steve placed his dad in a small part in the film *All of Me* with Lily Tomlin and his wife-to-be (or evidently not-to-be), Victoria Tennant. Glenn did in life what he had to do, and became one of the most respected realtors in California. But he always harbored some remorse for not being able to follow his passion.

I couldn't resist the temptation of asking him if he felt a vicarious type of success with Steve's ascension to the top of the entertainment field. "Naturally," he said. "Much more so than if I had never intended to be anything but a realtor." In the same breath, he admitted his obvious pride in Steve's accomplishments.

During the course of dinner, Mary Lee said that she would have invited Steve, but that he was a vegetarian and she really wouldn't know what to feed him. "Besides," she said, "I thought perhaps you would want to talk with us without Steve being here." The Martins had always been strong creatures of habit. When we were kids, and I would arrive at Steve's house to catch the bus, the Martins always had the same breakfast waiting for Steve. They would bow their heads and say the same blessing. They would each have a single piece of white toast, two strips of crisp bacon and two eggs. It was always precisely the same.

That night's dinner was topped off with apple dumplings cooked to perfection. We toured the rest of the house and chatted continually during the entire affair. In their exercise room were two corkboards with many wonderful photos of Melinda and Steve. Mary Lee was most generous and said I could use any photos I wanted in the preparation of this book. As I left the room, I noticed a photo in the hallway. It was a picture of Steve receiving his Emmy Award for writing for the first *Smothers Brothers' Show*.

Back in front of the fireplace and over a hot cup of coffee, Glenn told me again that Steve and he had never been close. When Steve had the rare occasion to speak confidentially, he would confide in Mary Lee. Glenn said that Steve seemed happiest when I was around or after he had been with me at Disneyland or my house. There were a few remarks Glenn made that were very enlightening to me. In talking about Steve's success, Glenn assured me that Steve had "tunnel vision." In other words, when he was a boy and he wanted to accomplish something, he would not accept "no" for an answer. At seven years of age, Steve decided that he wanted money and informed his mother and dad that he was going to get a job. At the time, they resided in Inglewood, California.

"He said he was going to get a job," Glenn stated, "and he came back with money and said that he had been employed by a gas station to sweep their floors. As a teenager, it was that same way with anything Steve did, including his magic. He would come home from working at Disneyland and go straight to his room and practice magic for hours."

Believe me, as I am his witness, this was absolutely true. Steve would set out to do something, and he would do it as well as it could be done. In reference to Steve's positive attitude towards his goals, his father told me that the most negative thing he ever heard Steve say was in 1975. Glenn and Steve met with Steve's lawyer, and Steve said to Glenn, "We figure that I'm good for about five years." This, of course, was in reference to his standing in the entertainment field, then as a comic. (Even though he was a rising star and could do no wrong.) To Glenn, it seemed almost out of character for Steve to admit that there was anything in his future but continual success. Coincidentally, and to document Steve's powers of planning and strategizing, by 1980, he had a number one movie and his stand up comic career was over, by his own choice. In other words, he wasn't saying that he was giving up in five years. He was just gauging and pacing his moves in an honest and calculating manner. So before his stand-up comedy career was on the decline, he had jumped trains and was onto an even bigger bonanza in "show biz."

What really bothered Glenn and Mary Lee about comments on Steve were all the references about him being an atheist. With sensitive indignation, Mary Lee said, "When Steve was in Sunday school as a young boy, he was extremely proud of his attendance record. He would come home with his chest protruding with pride. I don't care what anybody says, you can't take that away from him." She said that he kept that perfect attendance record until he started working at Disneyland. I looked at Glenn and asked, "Is Steve an atheist?"

He looked directly at me and announced, "I really don't know." Knowing I was to have lunch with Steve the next day, I asked him, "Do you want me to ask Steve if he is an atheist?"

"Yes," he said. "Ask him. I'd like to know." Steve admitted that he has always been secretive about his religious views, but it was never fair to assume that he was an atheist. Agnostic would be a better choice of words. Despite his great attendance record in Sunday school, Steve never had much use for organized religions. But I think it's an interesting observation to note that, out of all the famous stars and political and religious leaders, few have remained as morally righteous as Steve in their personal and public lives— especially entertainers.

Steve is a very spiritual person. He's a private individual and finds great solace in his freedom to be true to his own beliefs. He doesn't need to talk about them because, first of all, he's too smart, and secondly, he has more control over his spiritual aspirations if they are between just him and God.

After dessert, Glenn brought out a large cardboard box. "Steve keeps all his past photos and memories in this box. Would you like to look through it? You're welcome to use anything you want from it." He opened the box packed with photo memories of Stormie, Kathy, myself, and many others. Glenn said that Steve would quite often drag out the tattered, old box and look through it to remind himself of those youthful friends and experiences that he treasured.

We talked about Steve, the actor. Glenn felt that Steve hadn't utilized his acting ability near as much as he could have. Glenn felt that Steve didn't have a magnetic appeal in a dramatic situation. He recognized how easily Steve captured the audience's attention on the *1978 Entertainer of the Year Special*. "He came out on the stage, and for the first few seconds of his response to the award, he acted serious." Of course, that didn't last long, but what Glenn appreciated was the fact that the entire audience was hanging on his ever word. They broke up when Steve lit a cigarette with his gold plated statue. But Glenn's point was well founded. Steve had them in the palm of his hand, without the aid of comedy. At that time both Glenn and I looked forward to the day when Steve would have more opportunities in dramatic roles. Since then, we have been proven right. Although Steve has completed scores of movies to date, most of them comedies, Steve's true fans will have to agree that scenes from *Pennies From Heaven*, *Grand Canyon*, *Simple Twist of Fate*, *Father of The Bride I & II*, *Roxanne* and *The Spanish*

Prisoner all showed that Steve has the depth to be qualified as a great dramatic actor.

As I filtered through the last remnants of memorabilia in the cardboard box, I found our high school *Argobituary*. You know how seniors will traditionally leave a will and, more often than not, bequeath some ridiculous item to a fellow classmate or perhaps a teacher or underclassman. Well, this is the will that Steve left in the *Argobituary*:

"I, Steve Martin, being of all sound and no body, bequeath to the following: To Mr. Farrell, a recording of Hamlet in a Brooklyn accent; To Franz Sobejin, a piano and a pitch pipe; and to John McEuen, a Hindu pin."

Steve could have had no idea just how involved John and he would become as performers after that.

Our wonderful evening with the Martins was short lived. As with all good things, it had to come to an end too soon. Glenn and I were talking our heads off, but I could see that Mary Lee was getting tired. She would never say so, being the perfect hostess that she was, but it was getting late, and we had a long drive back to Hollywood that night.

Mary Lee and I had a chance to discuss many things that evening, and the primary conclusion was simply this: she adores Steve. She was proud and bewildered at his amazing success, and yet she and Glenn were very capable of handling any and all situations that might arise as a result of his career.

It was a real delight to spend an evening with these two wonderful people who I finally felt I knew after all those years. I was overwhelmed by their warmth, hospitality, and generosity. And when talking about how little they gave Steve in monetary terms or parental camaraderie, I'd be remiss if I didn't bring up the fact that they have always adored Steve, even when he wouldn't mow the lawn.

There is a reason why I haven't mentioned Steve's sister, Melinda, very much. After all, she is Steve's one and only sister. I didn't know her that well. I would see her at the house, but we didn't talk much. With all due respect to Melinda, I thought that in the process of writing this book a phone call to her would be in order. I wanted to know her reaction to Steve's success, among other things. She lives in Northern California with her husband and two children. Melinda was very charming, just as I remembered her in my youth. She seemed excited to talk to me and quite willing to help in any way that she could. We talked about Glenn, Mary Lee, and old times.

My first question was about Melinda's relationship with Steve when they were kids. Melinda admitted that she wasn't as close to Steve as she would have liked to have been. She recalls coming home from college and hearing Steve practice hour after hour on the banjo. Melinda always felt that Steve would be great at whatever he did. It seemed that feeling permeated all of the Martins. Each one of them, on different occasions, told me this.

Melinda said that people constantly ask her if Steve was funny when he was growing up. Here again, his really humorous episodes did not happen at home—which is the main place Melinda would see Steve. Being four years older than Steve presented a barrier most older sisters would understand. She was approaching adulthood when Steve was in intermediate school. She really doesn't remember very many humorous antics. She told me that she always thought I probably knew Steve better than anybody. In recent times, Melinda had gotten to know Steve better. Not because of his success, but because she felt that she had missed knowing him very well in their youth and she tried harder. I asked if her kids loved Steve and if they are proud of their uncle? "Of course," she insisted. "Rusty and Julie are his greatest fans." Melinda was so curious about my family and what we had been doing that before long it sounded like I was the one being interviewed.

Shortly after Steve had given Glenn a small part in the movie *All of Me*, in the 1980s, Glenn had a stroke. One side of his body became paralyzed, and the man I knew as Steve's father lost his magnetic good looks and physical appeal.

Mary Lee still lives in that beach house, and Glenn has passed on. Steve and I both felt that we had been cheated out of having fathers, so to speak. Mine was gone and his was there—but not there. But we had each other, and for that, we have always felt blessed.

The following is part of a letter I wrote to Steve after Glenn passed away. It was important to me to let Steve know how I felt about Glenn. I have avoided reprinting any of the letters Steve and I have written to each other over the years, but these thoughts are important if one is to understand the late Glenn Martin. They are deeply personal feelings about Glenn.

Dear Steve,

I am writing to convey my condolences regarding Glenn. You know, Steve, I had a very interesting perspective on your father. In my mind, even though I was not analyzing anybody much in those days, I saw Glenn as being a pretty amazing guy. I liked him a lot. I never had any reason not to.

He was tall, handsome and mysterious to me. I can't remember him ever saying anything to me that wasn't nice. He was always polite and kind. I admired him and I don't know exactly why, because, in retrospect, I know that I wasn't really allowed to know him very well. I don't think you were either. But there was an extremely intense person in Glenn Martin. I know that the main reason I loved your father was because he was your father. Steve's father. Just like you felt about R.W., I guess.

We hope and pray that the best of our characteristics and traits will surface in our children. In my case, I know my kids are superior to me, so I am blessed. I know Glenn felt the same way. You were able to achieve things and be things that Glenn could not.

Few people of those you know could say this to you now, but Glenn did the best he could do for you, Steve. In his mind, as a father he provided comfort and sustenance and love. He also sacrificed to do that. He didn't want to be a real estate salesman. He wanted to be an actor and that never changed. He wanted to be what you have become. He could only, in the final analysis, share vicariously those feelings.

We all have to move on to the next step in our spiritual evolution, and Glenn was ready. I know how intensely proud he was of you. He was, in his own right, a great man. I know you wished you could have known him better and that he hadn't been so aloof when you were young, but that, in itself, also helped set you up for success. It's a rocky road to understanding. I hope he died in peace.

I'm writing because of Glenn, but I am determined to stay out of your face as much as I possibly can, so I'll say this now. In all honesty, Steve, my greatest hope for you is that you can have a child before you die. In that event, you will finally feel the satisfaction of your greatest potential, short of true spiritual enlightenment.

Your Friend,
Morris

Steve Waitkus '76

Chapter 23

NEW YORK, NEW YORK

"Success is in the behind of the beholder."
—Morris Walker

The bitter bite of a Manhattan winter chilled me to the core as Kirk and I walked briskly to the old theater on Broadway. I was, for a short time (in between gigs when the kids were too young to perform), Director of Advertising for *Nevada Magazine*. Kirk Whistler was the publisher. He was smaller and much lighter than I, and he fit into the genius category, much like Steve. Only Kirk's talents were in statistics—facts and figures. A kind man with gentle thoughts, his voice was anything but aggressive or bold. Perhaps best described as your stereotypical, high school scientific type, he was hardly intimidating.

We were in New York City for a few days meeting with ad agencies. I had lunch with Rick Kendall, one of the old Fools. He now holds an executive position with HBO. How an Orange County boy winds up in New York City I don't know, but he took to it like a fish to water. We talked and our conversation, naturally, rotated around Steve for a while. He told me that he would occasionally visit with Steve when Steve was taking care of business in New York City. When he mentioned *Planes, Trains and Automobiles* was playing, I insisted we go, but he had already seen it. So Kirk and I planned to check it out after our rounds at the agencies.

It was late, but not quite dark. The Christmas season was pleasantly in full swing. "Silver Bells" echoed from the sound system of a department store. As we rounded a corner with bundled-up folks dashing in all directions, I noticed a group of people gathered in a loose-knit circle. Just then, a guy across the street hailed a cab; he wore a gray suit, felt hat, and overcoat. He reminded me of Steve, and I was momentarily taken back to past Christmases with Steve when he shared family times and turkey dinners with our family. Suddenly, a ruckus in the circle of observers snapped me back to reality. As Kirk and I peeked in at the edge of the group, it became quickly apparent that there was a serious altercation in progress. A black guy holding a broken two-by-four (with nails protruding from the end) had squared off with a Puerto Rican fellow. The Puerto Rican guy had a chain, he was bleeding from the cheek, and was screaming vehemently at his opponent.

"They're gonna kill each other," I said to Kirk.

"Stay out of it, Morris," he responded, touching my arm. There was a volley of all too recognizable foul language, punctuated with a series of intermittent Spanish words. It was a very interesting blend. I only understood the cuss words. But there was no misunderstanding the intent. The huge, burley black man swung the two-by-four at the other guy, barely missing him and then losing his balance. Then the shorter, leaner Hispanic doubled the chain over and began swinging it over his head, preparing to connect a devastating blow to the big black man, who was trying to regain his stance. I knew that if he connected with the chain, the black fellow, despite his size, would be severely injured. Once again, I heard the Steve Martin-look-alike hailing a cab—I glanced back quickly to see him climbing in. I wondered what Steve would do if confronted with saving these angry men from one another. I knew he wouldn't jump in the middle of the fight, and then it hit me like a blinding light. Stepping just inside the circle, at the top of my lungs, I burst into song.

"DECK THE HALLS WITH BOUGHS OF HOLLY FA LA LA LA LA LA LA LA LA, 'TIS THE SEASON TO BE JOLLY FA LA LA LA LA LA LA LA LA"

By the time I sang, "DON WE NOW OUR GAY APPAREL," the entire circle of onlookers was singing with me at the top of their lungs—no less than 100 people were singing loudly and directly at the two men. It sounded like the Mormon Tabernacle Choir on Prozac.

The fighters stopped and looked at us, and then looked at each other. Slowly, they simultaneously dropped their weapons and stared blankly at the crowd around them, who by now was entering loudly into the second verse, with people joining the group by the dozens. The black man looked straight at me—his face was distorted, confused, and angry, and then it went blank as he turned and quickly disappeared into the crowd. I don't know what ran through is mind, but I know that he was only seconds away from catching a chain in the head. I moved to the inside edge of the group and directed my new glee club. We sang boldly, with spirit and love and friendship pulsating through the group. A Santa Claus moved past me and began directing another section. I glanced back at the other brawler as he too wandered away, shoulders drooping, completely overpowered by the public's unexpected intervention. Everyone cheered and clapped and laughed together at the phenomenon before they began to disperse. I turned to Kirk, who was smiling pleasantly, and said with a broad smile, "I love New Yorkers!"

It was getting late, and we hurried on. The Broadway Theater was in a rather scary part of town for a couple of Carson City, Nevada guys, and as we paid and entered the building, we were quickly aware of the fact that we were the only "honkies" in the theater. Actually, I would not have been so keenly aware of that had the guy that sold us the popcorn not said, "You want your change, honky?" I wanted to go into a routine about who is the honky and who is the honker but figured the timing might be a little off. There were about a hundred people in the theater, and a low cloud of smoke hung above our heads, mixed with a strong scent of alcohol, pot, and just a hint of vomit. After we sat down, the large woman in front of Kirk turned around and asked, "Ya gotta light?"

Kirk leaned forward and spoke loudly in his most geeky voice (as he was usually very serious), "You shouldn't be smoking in the theater!" He said it like he was lecturing a class of sixth graders. No less than fifteen of the patrons turned their heads slowly. Her large, tough-looking Afro-haired companion put his arm over the seat and said, "Yo, muthafuckua...who the hell you think you are?"

I felt the room closing in; I wanted to point at Kirk and scream, "He's the Honky!" and run. Then suddenly, the lights went out, and the movie started without any previews or notices or anything. A moment later, the screen was filled with Steve Martin's silver watch and then his face. As always, the audience was instantly with him, and we were forgotten. We settled back in our seats. Kirk turned to me and said, "They really shouldn't smoke in here, you know!" I sank a little deeper; fortunately, nobody heard him.

This particular movie offered a very keen insight to Mr. Steve Martin. Steve likes to pair his new releases. It came out right after *Roxanne* which, by the way, had been his biggest hit since *The Jerk*. *Roxanne* earned $39 million at the box office and won Steve a Writers' Guild Award for best screenplay adapted from another medium. I remember Steve said, "That's one award I feel really great about, along with the New York and L.A. Film Critics, because you can't campaign for them."

Steve told me he was doing something different in *Planes, Trains and Automobiles*. He felt that playing this disgruntled ad executive "was one of the first real people" he ever portrayed.

Yes, the character was more like a real person and, in many ways, more like the real Steve. Whereas, John Candy was cast as a loud-mouthed, cigarette-smoking, obnoxious slob, Steve's character was a classic opposite. He was trim and well manicured, meticulously dressed, symbolizing the epitome of a middle-aged, rather uptight, boomer yuppie. This character was not a far stretch for Steve, without the negative connotation. He was put off with over indulgence and motor-mouthing strangers. He treasured his privacy, and his facial manners were easily realistic when a situation assaulted his sensibilities. His condescending nods and forced smiles were a perfect reaction to every ill-mannered action Candy so artfully carried off. John Candy, on the other hand, in real life was not, in any sense of the word, the crude character he portrayed. He was, in fact, one of the finest comedic actors Steve ever worked with. The magnetic attraction of character opposites on film was slowly unified into a loving friendship, and in the final analysis, there was a bit of all of us in John Candy and the conscientious spirit of human kindness that emerged from Steve's cold, calculating screen image in the movie. Nevertheless, there was a lot of the real Steve in that character. The scene that shocked me, because it was so totally out of character for the real Steve, was Steve reaming out the poor woman at the car rental store. He probably made cinematic history by repeating the word "fuck" more times (18) in the one minute monologue than anyone in the history of films. If nothing else, its shock value for the ultra-conservative character Steve was playing was profound. Regarding such language, I can say it would be completely out of character for the real Steve Martin to ever speak in anything close to this manner.

Obviously, for the sake of a show, Steve can carry off filthy lines. In the entertainment business, words are just words, tools of the trade. There is little or no morality involved in using them to portray a character. In Steve's personal life, however, profanity has never been a part of his common vocabulary. Not even when he was a kid. It's neither a moral nor a personal issue. It's just simply that, in personal conversations, his vocabulary is as eloquently appropriate as is his razor sharp wit. He just doesn't need to use such language to convey his point of view or to make an audience react.

When the movie ended (a happy, compassionate Steve Martin ending), the screen went dark and a dismal yellow light came on above us. Reality was back. The yellow smoke still hugged the ceiling and filled our lungs. We maneuvered down the aisle, with several of the people now giving us, what appeared to be, threatening looks. I was uncomfortable, and Kirk looked a little concerned as we moved past the snack bar towards the front door. Just as we approached the exit, a group of four tall, dark, bad-looking individuals, all towering above us, casually walked into our path. We were both looking at the ground, pretending we didn't see them and hoping that they would step aside. But all we saw were eight big feet and what looked like four-fifths of an inner-city basketball league team looking down on us. As I smiled a sheepish smile at them, I noticed three of them were the smokers that had been directly in front of us. Then my eyes locked on the largest member of the group, who was leaning on the shoulder of the one with the old-fashioned Afro. It was the guy who had, two-and-a-half hours earlier, been holding the piece of wood with nails protruding out of it, and facing off with the Latin dude. He looked like a cross between Mike Tyson and a grizzly bear. We stared. Eventually, I figured I would have to initiate some action. So I smiled. He didn't respond for just a few seconds, then smiled from ear to ear and said, "Merry Christmas, Man!" He took his buddy by the shoulder and walked away, as the other two followed.

We walked at a rapid rate once we made it outside. It was snowing heavily now, and the streets were dark and foreboding. "You worried, Kirk?" I said curiously.

"People get mugged here, you know!" he exclaimed.

"Not if you have the right defense," I replied.

"Yeah, like what?" Kirk asked.

I began singing loudly,

"DECK THE HALLS WITH BOUGHS OF HOLLY FA LA LA LA LA LA LA LA LA LA LA LA..."

Basil Poledouris & Bobby, Kathy Westmoreland, Steve, Doug Rowell,
Morris, Lynn and Starshine Rowell—"The Hollywood Reunion"

Chapter 24

KATHY, STEVE, ELVIS, PICASSO AND EINSTEIN

"It's a funny thing about life; if you refuse to accept anything but the best, you very often get it."

—Somerset Maugham

It was after the last show of the evening at the Hilton Hotel in Las Vegas. Steve had wowed the masses and earned himself a good night's sleep. He was exhausted. The crowd's spirited response had kept him going, but his schedule had been so horrendous that he felt like going back to his room and dying that night. As he was preparing to leave, his attention was drawn to the figure of a large, black-haired man entering his dressing room with a small entourage. Steve had never been so awed by anyone that you could notice an instant reaction in his expression. But on this particular night, he was visibly affected. There in his doorway stood The King, The Legend, The One-and-Only Elvis Presley! Steve's first remark was simply a disarming, "Hi."

The King smiled at Steve as he moved slowly across the room, holding out his hand. "I thought your show was really funny, man," he said as they shook hands.

"Thanks," said Steve, as he felt the rejuvenation of the superstar's compliment stimulate his weary body.

And then Elvis (still gripping Steve's hand) moved in closer and in a subdued voice gave Steve what he felt was a more sincere comment on his performance, "You have a very oblique sense of humor."

Steve thanked him. It was a well thought-out compliment. "Oblique" means simply "having a direction neither perpendicular nor parallel to some line or surface which is made the standard of reference." It's safe to say that Steve Martin's comedy was not similar to any standard of comedy the world enjoyed prior to Steve's success. The fact that Elvis Presley, who had seen and done everything that was available to man because of his exalted status, was interested enough to come backstage and tell Steve what he thought inspired Steve to even greater heights that night. Elvis liked Steve. And Steve had liked Elvis ever since we first tuned in to rock n' roll. According to Steve, I turned him onto rock n' roll music back in the '50s. I still remember talking him into listening to a rock n' roll station out of San Diego known as the "Mighty 690."

It seems apparent that Steve will be a legend in comedy, as memorable as Elvis has been to rock n' roll. Steve Martin, King of Comedy.

At that illustrious time in Elvis's career, he was just getting back into performing with a new tour after a ten-year hiatus. Our old friend, Kathy, had been discovered by Elvis and had become his lead singer. I wonder if Elvis ever knew that it was Steve who secured Kathy Westmoreland's first professional entertaining job for her? Several years before Elvis noticed Kathy's marvelous vocal talents in the Metropolitan Opera, Steve asked Kathy to come and audition at the Bird Cage Theater at Knott's Berry Farm. It was shortly after high school (I was playing bass and doing comedy with The Settlers, a folk singing group in Orange County). Kathy kept them spellbound at her audition, and for a time, Steve and Kathy did a comedy act together at the Bird Cage and a few other locations in Southern California. It was still another three or four years before Elvis hired Kathy to back him up at concerts and on his recordings.

When I contacted Kathy, she seemed elated to talk to me and was more than willing to get together and discuss the good old times she remembered with Steve. Lynn and I met Kathy at her parent's ranch near San Bernardino in southern California. Kathy looked great, and just as I had imagined, she was unaffected by her fame and fortune. She was genuine and down-to-earth and just as warm and wonderful as she was the first day Steve and I met her in high school. We talked all day about Steve and Elvis. Nobody had ever interviewed Kathy about Steve, but since the passing of Elvis, she has been bombarded with interviews, movies, and countless other Elvis-related offers. Kathy had appeared in a movie playing the part of herself, with Kurt Russell portraying Elvis. She said that Russell was uncanny in the part. I happened to see the movie just before we met, and it was the best portrayal of The King I had ever seen.

Kathy loved Elvis deeply and he loved her, but I felt there was some relief for her in talking about someone else for a change. Especially Steve. They had performed together on many occasions since the three of us had performed as Peter, Paul, and Almond Joy in high school. Naturally, they were close friends and admired one another's talents immensely. In reflecting back on our high school years, it was funny to remember that, despite the fact that Kathy possessed such a spectacular voice, Steve and she only performed comedy together. There were routines where Kathy would sing—but that was only for a laugh. Despite her tremendously powerful voice, she allowed her singing to take a back seat to Steve's comedy aspirations whenever she performed with us.

Kathy had this innate ability with timing, and the two of them put together a very clever show. Kathy says that Steve drove everybody crazy backstage at the Bird Cage Theater. Day after day, Steve would sit in what they called "the asphalt room" (a patio type of affair) and practice his banjo picking. If he wasn't practicing banjo, he was planting water balloons in precarious places so that they would fall on Kathy or Stormie or one of the other unsuspecting players. It got to be an accepted practice, after awhile, that someone would always get blasted with a strategically-placed balloon. Steve also caught his share of the balloon showers from Kathy and the others.

The owner of the Bird Cage Theater was an old thespian named George Stuart. He was a talented man who willingly passed on his dramatic knowledge to the young performers he hired to work at the Bird Cage. He had an unlimited supply of talented, minimum wage performers, and he provided the aspiring entertainers with excellent training. At times, it was more melodramatic than you would imagine. For instance, Kathy recalled one evening when she and Steve were acting, and her role called for getting shot in her bustle. She had been on stage and sniffed something burning. Her bustle had been penetrated by a blank fired by another player. Of course, he meant it as a joke, but before she got off stage, her dress somehow burst into flames. Steve quickly jumped into action with a stop, drop, and roll which left the two of them safe in the arms of laughter. Steve's put out a few fires in some hot numbers since then, I'm sure. Luckily, Steve's quick thinking saved her from injury and embarrassment, and allowed the show to go on.

Kathy told me that Steve sure liked to pull gags. She recalled that on one occasion she and Steve drove all the way to L.A. to buy some phony rubber bricks. As far as she knows, the only thing Steve did with them was throw them at her mother during rehearsals.

We talked about what an exciting time it had been in Steve's life as he was learning more about show business at the Bird Cage Theater; learning about women from Stormie; and learning almost nothing while attending Long Beach State. Steve enjoyed walking around Knott's Berry Farm barking at people. "Barking" was what old carnival folks did to try and get attention and draw people into their performances. He would be out there shouting things about the show to the tourists. "Hurry, hurry! You'll hear great songs like, 'When They Operated on Daddy They Opened Mother's Male!' or 'Get Out of the Wheat Field Granny, You're Going Against My Grain.' Hurry, hurry!"

Kathy's sister, Melody, also a wonderful singer and performer, had worked in Vegas for Wayne Newton and some other notable folks. Much to my surprise, Bobby Carter, another high school friend, dropped over to say hello. Her father was quite a fiddler and banjo picker. Steve and I went to hear him perform when we were in high school.

Since we were talking about the good old days, I couldn't resist asking Kathy a few questions about her experiences with Elvis. After all, Kathy had been with Elvis for over seven years. We talked about Ed Parker, Elvis' karate teacher. By the way, I learned that Elvis was an eighth degree black belt. He was very serious about his martial arts training, but, according to Kathy, many of his "Memphis Mafia" resented him and made fun of him behind his back. That really bothered Kathy because she loved Elvis. Kathy explained to me that Elvis was not a violent man. His life had been threatened so many times that he just had to take precautions. I asked Kathy if it was true that Elvis would actually pull out a .357 magnum and blow away TV sets. "Yes," she replied, "but it wasn't a violent act. It was just meant as a joke." I told her that I was of the opinion that if it was his TV in his house, then it was his prerogative to do whatever he wished. "Yes," she said again, "but what's just as important to understand is that he generally put on these performances for the benefit of his companions. It was meant as a joke when he'd shoot up a TV, and the punch line to this joke was, 'Take it to the graveyard.' " She smiled, as if remembering one of these episodes. "You see," she said, "Elvis really did have a graveyard for the TV's he had shot, and it was in the backyard of the Graceland Mansion." Now the humor became clearer.

Personally, this talk with Kathy told me more about Elvis than all the tabloids ever could. I never realized what a keen sense of humor Elvis had. A graveyard for his TVs! There have certainly been times when I wanted to blow up a TV set; on the other hand, Steve would never even touch a gun. Elvis, for some odd reason, felt he had to pull out an assortment of handguns, which he showed to Steve the night they met. Steve told me that he never really understood why Elvis did that.

"Did Elvis give you a new car?" I asked Kathy before we left.

Kathy answered by explaining that one late night at his Graceland Mansion in Memphis (Elvis and his entourage lived by night and slept by day), Elvis asked Kathy, "What kind of a car do you think I ought to get next year?" She discussed Mercedes and Cadillacs and a few others, not really committing herself to any of them. Finally, she explained, Elvis decided to stop beating around the bush and just asked her point blank, "What kind of a car would you like if you were going to get a new car?"

Kathy told us that she felt a flutter of butterflies for a minute and stuttered, "A Lincoln Continental."

Elvis grinned and announced, "You got it!" She then told us that Larry Geller (Elvis' hairdresser) laughed at Kathy's reaction, and Elvis then wheeled around, pointed to him, and said, "Okay, you got one too!"

Kathy explained to us that she wanted a black Lincoln, but Elvis insisted that black was too "evil" for such a sweet lady, and, despite her wishes, he surprised her one night at the mansion with a brand-new, white Continental. She said when she thanked him, Elvis looked down at her, put his arm around her shoulder, and said with a smile and the sincerity that was Elvis, "Kathy, don't put my name on it. All gifts come from God!" True to character, Elvis was a benevolent King.

In 1988, Kathy published a book called *Kathy and Elvis*. The first photo in the book was of Kathy, Steve Martin, and myself doing "Peter, Paul, and Almond Joy."

Steve Martin began writing plays a couple of years ago. One particular play made it to Broadway. It was called *Picasso at The Lapin Agile*. The year was 1904, and the setting was a bar in Paris. The chief protagonists were a young Albert Einstein (played by Mark Nelson) and a young Pablo Picasso (played by Tim Hopper)— both of whom stand on the threshold of international fame. Low and behold, there is a dream sequence in which a young, slim, narrow-hipped Elvis Presley appears in a beam of light. The infusion of Elvis was a delightful highlight to a play that deals with intellectualizing as a source of humor. One could deduce that this was Steve's little reaction to his memory of Elvis. Elvis brought Steve to life one night in Las Vegas, and Steve now had his opportunity to bring Elvis to life one night in New York.

Steve reading my original manuscript, early 1979

Chapter 25

THE "GREAT" STEVE MARTIN

"Only by recognizing greatness in others may one manifest greatness in their own life. You cannot become something that you cannot perceive."
—Morris Walker

Some things never change. Steve's favorite word, and at the same time his highest compliment, was and always will be simply the word "great." To Steve, the word "great" has always meant awesome, spectacular, interesting, intense, fine, beautiful, wonderful, rewarding, and magical. I can't begin to tell you how many times he would get a look of sincere wonderment in his eyes and simply say, "That's great!" It could be something as simple as an onion that brought tears to his eyes or the King of rock n'roll complimenting his style. I realize it's a word that anyone can use, and that everyone does. But you have to understand that, with Steve, it was his highest praise.

Wiley Britain, a straw-haired wheeler-dealer who attended Rancho Alamitos High School with Steve and me, had a way with words. He either became a great real estate salesman or is doing time in some forgotten prison. Wiley had a banjo. I was kind of interested in seeing it, as I was a Kingston Trio fan and curious about the thing. It was a nice, old tenor banjo with a warped neck. I gave Wiley a Spalding baseball mitt and fifteen dollars cash for the old, four-stringed banjo. The neck was warped so much that it almost looked as though the strings were bending it like a bow. He made a point in explaining that it was okay if the neck was warped inward, because the strings didn't lay across the frets. "On the other hand," he further explained, "if it was warped in the opposite direction, you couldn't play it!"—and I believed him! After plucking a few notes for the next night or two, I took the banjo over to Steve's house on Brookside Lane. It was our senior year. Steve's eyes lit up like a Roman candle. He had never played an instrument in his life, but as he gently took the banjo into his big hands, a sense of awe embraced him. He handled it like a great work of art. It caused the same facial reaction I had witnessed in his expression when he used to watch Wally Boag do his balloon tricks at the Golden Horseshoe Theater in Frontierland. I knew what he was going to say.

"This is great!"

I left the banjo with Steve for a couple of weeks. As a matter of fact, I decided to give up playing banjo after that and started playing bass. I knew intuitively that Steve was going to play banjo, and he was going to be "great." He gave the old four-string back and thanked me immensely, and before long, had picked up a five-string banjo and began listening to Flatt and Scrugg's records. God, he was intense. He never had a lesson. He would put those 45 records on 33-and-1/3 speed, and he'd listen to each of the riffs. He slowly figured out the entire picking patterns to extremely complicated tunes like *Foggy Mountain Breakdown*.

Steve won the Topanga Canyon banjo and fiddle contest when he was twenty-years-old.

Lynn and I visited Steve in Aspen a couple of times, and on one occasion, met with some old high school friends at the Aspen Recording Society Studio, around 1977. This society was organized by Steve and our two friends, John and Bill. John McEuen, by his own admission, was a "nerd" in high school. Steve and I met him at Disneyland when he worked at the Magic Shoppe with Steve. To Steve, it didn't matter if everyone in the school thought someone was a dweeb or a nerd. If Steve perceived characteristics that he appreciated, that was his only criteria for friendship. John was an exceptional guitar player, and after high school, Steve and John spent long hours together playing banjo and guitar. Not too long after those intense jams, John formed the *Nitty Gritty Dirt Band*. He became extremely proficient on practically every stringed instrument he touched. He told me a few years ago that he played twelve instruments, and then he said, "I also play bass." I asked him why he just sort of added the bass on to the list like that and he said, "Any idiot can play bass." After catching a session with John and some of his band members, we had quite a long visit with him. As long as John's older brother, Bill, was Steve's manager, most everything Steve did was produced as an Aspen Recording Society project.

John told me that he met Steve and me at Disneyland between our sophomore and junior year. I didn't remember, but he elaborated on the fact that he was another young Disneyholic. He told me he spent so much time there that Disney gave him a job, because they figured if they paid him, he would have to go home sometime. He spent a lot of time with Steve at the Fantasyland Magic Shoppe. When he was first getting to know Steve, Steve was working in Adventureland. Employees of the Magic Kingdom, in those days, seemed to move from job to job and, therefore, from land to land. Steve and John went to Tomorrowland for a burger, and Steve told John that he owned a Magic Shoppe in Long Beach, and that if John dropped in, Steve would give him a job. He gave John the address, and John drove thirty miles to find an empty lot.

The following year (our senior year), Steve and John worked at the Fantasyland Magic Shoppe, played chess, and started getting more interested in music. As John began to tell me more, he filled in a lot of gaps for me in how his relationship with Steve developed. After I loaned Steve his first banjo, he and John heard a group called the "Mad Mountain Ramblers" and tried to figure out how to play "Cripple Creek" on a four-string banjo.

John and Steve both became quite proficient on well known bluegrass tunes, but as John focused more on traditional tunes, Steve actually learned to play classical tunes on the banjo. That was truly amazing.

I remember Steve learning a poem called the "Mountain Whippoorwill," and playing banjo back-up while he would recite the thing. John had recollections of the tune also, and remembered himself and Steve doing a duet at Bolsa High School and getting their first standing ovation.

Bill also became close to Steve and actually started managing him (part time). Steve was breaking away from college and planning to work the clubs. When Steve became a comedy writer for the *Smothers Brothers* and other shows, he didn't need Bill's services, but he eventually returned to the fold when he wanted to hit the road.

As time moved forward, as I have mentioned before, Bill also managed John's new group, the Nitty Gritty Dirt Band. They climbed the charts quickly with "Mr. Bojangles," and eventually became the first American rock group to tour Russia.

John remembered times on the road when Steve was the opening act for the Dirt Band and flopped time after time. But he also witnessed Steve trying different things on stage and, slowly but surely, ferreting out the routines that worked and trashing the ones that didn't, until eventually, he had a tight act of well rehearsed material. One of my all time favorite lines was an idea that Bill actually came up with. Steve told the audience that he was in a restaurant, and the guy next to him said,

"Mind if I smoke?"

Steve responded with, "Mind if I fart?"

John saw Steve fail, but he also saw the birth of Steve's "Pied Piper" routines where he would take the entire audience out in front of the club, withdraw a straw, and announce, "I'm going to do something that has never been done before. I'm going to suck this car into my lungs." Then he would put one end of the straw up to the car, and the other end to his mouth, and stand there for about two minutes, perfectly still. He knew just how long to do that to make the people start laughing.

Steve would take a couple hundred people out into the street and flag down a policeman and ask him loudly, "Do you know where I can score some drugs in this town?" John told me that he had been extremely jealous of all the antics Steve and I pulled in high school and how much he wanted to be on our side of the microphone. He told me about routines we did that I had completely forgotten.

Several years later, I saw John playing a gig at the Holiday Inn in Frisco, Colorado. My family band, the Earthwalkers, was on tour, and since my son, Skye, plays banjo, I knew he would enjoy seeing John perform. It was a little sad. John had hit the big time with the Dirt Band, and now he was doing gigs for a couple hundred bucks a night. I've done a thousand of these two-bit shows, but it seemed like a big step-down for him. Nevertheless, he gave a great performance and even did his banjo recital of "Whippoorwill" that Steve had taught him twenty-some years earlier. Whether he ever surfaces as a mainstream star or not, his incredible acumen for playing will always keep him in demand as a studio musician. His CD, *String Wizards*, is excellent.

The one thing John told me about Steve that truly shocked me was that Steve had been celibate for a year. I found that to be the most amazing accomplishment of all. I know that Steve has never been a womanizer—never "over-sexed," never gay—but to not have any sex for a year put him on a par with a monk or someone with mystical strengths and convictions. But with Steve Martin, the word "impossible" is not applicatory. If you had asked Steve what he wanted to be in this world when he was a youngster, short of career options, I can promise you he would have said, "Something great!" One thing that makes Steve so great is his drive. He just keeps on going and going and going.

Chapter 26

WHY ANTEATERS DON'T GET SICK

"There is no way to prepare for the past."

—Morris Walker

Now, as I begin to write, I feel my eyes tearing up just slightly. You know what I mean; I'm not going to cry, but just like clouds that threaten rain that never comes, it seems as though the drops are imminent.

This story is about Steve Martin. By now, you know a little bit about my family, the Earthwalkers, "The family band that's sweeping the land." It would be impossible to tell you this story without relating a little bit more about what we were doing at the time these incidents transpired. I have to bare my soul a little bit here. I have to shed some pride. We were broke. This is not an unusual scenario for most "professional" entertainers. Most of us "entertainers" spend our lives doing what we love and scraping by so closely we walk the edge of homelessness as comfortably as an investor plays the stock market. We never considered ourselves poor. We just

never owned a home or had much to speak of. We were on the road
day after day, month after month, year after year. We were always
struggling, always happy, and always close. We rode the roller
coaster of life in the front seat, with our fretting fingers dangling
near the rails. When our kids were old enough to learn our trade,
we took them on the road. They quickly became dynamic performers at an early age. We home schooled them as we traveled the
country doing shows for schools and little communities. If we
made $140 on a show, our agent would get about a third or more.
We had to do three to four shows a day just to make enough money
to get to the next town and camp out or get a cheap motel. We were
in our element on stage and with our family all the time. We were
happy. The kids didn't feel the stress that Lynn and I did, but they
felt something. We had no resources, no credit, nothing. We often
would have just enough money for gas, an evening meal, and that
was it. The next morning, we would do a show for a school, cash
the check, and have a good meal. In the summertime, we would
stop and rent an inexpensive cabin in a bucolic setting and pick up
little gigs nearby. I would augment our meager income by painting
signs or murals or whatever I could to keep our boat afloat.

It was a summer like that—we were just scraping by but, nevertheless, glad to be in a one-room cabin on a lake in Oregon. As the
summer drew to a close, we knew we had to start our tour in Illinois
in a few weeks, but it was questionable whether we would have
enough money to even get to our first gig. I was feeling pretty desperate then, and wanted to stop the touring, but there just wasn't an
opportunity for us that would support us through the winter. We had
to go back on tour. Steve had made several movies and had been a
millionaire for years by then. I envied Steve, more for his business
savvy than anything. I wished some of it, even just a fraction of it,
had rubbed off on me. He was out of the country at the time, and I
knew it. But before we left, I wrote him a letter. I was bitching and
moaning to him about how tight things were for us. And telling him
we had to go back on tour, and that it was killing us, and so forth and
so on. Over the years, we have bared our souls to each other in letters from time to time, and in this case, I just needed to tell someone
how bad it was. It was fair, he had written to me and complained
when times had been tough for him, so it was okay. I signed it, Your
Friend, Morris, sealed it, stamped it, sent it, and forgot it.

We hit the road with our van, a little fifteen-foot trailer, a P.A. system, some instruments, and each of us surrounded by enough love to carry an army. We were barely making it but not lacking in the family love department.

We made it to the first gig and many more. One day after our shows, due to flooding and very inclement weather, we had to take a long detour to the town where we were performing the next day. I only had about fifteen dollars left. We had been traveling for a couple of months, and things were worse than ever. I had developed a really bad cough that would not go away, and we were all exhausted. I was depressed, feeling fate was too hard on us and we deserved more in life. I was in my forties and feeling road weary beyond imagination. Lynn never complained but dreamed of her own garden and a humble home. My self pity was only mollified when I glanced around at my family and felt the value of having the best life could offer me at that moment. I never told the kids how bad it was. I knew we had enough gas, but the money in my pocket was all the money we had until we did the show the next day. I told the kids we would stop for french fries only and eat when we got to our destination. Everyone approved instantly, as we pulled into a Burger King just off the freeway.

The alternate sleet and rain was not heavy, but icy cold, and the dismal skies added to my depression. As I washed my hands in the rest room, I noticed a middle-aged man, about my age, as a matter of fact. His clothes were old and badly frayed, and his battered cane was leaning in the corner as he was attempting to tuck in his tattered shirt. His graying beard had not been trimmed for some time, and hard times were written deeply in the lines of his face.

As I dried my hands, he picked up his cane and leaned closer to me, with an impish smile belaying his obvious problems. I smiled a shallow response, and for a brief second in time he looked like a high school kid Steve and I used to know. A kid named "Whitey" who had been killed in Vietnam. And then he spoke to me as if I was an old classmate he had talked to a hundred times.

"You know why anteaters don't get sick?"

Now I smiled a real smile. "No," I said. "Why don't anteaters get sick?"

He leaned even closer to answer. "Because they are filled with little antibodies."

I laughed. I needed to laugh; I was having a bad day. Then I looked at him again as his smile faded, and he turned and limped out the door. God knows, he had not chosen to be so compromised in life. Life is full of shitty tricks, and this guy was really down.

A few minutes later, after I had paid for the kids' french fries, my daughter Amoris pointed to him inconspicuously and said, "Dad, you know what that man said to me?"

"No," I responded, looking at the man again briefly.

Now she smiled, "You know what Buddha said to the hot dog vendor?" I shook my head as my lips turned up slightly in anticipation. She held her hands in front of her face as if in prayer, looked me in the eye, and said, "Make me one with everything!"

I laughed outloud.

I looked around again, and our ragged friend had moved to the end of the counter where he had removed the contents of his pockets and was perusing the items. It appeared to be mostly crumpled-up papers and unidentifiable bits and pieces of pocket trash. He continued to search his pockets, as if hoping to discover some long lost coin or bill.

I walked up to him and asked softly, "How's it going for you?"

He granted me another smile, although strained, not giving way to admitting destitution. "Not very good, I'm afraid."

He began putting the scraps back in his pocket. I knew he had nothing. Torrents of rain began rolling across the parking lot as we both peered momentarily out the window. I had the best things in life: a lovely, loyal wife and two beautiful and healthy kids. All the love and care and camaraderie anyone could desire. Plus, I had a whole bunch of gigs right around the corner. I had it all, and he didn't even have a friend. I felt rich.

I reached in my pocket and pulled out our last ten-dollar bill and handed it to him.

He took it slowly, as if it were hard to accept.

"Don't tell anybody," he said, "but your heart is showing."

Now you see, there I go. My right eye is a little wet. Why is that?

I've spent a lot of money on a lot of things, but nothing else has ever came close to approaching that feeling.

A few minutes later, I gathered the kids together and started out the door. He was standing near the exit with a hot cup of coffee in his hand and motioned for me to step closer before we left.

"You know why anteaters don't get sick?" he asked softly.

"Yeah, I know."

In our trailer that night, I lay awake and wondered in desperation how in the hell we would ever get off the road. Lynn and I had always been on the road, but now the kids would soon be teenagers. They were gifted entertainers, but we had an aging agent who never booked anything but these low paying gigs at schools, prisons, churches, etc. No manager, no money, no home. We couldn't afford to stop. We were trapped in an endless cycle of gigs—like we had been, it seemed, since forever. We had nothing. We had only each other and the shows we loved and "the road," which looked dismally dark and interminable that night. I never did get to sleep.

Our first gig was at 8:30 a.m. for a middle school in a small town somewhere southeast of Peoria. The second show was at a junior high school in the same town. Everyone was hungry, and I was exhausted and cranky. I needed to cash the check I received from the superintendent before we could eat. After mailing off the commission to the agent, we would net less than a hundred bucks for the two shows. But it was gas money and sustenance, and we were alive. I know Lynn and the kids were worried about me, as my cough was getting progressively worse, and I could hardly talk, let alone sing.

I had to stop in the post office and pick up our mail, which was forwarded to our different mail stops twice a week. Sometimes we missed a mail stop, and it was sent back to the agency, and we wouldn't get it for weeks. There was a short letter from Steve and a check. A check! I was dumbfounded. Steve was sending me money, and it couldn't have been at a better time. It was enough to pay some bills and keep us ahead until we finished the tour. It simply said, "I hope this will help you through these times. Regards to Lynn and the kids, Steve." I remember that moment like I was hit by lightening. I remember thinking, "Don't look now, Steve, but your heart is showing." I could breathe again. We were able to finish the rest of the shows that month and afford to stop touring and settle down. We returned to the West Coast, rented a house, and regrouped. The kids had their own bedrooms for the first time in years and were thrilled at the prospect of staying in one place and making friends and going to school. Public schools get a bad rap these days, but you know, that's where I met that young magician, Steve Martin. The check would have been there sooner but it had been rerouted several times trying to catch up with us on the road. But the timing couldn't have been better. Even when we finally settled down, it took almost two years to recover from that cough I thought was going to kill me. I would not have recovered on the road. We all have our crosses to bear, and Steve and I have found ourselves at distant ends of the same stick. Same stick, extremely long with vastly different surroundings. He has felt compassion for my lack of material needs and success, and I have been concerned about his lack of connubial success.

On the cover of the April 1996, issue of *Esquire Magazine*, Steve was standing on a miniature sand island with his arms stretched out. In garish pink and yellow letters set crooked against a clouded background it said, "STEVE MARTIN NEEDS A HUG." The article was titled, "MISTER LONELY HEARTS." The photos were artistically designed, showing Steve in different scenarios with a lonely, desperate look in his eyes. He is posed as if he were a part of one of his highly collectable paintings. He is ostensibly paying homage to one of his favorite artist's paintings. The artist—Edward Hooper, the painting—*Excursion Into Philosophy*. What surprised me most about the article was a reference in the first paragraph to Steve arriving "loose and relaxed, fresh from a visit with his therapist." On my end of the stick, we could go absolutely stark-raving bonkers and never consider "a therapist." I suppose therapists are the penchant of the rich, and it was only a matter of time before Steve was convinced he needed one. The article quotes Steve as saying, "I feel like I'm in an interim period, and I'm fifty, this is my last viable decade." He talks about how he is dealing with being a bachelor and his fear of eventually turning sixty, having thirty-five "middlebrow family hits in the can, and starring in *Father of the Bride VI*." And another bitter divorce.

The article painted a dismal view of the future as Steve saw it in one of his more morose visions. "It is a vision of hell, as complicated and horrifying as one of his paintings by Hieronymus Bosch. As empty as an Edward Hopper and as self-absorbed as a late Rembrandt."

Listing a few paragraphs under each of ten categories, the writer summed up hours of recorded conversations into, what she felt, was

Steve's ten point plan for solutions in his midlife confusion.

STEP NUMBER ONE: KNOW THAT YOU DON'T KNOW

He learned that from his philosophy adventures at Long Beach State.

STEP NUMBER TWO: GIVE YOURSELF PERMISSION TO FALL APART

A well known "workaholic," it sounded like some good advice from his therapist. But on the other hand, I could not imagine Steve falling apart as a result of pressure. I think, possibly, the best thing he could do would be to peel a bunch of onions with an old friend.

STEP NUMBER THREE: BUY A DOG

From this old Gopher Boy, that is probably the most important remedy of all. There is no better example of unconditional love than a dog. Steve has always been a cat kind-of-guy, and cats are great, but cats don't follow their master into hell. They stand back and say, "Good-bye, master. I loved you but it's too hot down there." Dogs say, "It's hot but if you go, I go!" To get a dog is a quantum leap for Steve in dealing with the pressures of lost and questionable love in his life and life in general. Roger is a yellow Lab. A big, fluffy, sloppy, soft cure-all. We have always had dogs; Yin, Yang, Taiho, Clyde, Lola, Shy, Lakota, Dumbo, Cognac, and (as if to suggest that every portion of my life relates somehow to Steve Martin) we had a dog named Cyrano. But that was long before *Roxanne* (not the dog... the movie).

STEP NUMBER FOUR: REMEMBER, YOU HAVE FRIENDS

No doubt. Steve's friends are like a who's who of Hollywood and other worlds—Brian Grazer (who produced *Bilko*, *Apollo 13* and others including, of course, more Martin movies) and other pals like Lorne Michaels, Tom Hanks, Mike Nichols, and the list goes on. Somewhere on the other end of the schtick, we find me— the oldest of the friends. And although no longer in the close circle Steve said he drew around him as a boy, still a friend.

STEP NUMBER FIVE: EXAMINE THE PAST

Here the article quickly summarizes Steve's entire past, including everything in this book, into a few lines. And at that junction, I take exception with both the writer and the solutions. I believe that the secret to Steve's cognizance of happiness lies in his past, not in the opulence of his future. It was as a boy and a teenager that Steve reveled in the glory of living. He knows it, and I know it. But the therapist only needs to know that Steve Martin as a client is a rocket in his pocket, and that's where he probably wants to keep him. Do we believe that perhaps the benevolent therapist is hoping and praying that Steve can soon be cured and never return for another session for more money per hour than the average American takes home after taxes in a week!? I don't think so. I believe the therapist is more like a mental masseuse, and Steve and all the other actors that pay a great amount of money to these professionals leave with their id well oiled. And if it feels good, they keep doing it.

STEP NUMBER SIX: OPEN YOUR HEART

Now, Steve is making more references to the dog again. Good point. I think that Roger is already more effective than the therapist.

STEP NUMBER SEVEN: QUIT TRYING SO HARD

Steve was quoted as saying, "First, you work hard to prove you aren't a flash in the pan, then you work to show other things you can do. And you write to show something else. It's showing and showing and showing. And pretty soon, you realize there's a kind of emptiness left, and it's traumatic. And I realized that, unless I was continually working, I felt people wouldn't like me."

Steve is a driven man—so driven, perhaps, that he can't see exactly how his friends perceive him. He is more loved than he understands. Steve is the ultimate nice guy. Everybody knows some jerks. And for being the most famous Jerk in history, Steve is anything but a jerk. I'm not saying this just to stroke Steve because he has been my friend for so long. It's just the truth. But ironically, I don't think he knows this as well as everyone who knows him.

STEP NUMBER EIGHT: LEARN FROM MISTAKES

It was at this point that the writer summarized Steve's relationship with Victoria Tennant, who instantly gave me painful vibes in the old "tookas"! I still remember how Steve was ever so genteel when he said that he would not have described her as "Sweet and Kind;" rather, he told me, "My wife was strong and, uh, nice." He also stated, "But those wouldn't be the two words that would come to mind to describe her. No."

What a diplomat. Later on the article explains that Victoria has finally remarried a man named Kirk Stamble, a young (eight years younger than she) Warner Brothers Executive. Then it discussed how Steve had an affair with a twenty-five-year-old beauty named

Anne Heche. "The Heartbreak Kid," as Martin's Hollywood friends described her. It was a "torturous love affair" and when it was over, he found himself forty-nine, alone again, and wondering what life was all about.

I empathize with Steve's situation. I even identify with it, but from this end of the stick, the love and companionship have always been with me since I met Lynn. The agony of not enough money has also been a constant companion. Everything Steve ever touched turned to gold, and, unfortunately, most things I ever touched turned to mush! But I'm still out there plugging away, learning from my mistakes, and trying to do the best I can for my wife and family.

The real heartbreak for Steve was his girlfriend, Stormie. After her, the loner side of Steve took precedence. The businessman, tunnel visioned, dedicated achiever took over, and love was just never the main goal. Love was just a sidebar in the pages of Steve's life. He has been so determined to accomplish and achieve and collect and be the best at everything, that he has not really been open to more subtle types of success. Like true love. Although, he thought he had it with Victoria. He was half right. Eventually, he "had it" with Victoria.

I believe that true love is critical. But it's not something you "accomplish." You have to spend a lot of serious time in your life going out and hunting for it.

STEP NUMBER NINE: TURN MISERY INTO ART

Steve talks about spending a year recovering from that crushing love affair. Steve is anything but shallow. While many rich and famous men caught up in the weirdness of Hollywood would just keep gobbling up the lines of wannabe young lovers, Steve was crushed, and that's how he behaved after the divorce. Other Hollywood stars would leave a line of broken hearts and rely completely on their success to attract more candidates to fulfill fantasies and imagined realities of love. But these types of people stink! As Elizabeth Taylor once said, "There is no deodorant like success." But Steve Martin has never traded on his success to meet or impress his female friends. Love, for him, is not a one-night stand with a drop-dead beauty. Steve is just not cut from that sort of cloth. I'm not saying it hasn't happened. But it's not his obsession. I believe that he has just been looking for love in all the wrong places.

Steve tells about a play he wrote as a result of the affair with Heche. It's called *Patter for a Floating Lady*. In the play, a magician appears onstage and levitates a young woman named Angie. At the end of the play, after the audience realizes that these two had loved each other and never quite trusted each other, causing each other great sorrow, she says, "Now I wait for a man my own age who will stand before me at arm's length, and I will hand him unimaginable joy, and he will not move forward, nor move back. Then I will hand him unimaginable pain. And he will stand neither moving forward nor moving back. Then, and only then, I will slit myself from here to here (she indicates a vertical line from her neck to her abdomen), open my skin, and close him into me."

The Angie character is "very beautiful" in her plainness. Steve's admitted that he is not attracted to really beautiful woman. He has told me that he finds them scary. The truth is, Steve is attracted to something deeper than beauty. His friends say he shows up with lovely young women who don't say much at parties. I don't believe Steve is going to find true love with a young woman. Why? First of all, that's not the important qualification for the job. And because Steve is a man in his fifties, mature beyond his years like he always was, he is not looking for a party-doll type. This is not to say that younger woman can't be mature for their age, but they had better be prepared to understand that there are endless, deep recesses within the mind of Steve Martin; he can be sitting right there and still be somewhere in the "in-between-world" thinking about a character for another movie. In our fifties, we are different. When Oprah Winfrey had Steve and Dan Akroyd on her show before *Bilko* was released, she asked him about aging. She mentioned, of course, that he doesn't seem to change. And it's true. His skin, his waistline, his face. He is amazing. But she pursued this line of questioning. "How do you age, Steve?" He politely responded, matter-of-factly, with, "You mean are my testicles hanging lower?" (As if to suggest that she had noticed) and then he said, "You can say anything on daytime TV, can't you?"

Getting older is a fact of life. Forget denial. Steve's no kid anymore. He doesn't need just a woman. He needs a soul mate. And they don't come easy, or necessarily when you need them.

STEP NUMBER TEN: BE OPEN TO NEW THINGS

Steve has a new house, a rambling ranch house instead of a

stark, white, plush prison. He's got a dog. Brian Grazier says, "Before, it was about his work and the art world. Learning more about art. Being ahead of the art curve. It was always about more tangible stuff. Buying the right art. Being brilliant in another movie. Being in another hit. You know. And now he's trying to be reflective and find a balance."

There is only so much stuff you can get in life. If you are so disposed, and if the drive and the money are there, you can get anything. But, of course, you can't buy love. Steve had been going through a lot of changes when that article was written, and the writer sucked up all the confusion possible and neatly categorized it. One of Steve's greatest fans called me from Canada and told me how sad the story was.

Steve keeps close reins on whatever is written about him. This magazine article came out, no doubt, as a result of his publicist lining up promotional ideas for Steve's movie *Sergeant Bilko*, which was released weeks after the article came out. The most interesting aspect of the article was that there was a vague bottom line as far as why Steve wanted to expose himself quite so blatantly. It has been his practice to keep his private life private. I think that might be the last time he will be quite so frank.

Steve mentioned to me a couple of years ago how much he would like to talk to Ratty, his high school sweetheart. I tracked down her number and called her. She has been married for almost thirty years but talked fondly about Steve and the old days. Ratty was the quintessential "beautiful in her plainness" type of girl. I believe she set the precedent that Steve is still pursuing. I asked her if she minded if I gave her number to Steve. She said no, but indicated that she didn't understand why he would want to talk with her. But Steve is a softie. Memories are important things—real things that stay with Steve, and he treasures them, like an older woman treasures her cat or a family scrapbook.

There is no way to prepare for the past. But we can examine it, and, with luck, it helps us deal with the here-and-now and the future. If there is a perfect woman for Steve, I surely hope he finds her soon, because, in my opinion, living as a single person causes one to get eccentric. And rich and famous people have more eccentricities than others to begin with. Steve would, obviously, find peace and joy in the arms of the right woman, and if he could ever see his face in the shining glow of a baby, his whole reason for living, his focus, and his movies would never be the same. If Steve is feeling lovelorn, I wish more than ever that he would find the right *aardvark*!

I've known Steve for more than forty years, and I have generally felt like I was inside his head and could understand him. In most cases, I know that's true, but now, because there is a therapist in the picture, I know that Steve has taken a step into Hollywood's weird world of self-doubt. This is a place I never imagined Steve would belong. He is everything he appears to be, but there are some long, deep voids in that wild and calculating mind. I know that he hasn't forgotten his past, but he has buried the Gopher Boys and traded his youthful delights for the new group of "friends" that fill his sacred, inner circle now. But Steve never forgot his friend when I needed help, and he saved my family and me from some awfully bumpy roads.

Perhaps it's because he has been so ubiquitous in my life that, over the years, I have vacillated between feeling like he would always be my closest friend and feeling like I wish I never knew him. Maybe he feels the same way. He once said I was like a Jewish mother to him. On another occasion, he sent a photo to me with this written on it: "The laughter we shared as children is priceless."

When we are withered old farts, and our life lights are blinking on and off and there is no distance between us, I'll tell him, "Although the strobe hasn't started blinking, it won't be long now." And if I don't happen to get his reaction to this comment before one of our lights is snuffed out, I will tell him in that in-between world where everyone is a blob (even the *aardvarks*), "Life is an unfulfilled dream, and there are no therapists."

Greg Gorman photograph

Chapter 27

"I Love You"

"Of all things which wisdom provides to make life entirely happy
much the greatest is the possession of friendship."

—Epicurus

Twenty years before this book was published, I decided to write my memories of what it was like to grow up with Steve Martin. My recollections were more vivid then, and I spent a year (off and on) gathering thoughts and talking to old friends and "fools." That original manuscript has formed the roots of this book.

Since then, we have traveled a million miles in our quest to entertain and bring our music and humor forth in a fight against mediocrity. I thought back then that I would publish the book soon. But the fickle finger of fate has pressed hard on this old "fool," and time left wrinkles and splotches on my face, not to mention the fact that a lot of my hair fell out. My kids grew up, and time waged a war of joys and tears against this family of performers. During those years on the road with Lynn, and then with Lynn and the kids, I kept making notes and adding to the original book. Way back then, when I finished the first draft of the manuscript and

Steve was *only* the number one stand-up comedian in the country, I decided to have a little get together with Steve and some of the people I mentioned in the book. I met him at his apartment in Hollywood. He had six or seven gold and platinum records on the floor and leaning against the wall. I gazed at them for few minutes. Perhaps I was shaking my head in disbelief. I said, "Steve, do you ever look at these things and just…" I motioned towards the records and lifted my arms in a way that showed I apparently had no words for this type of super stardom.

He glanced at the objects of my attention while he was pulling on his baggy wool slacks. "Those I look at more than anything else," he said sincerely. "You know" he paused "…what they represent."

I looked again at the trophies and nodded my understanding. I picked up an 1850 New York Martin guitar that was lying on a table by the door and strummed a few chords. It was a magnificent instrument, a real collector's item and also the mellowest sounding box I ever heard. I noticed that there were several oil paintings there that I hadn't seen before, all apparently nineteenth century creations. I was going to ask more about them when Steve announced he was ready to go. Steve kissed his cats goodbye, and we strolled down the hall towards the elevator.

We waited while the valet brought Steve's Jaguar around to the front. As we cruised through the back streets of Hollywood to avoid traffic, we talked about the past, Steve's life, and life in general.

He seemed so casual, genuine, and relaxed. When we finally ascended the narrow street that led to our destination, we noticed a sleek, white Continental cruising slowly in front of us. Momentarily, I recognized that it was Kathy Westmoreland, and we pulled up beside her and told her to follow us to the house. She thanked us, and when we finally arrived in front of the house, she admitted she was a bit lost.

Doug Rowell was already there with his daughter, Starshine. Basil Poledouris arrived with his wife, Bobby, and our little re-union was complete. Our friends, Ned and Sally Simonds, had a wonderful home overlooking the Hollywood sign in those days. We had a small vegetarian dinner party with old friends so that Steve could read the manuscript. He had three helpings of delicious veggie cuisine and charged through the book one chapter after another.

He said, "It is like a dream." He added, "How did you remember all this?" He read the entire manuscript that evening amidst old friends, sipping wine, reminiscing and totally enjoying everyone's company. When he finished reading, he commented that it was, "Lucid and...great!" That's all I needed to know from Steve.

Ned took some group shots, and as we all stood in the doorway saying farewell, there was a short chain reaction of emotion flowing through the group—a feeling time and space could not erase.

I really had no intention of suggesting that Steve sit and read the entire book, but that's exactly what he did. He said, "If it's interesting to me, it should be interesting to anyone who thinks they might want to read it."

Steve waved goodbye to the others, and he and I cruised slowly downhill in his car together. A strange thing happened.

I said, "Steve, when you are cruising around like this in Hollywood, do your fans ever notice? You know, wave or something?" Of course, I assumed they did, but I wanted to hear what Steve had to say about it.

He merely nodded his head (as if to acknowledge the obvious), and said, "Yeah, sometimes." I thought he was just being modest about how often it actually happened. Just then we pulled up to a boulevard stop and sat there waiting for the light to change. I looked out of my window at a Toyota in the lane next to us. The driver was a middle-aged man, and his passenger was a teenaged girl, who was probably his daughter. As I looked at them, I saw all of Steve's public represented in the expression on that one beautiful, young girl's face. She leaned awkwardly across her father's lap, staring at Steve, practically mesmerized, her lips silently repeating over and over, "I love you, I love you, I love you..."

As the light changed and we proceeded, I bumped Steve's leg and motioned to the girl in the car. He glanced over at her and smiled as we pulled away from the Toyota and the enchanted fan. His eyebrows knitted slightly in the middle, in a way that would indicate things like that happened more than just a few times. But his mouth did something unusual. The right side turned up, as if to smile, and the other side stayed straight.

The expression summed it up for me. Even now, he is simply proud, happy, successful, confident—and really no different than the young numismatist I met over 40 years ago, except now he's got more coins.

Chapter 28

FINALLY, SOMEONE
WITH A VISION

"You see things, and you say, 'Why?'
But I dream things that never were and say, 'Why not?'"
—George Bernard Shaw

Growing up with Steve Martin never stopped. Growing up with Steve Szalay or growing up with Greg Magedman ended with high school. I knew them, they knew me, and that was all there was to it. Age doesn't necessarily compliment us but it does humble us. We all go through some monumental changes over the years. I respect and admire Steve now, but no more than I did than when I was a kid. I've enjoyed the ride. If I could choose one word to describe him, it would be "great." We were intense friends, and then he went to the top. I have seen his face in thousands of towns, at corner newsstands, in magazines, in newspapers, on television, in the movies, on videos, in my dreams, on bathroom walls, record albums, tapes, cassettes, megaphones.

He has been an undeniable presence in my life. I never could have predicted his amazing future when we were simple Gopher Boys, but if you would talk with him, he would simply tell you that his story is no more important than yours. He is no greater than the vision he fulfills in his own life. He has the highest respect for every person on the planet and doesn't consider himself to be any better than anybody else. There are many Hollywood egos out there that will never accept this simple truth.

My life has been filled with love. Neither fame nor fortune has been my destiny thus far, but I have lived many fall-down-funny, exciting, and dangerous moments. I've shared passion and love and procreation with my darling wife. The sun rises and sets on my daughter, Amoris, who is stronger than Atlas and much braver than I. She is a wealth of talent and beauty and more precocious than I want to believe. She helped me edit this book, as did Lynn. My son, Sherlock Skye Walker, is the most talented comedian and impersonator I have ever worked with or known. He is an intense artist who created all of the pen and ink renderings in this book. My wife, Lynn, did over 9,000 concerts with me before our kids joined the act, and in the last five years, we have done more than 1000 live concerts with them. Lynn has endured unbelievable hardships, and done so with the grace and beauty that first attracted me to her almost thirty years ago. Her acting and singing talents are simply incomparable.

Steve and I were together almost all the time when we were young, but he had moments when he would just walk off into a zone of his own, and I didn't understand it. Any women who ever had or intended on having a meaningful relationship with Steve would eventually learn that only part of his existence is open to companionship. The other part is in a mystical in-between zone that no one else could understand. Steve adores his privacy and does not want anyone to intrude.

Which reminds me of one last story in which a major Steve Martin event was never made public. Prior to the release of *The Jerk*, Steve and Bill McEuen organized a nationwide contest called the "STEVE MARTIN LOOK-ALIKE, SOUND-ALIKE CONTEST." The purpose of the contest was to find an impersonator that could pass for Steve from a distance. Steve planned on using him in a TV special or a future movie. They had the final competition at the Comedy Store on Sunset Boulevard in Hollywood. I'm mentioning this now because I remember how secretive Steve and Bill had been in organizing the event. They didn't want the public to know that Steve was going to be there that night. They would have been overrun by fans. It was by invitation only. The price of fame is seclusion, and public events must be private if you don't want chaos to ensue.

I arrived with my good friend, a photographer, Ned Simonds.

We met briefly with Steve, who, contrary to popular expectations, was wearing a new $2,000 pink suit. I guess he didn't want to be confused with the impersonators. As the show kicked off, Carl Reiner gave Steve's new movie a solid plug, and the contest was under way. There were six finalists; all but one of them had gray hair. In fact, they all had tight white suits on, just as the organizers had expected. Some contestants were good. Most of them copied routines off Steve's albums, *Let's Get Small* or *Comedy Isn't Pretty*. One stark realization was that Steve's material wasn't necessarily funny when performed by anyone else. After one particularly bad attempt by a poor impersonator, Steve stood up in the front row, turned around and looked at the audience, and shouted, "Some of this stuff isn't my material!" That got more laughs than all the look-alike and sound-a-likers put together. A research scientist named Mark Phillips from Nashville, Tennessee won the contest. There was a cash prize and an appearance on another of Steve's television shows, where viewers were deceived by the ruse for a few minutes.

I have mentioned my family briefly in these pages. They are my life. There is a series of circumstances that have produced a very interesting reality, relative to Steve Martin and my son, Skye. He was born just before I started writing this book in 1978. What I haven't mentioned in detail is that he is also a banjo player and, as time and circumstances would have it, he is the best Steve Martin (Wild and Crazy Guy) impersonator in the world. (Well, excusssssse me for saying so!)

Skye won the Disney Talent Search in Hawaii, in 1989, performing Steve's antics on Hawaii PBS-TV. Not one of those Steve Martin look-alike contestants at the Look-a-Like-Sound-a-Like Contest even played banjo or had Steve's moves down like Skye did. Skye learned to impersonate Steve, at my request, very early

in life. He is just as comfortable imitating anyone, from Sean
Connery to Bill Clinton to Jim Carrey.

It is hilariously entertaining and incredibly ironic. If I ever
write another book about another man, it will be about Skye. Oh,
by the way, Skye was not named after the Star Wars character,
(Luke) Skywalker. He was given the name Sherlock Skye McLeod
Walker after the McLeod clan on the Isle of Skye in Scotland.

What you've read in this book have been my impressions of
Steve as a lifelong, personal friend. I could have gone out and done
years of research and given you a lot more information about his
movies, statistics, producers, etc. You can go to the World Wide
Web and start clicking on Steve's stuff, and your printer will have
a wild and crazy hernia. You can get everything from sound bites
and publicity photos, to entire movie scripts, the writers, cast members—the works. Steve's material on the Web is in the top five per-
centile of material folks like to look at.

But just as Steve has blasted into the galaxy of stars, he is
imploding into the microcosm. The bigger he gets, he still manages
to "get small."

It's interesting to note that since Steve made it big, his personal letterhead had a simple Helvetica type face at the top of the
page, which read "Steve Martin" in clear, embossed, capital letters.
Then, around 1990, Steve's traditional letterhead changed. He still
had that same simple "STEVE MARTIN" at the top of his beige
linen stationery that he used for 25 years, but this new letter I
received had a new phrase:

STEVE MARTIN

"Finally, someone with a vision"

Glenn Martin knew what the vision was since Steve was a
baby. On a number of occasions, Steve told me he had it. And anyone who ever worked with Steve, saw him perform, or watched
him attempt to do anything he set his mind to was keenly aware of
Steve's vision. It's tunnel vision. But as I've mentioned many times
in these pages, Steve is a very private person. His tunnel vision is
an obvious manifestation of his aspirations. It's the method by

which he accomplishes anything and everything. But it's a long tunnel, and the distant light at the end is only a glimmer to even the greatest visionary. Only Steve sees his visions as they will one day exist.

We can only guess what else this creative genius is working on. But there is one thing that has always been an integral part of the Steve Martin mystique—magic. Whatever he touches with his Midas touch, whatever dreams he envisions, whatever he wants to accomplish, he will. And the final product resulting from those efforts will be magic. Incredible, enchanting, mystical magic.

Perhaps someday Steve will write his memoirs. He loves writing. It seems that writing allows Steve the opportunity to express himself without compromise. As much as Steve has controlled his career more than many superstars, there is always the need for compromise. No movie is entirely under his control, nor could it be. But with writing, it's between him and his computer screen. Somebody will proof and edit, delete those dangling participles and dot those i's, but nobody will force him to compromise the words.

The real Steve Martin will be found between the lines of his plays and his essays. If he does finally decide to write his story, it will be an instant hit. It will be funny, because Steve is a true humorist. It will be magical, because his life has been magical. There will be romance, for he has loved, and he has loved and lost. There will be art, for art is the uncompromised passion of his existence. And there will be a few friends mentioned along the way. Friends that have been carefully and sensitively chosen to fit in a very small circle around a man with a very big influence. It will have a mystical title, perhaps "The Tao of Steve Martin." Or better yet, "Dow for a Booberday!"

I wish Steve the best in life. I always have. And whether he takes home a Golden Globe, a little Oscar guy, becomes the first celibate President of the USA, is knighted Sir Steve or finally turns out to be the Cinema Saint of the Century...the title I will always most enjoy placing before Steve Martin's name is "My Friend."

THE INANE INDEX TO A GOPHER BOY'S VOCABULARY
(The Fools Glossary of Terms For a Booberday)

This index has a special purpose… to enhance a Gopher Boy's vocabulary.

1. Aardvark...............................a girl for whom every Gopher Boy had a special purpose, not to be confused with: a burrowing insectivorous mammal of South Africa with a stocky, hairy body and a long-tubular snout

2. Arbigan................................synonymous for a dow for a booberday

3. Babo of the Orient...............Steve's sultry magic assistant

4. Bo Bo Skee Watten Dotten ..Argonaut cheer

5. Comedian............................one who tells stories funny

6. Comic..................................one who tells funny stories

7. Crebin.................................anything in Webster's Dictionary

8. Dow for a Booberday..........a life's work; philosophical jargon for useless verbiage DOW (TAO); also has very deep spiritual meaning, if one looks deeply enough

9. Double Talk........................nonsensical words delivered with the intention of sounding like real words

10. Farly...................................double talk used in *Three Amigos!*

11. Fedelforinstaf.....................check synonym for "Dow for a Booberday"

12. Ferbin.................................a small, fuzzy wart on an Arabian muskrat

13. Flydini ....a magician with a special purpose

14. Fools ....member of a very elite club

15. Fools Unlimited ....you and everyone else in the world

16. Frazen ....like a rebuff meter

17. Gag ....to pull a trick on some uninitiated tourist or observer

18. Goggles ....kid with glasses

19. Googlee Eyes.......................boy who hangs out with a kid with goggles

20. Graduation.............................maturity level for certain "Aardvarks"
21. Happy Feet............................size 12
22. Heola ....railroad crossing salute
23. Hoofer.................................vaudevillian ad-libs
24. Hoot or hootenanny..............a gathering of folksingers, singing
25. "La Crapola
    De La Flambay" ....priceless work of art
26. Nayem, Nauyem...................double talk in soundless music for Sound Explosion
27. Numismatist........................a coin collector
28. Prank..................................fake
29. Rebuff ....a double talk word, used frequently until we found out it was a real word
30. Rebuff Meter........................see stagmas
31. Regal..................................legs on an "Aardvark" that go all the way up
32. Schlept...............................sloppy moving
33. Schlepping..........................moving sloppy
34. Schmaltz.............................not used in this book
35. Schstick ....stick spelled with an extra sch
36. Sexy ....peddle-pushers with ponytails
37. Stagma...............................see frazen
38. Special Purpose....................."It," "Your Thing," "Wang," "Tallywhacker," "Tweeter," "Dingus," "Dick," "Peter," "Pecker." "PeePee," "Willy," "Private Parts"
39. Squash Blossom ....large gaudy turquoise jewelry in a silver necklace
40. TAO ....(pronounced dow) the path of life and the order of the universe
41. Thespian.............................one who loves to perform
42. Tookas ....bum, bummy, butt, ass, rear-end, cheeks, fanny
43. Vamp..................................to scratch someone's back
44. Vignola ....sacred sign for railroad crossings

MARTIN MANIACS
MOVIE UPDATE

FEATURE FILMS

Novocaine	2000	Artisan Entertainment
Joe Gould's Secret	2000	October Films
Fantasia	2000	Disney
Bowfinger	1999	Universal; screenwriter, actor
The Out Of Towners	1999	Paramount
The Spanish Prisoner	1998	Sony Classics
Sgt. Bilko	1996	Universal
Father of the Bride Part II	1995	Touchstone
Mixed Nuts	1994	
A Simple Twist of Fate	1994	Touchstone; screenwriter, actor
Housesitter	1992	Universal
Leap of Faith	1992	Paramount
Father of the Bride	1991	Touchstone
Grand Canyon	1991	20th Century Fox
L.A. Story	1991	Carolco-TriStar; screenwriter, actor
My Blue Heaven	1990	Warner
Parenthood	1989	Universal
Dirty Rotten Scoundrels	1988	Orion
Planes, Trains and Automobiles	1987	Paramount
Roxanne	1987	Columbia; screenwriter, actor
Little Shop of Horrors	1986	Warner
Three Amigos!	1986	Orion
Movers and Shakers	1985	
All of Me	1984	L.A. Films
The Lonely Guy	1984	Universal
Man With Two Brains	1983	Warner
Dead Men Don't Wear Plaid	1982	Universal
Pennies From Heaven	1981	MGM
The Jerk	1979	Universal; screenwriter, actor
The Muppet Movie	1979	
The Kids Are Alright	1979	
Sgt. Pepper's Lonely Hearts Club Band	1978	
The Absent Minded Waiter	1977	

TELEVISION

American Comedy Awards	2000 Fox Career Achievement Award
Scene by Scene with Steve Martin	1998 series
The Simpsons	1998 animated series, episode
The Tonight Show	1975-98 frequent appearances and hosting
And The Band Played On	1993 TV movie
Shelley Duvall's Bedtime Stories	1992 "Tugford Wanted to Be Bad" episode
Toonces, the Cat Who Could Drive a Car	1992 special
Leo & Liz in Beverly Hills	1986 Series: creator, director, executive producer
Saturday Night Live	1975-94 frequent appearances
Domestic Life	1984 executive producer
The Jerk, Too	1984 movie; actor, executive producer
Steve Martin's The Winds of Whoopie	1983 actor, executive producer
Twilight Theater	1982 special; actor, executive producer
Steve Martin's Best Show Ever	1981 special
All Commercials, Steve Martin Special	1980 host
Steve Martin: Comedy Is Not Pretty	1980 actor, writer.
John Denver: Rocky Mountain Christmas	1975 special, writer
Half the George Kirby Comedy Hour	1972 series, writer.
Ken Berry "Wow" Show	1972 series, writer, actor
Sonny and Cher Comedy Hour	1971 series, writer, actor
The Ray Stevens Show	1970 writer
Pat Paulsen's Half a Comedy Hour	1970 series; writer, actor
The Smothers Brothers' Comedy Hour	1967-69 1969 Best Writing Emmy

STAGE

Picasso at the Lapin Agile	1994 playwriting debut
Waiting For Godot	1989

BOOKS

Shopgirl	2000 amazon.com
Pure Drivel	1998 Hyperion Press
Cruel Shoes	1979 Putnam Publishers

MUSIC

The Steve Martin Brothers	1982 Album.
Comedy Is Not Pretty	1979 Album.
A Wild and Crazy Guy	1978 Album: hit single "King Tut" Grammy
Let's Get Small	1977 Album; Grammy

ABOUT THE AUTHOR

Morris Walker is a consummate raconteur. His short stories and stage antics have been appreciated by millions of folks over the years. In the words of Steve Martin, "Morris is a natural humorist and an excellent writer!"

Morris and Lynn, along with their talented children, Skye and Amoris, have performed as "The Earthwalkers" in thousands of live concerts across the United States and abroad. Morris' scripts, books and original comedy dialogue are unique creative reflections sharpened to a comedic cutting edge through years of hard knocks and performance experience. Today, as the owner and CEO of his award-winning video production company, Morris continues to nurture and expand his multi-faceted accomplishments in the entertainment business. He writes daily, performs periodically, and produces nationally acclaimed video productions. He and his family reside in Corvallis, Oregon.

magicyears@hotmail.com